THE HISTORY
OF
THE MANSION HOUSE

GEORGE DANCE, THE ELDER
By kind permission of Miss Dance of Bath
(not previously published)

THE HISTORY

OF

THE MANSION HOUSE

BY

SYDNEY PERKS

F.S.A., F.S.I., F.R.I.B.A.

CITY SURVEYOR TO THE CORPORATION
OF THE CITY OF LONDON

CAMBRIDGE
AT THE UNIVERSITY PRESS
1922

CAMBRIDGE
UNIVERSITY PRESS

University Printing House, Cambridge CB2 8BS, United Kingdom

Cambridge University Press is part of the University of Cambridge.

It furthers the University's mission by disseminating knowledge in the pursuit of education, learning and research at the highest international levels of excellence.

www.cambridge.org
Information on this title: www.cambridge.org/9781107456532

First published 1922
First paperback edition 2014

A catalogue record for this publication is available from the British Library

ISBN 978-1-107-45653-2 Paperback

PREFACE

WHEN it was decided in 1728 to build the Mansion House a Committee was formed and it was known as the Mansion House Committee, the name was altered to the General Purposes Committee in 1789, and that Committee is still entrusted with all matters arising in connection with the building, but in addition it has, as its name implies, other duties.

For many years I had considered the idea of writing a history of the building and had collected material, and when the War broke out, the customary holiday in France or Italy became impossible, and I had time to devote to research work in London, Oxford and elsewhere.

In 1916 the Chairman of the General Purposes Committee kindly mentioned my work to his Committee, which resolved "that permission be sought for him to search the records in Guildhall, and also have permission to search the records at the Mansion House at any time convenient to the Lord Mayor." Consequently I had exceptional facilities for carrying on my researches.

I am very grateful to many people for kind assistance and particularly to Mr J. H. C. Evelyn; Mr J. Bevan, the Secretary, and the Burlington Fine Arts Club; the Governors of the Bank of England; Mr C. F. Bell, Keeper of the Ashmolean Museum, Oxford; Mr J. P. Gilson, M.A., and Mr Reginald A. Smith, F.S.A., of the British Museum; Mr Alfred Conder, F.R.I.B.A.; Mr P. M. Evans and the Clothworkers' Company; Miss Dance, of Bath; Miss J. Broadwood; Miss E. M. Thompson; Messrs Devonshire, Monkland & Co.; Sir Charles W. C. Oman, M.P., and the Authorities of All Souls College, Oxford; Mr Edward Tanner, Solicitor to the London County Council; the Medici Society; Mr R. W. Bobbins, Renter and Registrar of Guy's Hospital; the Trustees of Sir John Soane's Museum; Mr R. V. Somers-Smith and the Grocers' Company; the trustees of the Radcliffe Library Museum, Oxford; Messrs Mackrell & Ward; Mr Francis W. Reader; Captain Arthur Anderson of

York; Mr Edward R. Warre and the City Parochial Foundation; Sir William Treloar, Bt; Mr F. W. Spurr, City Engineer of York; and to Messrs J. H. Willett, F. J. Craker and J. F. Coldwell, of the Guildhall.

I am also much indebted to Mr F. Madan and the Assistant Librarians of the Bodleian Library, Oxford; to Mr Bernard Kettle, the Guildhall Librarian; to Mr Thomas, Records Clerk at the Guildhall; to Mr Robert Harrison, Librarian to the Royal Society; to Mr A. Cecil Piper, City Librarian, Winchester; to Mrs J. Lindsay-Wood for assistance in London and at Oxford; and to many others, for it is very gratifying and encouraging to find so many people interested in research work.

The City of London has many sites and buildings of great interest; and we have many little guide-books giving a short description of a building on one page and a photograph opposite. Books of that description show little, if any, original research work; inaccurate statements are handed on from one edition to another, and inaccuracies like those originated by Elmes are hard to kill. The training of an architect is of great value and there are many opportunities in the City for energetic men who are interested in the subject.

S. P.

CLARIDGE HOUSE,
   SEVENOAKS.
      14th March 1922.

CONTENTS

CHAPTER I. THE WALBROOK

Roman Londinium. Levels of Roman pavements. Level of Roman London and London to-day. Roman wall recently discovered by the author under the Mansion House. The Walbrook stream in Roman times, and in the middle ages. References to the stream in the Letter-Books. An account of City Sewers written in 1834 and 1840. Depth of the Walbrook. Position of the Walbrook. The present stream

CHAPTER II. THE STOCKS MARKET

Market laws in the first century. St Mary Woolchurch-haw. *Liber Custumarum.* Charter of 1268. Deed of 1285. *Liber Horn*, 1305. Corporation Letter-Books. Egerton MS. 1324. Charter of 1327. *Letter-Book E*, 1346. Egerton MS., the butchers, etc. in 1360–1. Ancient Statutes of Fishmongers. The erection of the Stocks building, 1384. "Right to light" in 1441–2. St Stephen's Walbrook agreement in 1484. Water supply to the market. St Stephen Walbrook. Sale of cloth and merchandise at the Stocks Market. Lease of the Stocks Building in 1524. City Companies to survey the market in 1534. Lease of the Stocks building in 1536. Rent of the Stocks Market and Chambers over in 1542. Cost of meat in 1544. Market rights in 1546. Twelve chief Companies to survey the market in 1551. Lease of the building in 1557. Lease in 1576. Vegetable in fruit market in 1592. Building in bad repair in 1601. The great stone house called the Stocks in 1601. One butcher one shop. Rent of the Chambers in 1602. "The Committee for leasing of the Cities Landes" in 1602. Sewer in 1606. Herb women in 1631. Lease of the market in 1645. Petition by the Goldsmiths' Company in 1657. Street obstructions. Sewers in Walbrook and Poultry. Decision of the Court of Common Council with reference to the obstructions in 1657. Notes on the Walbrook 1277 to 1477 . . . .

CHAPTER III. MARKET RENTS AND TENANTS

Shop rents in Walbrook and Berebynder Lane in 1357. Description of the Stocks Building and rents in 1357. Sales outside the building. Accounts of rents for years ending Michaelmas, 1382 and 1395, and reference to sale of cloth. Tenants in 1357. *Chronicles of London Bridge*: incorrect translation of ancient deed. Deeds at the Record Office. Bridgemasters' Accounts, 1424, 1460, and subsequent dates in the fifteenth century. Accounts during the sixteenth century, and part of the seventeenth century. Accommodation in the building—Leake's map. St Mary Woolchurch-haw and Parsonage. Public right of way. Parish stocks and "whiping poste." Building re-erected in 1410. Analysis of number of tenants from 1460 to 1562. Sixteenth and seventeenth century maps. Position of the Mansion House with regard to Stocks Building . . . .

CHAPTER IV. ST MARY WOOLCHURCH-HAW

CHAPTER V. ST STEPHEN, WALBROOK

CHAPTER VI. THE STATUE

CHAPTER VII. THE STOCKS MARKET
AFTER THE FIRE

CHAPTER VIII. THE SURVEYS AFTER THE FIRE

Act of Parliament to deal with difficulties in consequence of the great fire. Streets to be widened. Surveyors appointed to set out boundaries, etc. Three Surveyors appointed by His Majesty: Wren to act with them, and not as their superior. Salary of the Surveyors. J. Oliver appointed a Surveyor. Cash received for surveys, total amount. Robert Hooke and his work. Death of Peter Mills: salaries of the Surveyors raised: death of Jerman: Robert Hooke's "profits." Total cost of the work by the City Surveyors. Properties surveyed near the Mansion House site. Total number of surveys. Survey books in the Guildhall Library: Oliver and Mills. Dates of surveys. Oliver's work: Mills's work: Dr Hooke. Awards by the Viewers . . . .

CHAPTER IX. PURCHASE OF PROPERTY

Purchase of property before building the Mansion House: Parsonage of St Mary Woolchurch-haw. Perpetual rental. Private Act of Parliament, 1737. Site of the Parsonage. Deputation to the Bishop of London: Calvert's property. The Swan Tavern. Clothworkers' Company. Ryder's property. Letter by Mrs Ann Hill dated 12th June, 1744. Duke of Bedford's property in the Poultry and Walbrook: proposed coach house and stable for the Lord Mayor. Property of the Clothworkers' Company. Total amount of purchase money. Thursby's interest. Lord Micklethwaite's property . . . .

CHAPTER X. THE PLANS FOR THE MANSION HOUSE

References to the Lord Mayor's House. List of private residences from 1246 to 1679. MS. dated 1609 giving particulars of residence, etc. Proposal to build a Mansion House in 1670. A reference in 1679. Committee appointed in 1689. Assessment of the Markets in 1697. Committee appointed in 1728 to find a site for the Mansion House. Fines for not holding the office of Sheriff. Committee appointed in 1734 to obtain designs, etc. Pamphlet written objecting to the present site: the reply. Sketch plan by the Sword Bearer and the Common Crier. A limited competition. Letter signed "Hiram" and one by Batty Langley dated 18th March, 1734. Articles in the *Grub St. Journal*. Gibbs and Leoni submit schemes. Gresham College and Leadenhall Market sites considered. Schemes by Leoni, James and Gibbs. Letter from Batty Langley, he is asked to compete. Dance also invited to submit drawings. Report of the Committee upon the Stocks Market site. Architects submit plans for Leadenhall Market scheme: letter from Captain De Belain. Report by Committee recommending the Stocks Market site. Report upon the designs of Leoni, Gibbs, James and Dance, also reference to Ware. Recommendation of Dance as architect. James Ralph's *Critical Review of the Public Buildings*. The Palladio story: Lord Burlington's drawings. Description of the designs by Isaac Ware, John James, James Gibbs, and Batty Langley. Press references. Payment to competitors. Notice to close the Stocks Market. Fleet Market. Committee bills, 1738. Hostile criticism of Dance's design: the Dance family . . . .

CHAPTER XIII. THE ROOMS IN THE MANSION HOUSE. THE DANCE FAMILY

LIST OF ILLUSTRATIONS

PLANS

Plans 63–67 are available from www.cambridge.org/9781107456532

Chapter I

The Walbrook

THE site of the Mansion House was in the centre of Roman Londinium (see Plan 63) just as it is in the centre of the London of to-day. Before the Roman walls were built there were probably fortifications enclosing an encampment, and the site in question was just outside those boundaries on the western side, and near the eastern bank of the Walbrook stream.

The level of Roman London is ascertained from the discoveries of streets and pavements of houses, which as a rule may be assumed as about level with the roadway. In St Paul's Churchyard (Plan 63, 196) the pavement of a domestic building was found at a depth of 18 feet below the present level of the ground. At Warwick Square remains of a building were found at a depth of 17 feet. Then further east at Bow Church (176), as is recorded in Wren's *Parentalia*, there was a Roman causeway at a depth of 18 feet, this was 4 feet thick and was used for the foundation of the tower of the church. Opposite Bow Church (174) some paving was found about the year 1615 at a depth of roughly 15 feet. At the north-east end of Queen Victoria Street (125) a fine mosaic pavement was found at a depth of 19 feet, this is preserved in the Guildhall Museum, and probably formed the flooring of a room of a villa overlooking the Walbrook. In the Poultry (118) part of a pavement was found at a depth of about 18 feet below the surface. When the National Safe Deposit Buildings were erected a timber staging was found running north to south, parallel with the west front of the Mansion House at a depth of about 25 feet, this is supposed to have been a landing stage but the evidence is slight, and if so it was probably slightly above the level of the stream. In Bucklersbury, on the south side of the National Safe Deposit Buildings, there were remains of a macadamized road at about 25 feet in depth, this roadway

had a gap, and it is thought the gap indicated the position of a
bridge over the Walbrook. We learn that a bridge was there
long before 1291 (see page 4). At the corner of Lombard
Street and King William Street, paving was found in the year
1785 at a depth of 10 to 15 feet (87) and further east at a
depth of 17 to 18 feet. In the same street at a depth of 8 feet
some paving was found, and it has been suggested that as it
was so near the surface it must have been of late date, but there
is no reason why it should not have been the flooring of an
upper room, especially as some paving was found adjoining at
a depth of 17 feet. If the paving was that of an upper room it
might naturally be expected that remains of the lower floor
would be present, but these are not mentioned.

Still further east in Leadenhall Street (44) pavings were
found, one at a depth of about 9 feet, the other at a depth of
about 19 feet 6 inches, no doubt there were either two floors
of a house as explained by Sir W. Tite[1], or 9 feet was a mis-
print for 19 feet. In the Minories (18) heating flues were
found at a depth of 18 feet. It is stated[2] that "an ancient paved
causeway" was found in Lower Thames Street at a depth of
20 feet, and that it was uncovered by labourers making the
sewers. This is difficult to believe as the invert or bottom of
the sewer in Upper Thames Street is about 11 feet 6 inches
below the pavement and 10 feet above Ordnance Datum. If
such a paving existed at about Ordnance Datum it would have
been flooded at high tide to a depth of about 14 feet, but as low
tide would be about 6 feet below Ordnance Datum the paving
might have been a causeway at right angles to the river, used
for loading ships, and not a street parallel with the river as at
present. According to recent information from the foreman of
the sewer works an old cobble road was found at a depth of
about 13 feet 6 inches.

The Romans occupied London for about 450 years, and it
seems improbable that the level of the city should rise 10 feet
in that time, and that the lower remains were constructed at
the very beginning of that period and the remains at the higher
level just before they withdrew. There are far fewer remains at
a high level than at a low level, and in the ordinary course of

[1] *Archaeologia*, vol. XXXIX, p. 494.
[2] *Gentleman's Magazine*, 1832, Part 2, p. 11.

PLATE I

SKETCH SHOWING ROMAN WALL UNDER THE MANSION HOUSE

events the building operations should have been greater at the later date. The Romans had upper floors to certain buildings, particularly the "insulae" or blocks of dwellings for the working people. Flats were built in Rome as early as 455 B.C. Dionysius relates that "the plebeians agreed to divide among themselves *bona fide* the building lots of the Aventine, each family selecting a space in proportion with the means at its disposal, but it happened also that families, not able to build independently, joined in groups of two, three and more, and raised a house in common, one family occupying the ground floors, others the floors above." Plutarch in his life of Sylla states: "I am an old acquaintance, we lived long under the same roof, I hired the upper apartment at two thousand sesterces, and he that under me at three thousand." This obviously refers to a building of more than one storey. Further particulars are given by the author in his book on Residential Flats. A pottery lamp found on the site of St Paul's Cathedral illustrates buildings with upper floors[1].

About the year 1900 excavations were made at the Mansion House, in consequence of certain settlements, and I heard a rumour that some old work was encountered but not exposed: an opening made in a disused cellar proved that the rumour was no "lying jade," and Plate I and Plan 1 show the result. A small portion of the wall was exposed, noted, and the earth filled in, but further excavations should be made towards the north as that end of the wall was not exposed. It will be seen from the illustrations that the bottom of the wall and top of the piling are about 17 feet below the adjoining road level of Walbrook: and that the black earth is about 17 feet 2 inches below that level. One face of the wall is rendered in cement and there is an off-set with tiles laid at a slope, the tiling and cement were probably on the outside of the wall and built for protection against bad weather. It is impossible to state if the sloping tiles went further or were level beyond the point shown, which is 14 feet 5 inches below the present road level.

Plan 63 was prepared by Mr Francis Reader; shaded lines show the extreme limit of the Walbrook stream during its history: this does not mean that in Roman times the river was nearly as wide as the Thames, but that it had changed its

[1] *Victoria History of London,* vol. I, p. 25.

THE WALBROOK

limits of the black peaty earth. Unfortunately we know comparatively little about the Walbrook in Roman times: it is clear
it was a narrow stream in the middle ages, and the Bucklersbury
macadam roadway indicates that it was narrow in Roman times.
On the west bank of the stream there was a villa which is referred to above, and there was a Roman building on part of
the site of the Mansion House on the east bank of the stream.

Mr Loftie, in his well-known book on London, gives a
description of Roman maidens tripping down steps to the Walbrook stream, one wonders what his authority was for doing
so; the depth of the two approaches to the bridge at Bucklersbury and the piling at about the same depth, lead us to assume
that the level of the water was about the same as that of the
adjoining land. Perhaps the steps belonged to the houses.

In an article in the *Morning Post* of May 23rd, 1886, it is
stated that

this river ran between steep banks and the land on which the Mansion
House stood would then have been at a considerable elevation. During
recent excavations the ancient Roman landing stage was discovered at a
depth of 20 feet, and boats would thus have been enabled to come up
from the Thames.

This statement was made at a meeting of the Middlesex
Archaeological Society: one would be glad to learn on what
authority.

The Walbrook in the neighbourhood of the Mansion House
was covered over about the year 1473, and this portion of the
stream is not shown on any of the old maps. Agas's Map, made
circa 1570, is the earliest known; it shows a portion of the
stream north of the wall.

When 12 Tokenhouse Yard was built, in 1870, a portion
of some vaulting over the stream was discovered, the span was
8 feet and is described as Tudor work.

The following are extracts from the Calendar of Letter-
Books[1] of the City of London.

Friday the Feast of St. Margaret (20. July), 19 Edward I (A.D. 1291).
An inquisition was made as to who is or are bound by right to repair
the bridge of Walebrok near Bokerelesbere, and who had been accustomed to do it and in what manner, &c. The jurors say that a certain

[1] The Letter-Books are not books of letters, but form a series of which the
different volumes are distinguished by the letters of the alphabet.

tenement formerly belonging to Richard de Walebrok, and now held by Thomas Box; another tenement in the same street formerly belonging to John de Tulesan, senior, and now held by John de Tulesan, junior; another tenement formerly belonging to Laurence Fitz Michael, and now held by the Society of Luka and John le Mazerer; and the tenement of Bokerelesbere held by the heirs of Roger Beyvyn, are bound to repair the bridge aforesaid, and have been accustomed so to do in common. They further say that of old four stones used to be placed opposite the aforesaid tenements, one stone before each tenement, in token of their duty to repair the bridge; but these were afterwards removed by Walter Hervy, the then improver (*aprouator*) of the City; and at that time he caused the bridge to be repaired at the cost of the tenants of the tenements aforesaid, &c. Therefore precept was given to the Sheriffs to distrain the aforesaid tenants of the said tenements for the repair of the said bridge, &c.

Calendar of Letter-Book A, p. 178.

Tuesday after Feast of Purification B.M. (2 Feb.), 20 Edward I (A.D. 1291–2).

Edmund de Byre, Mabel his wife, Anselm de Thele and Edyth his wife demised to William de Evre a tenement formerly belonging to Ralph Lupus in the parish of St. John upon Walbrok (except a house occupied by the aforesaid Edmund and Mabel adjacant to the parish church), situate between the church towards the south and Candelwystrate towards the north, and between the course of the Walebrok towards the west and Walbrokstrate towards the east.

Calendar of Letter-Book A, p. 190.

Thursday the Feast of SS. Simon and Jude (28. Oct.), 5 Edward I (A.D. 1277).

It is agreed.... that the course of the Wallebroke shall be entirely freed from dung, rotten matter, and other obstructions and nuisances, and that gratings (*rastalli*) be replaced at each tenement on the course aforesaid from the Moor of London down to the Thames, under penalty of 40*s*. to the use of the Chamber of the Guildhall of London.

Calendar of Letter-Book A, p. 212.

The Assizes of the City of London read by the Mayor and reputable men A.D. 1276–7 and 1277–8.

Also the course of the Walebroke and all the King's road shall be freed....   *Calendar of Letter-Book A*, p. 217.

Inquisition taken before the Mayor on Wednesday the morrow of the Translation of St. Benedict (11 July), 28 Edward I (A.D. 1300), as to who are bound to repair the covering over the water-course of Walebroc, over against the chancel-wall of the church of St. Stephen de Walebroc. The jurors say that the parishioners of the said church of St. Stephen are bound of right to repair the said covering.

Calendar of Letter-Book C, p. 71.

Wednesday before the Feast of St. George (23 April), 19 Edward III (A.D. 1345).

William de Iford, John de Enefeld, John de Westwyk, David de Kyngestone, John atte More, Richard Kisser, John de Thrillowe, William de Bray, and William Tithynglombe sworn to see that the water-course of the Walbrook be not impeded.

Calendar of Letter-Book F, p. 120.

Indenture of grant by Adam de Bury, the Mayor, the Aldermen, and John de Cantebrigge, the Chamberlain, to Thomas atte Ram, "brewere," of the Moor and the keeping of the water-course of Walle-broke for a term of seven years, quit of any rent, but on condition that he well and honestly safeguard the Moor and keep the said water-course clean.

Dated in the Chamber of the Guildhall, Thursday the morrow of St. James (25 July), 48 Edward III (A.D. 1374).

Calendar of Letter-Book G, p. 324.

Common Council held in the Chamber of the Guildhall on Wednesday, the 6th. May, 6 Richard II. (A.D. 1383).

Also that the Aldermen of the several Wards of Colemanstret, Bradstret, Chepe, Walbrok, Vintry, and Douegate, through which the water-course of Walbrok runs, take steps to prevent it becoming stopped up by refuse, &c.   *Calendar of Letter-Book H*, p. 216.

The Feast of the Assumption, 15 Aug. 8. Richard II. (A.D. 1384).

A proclamation made against covines and conspiracies; against walking the City after 9 o'clock (at night), except officers of the City and those engaged in preserving the peace; and against throwing rubbish into the Thames, the Walbroke, and the Flete.

Calendar of Letter-Book H, p. 247.

2 July, 3 Henry V. (A.D. 1415).

Ordinances by the Common Council to the effect (1) That the little postern built of old in the City Wall and leading to the Moor should be pulled down, and a new and larger one built to the westward of it, *with a gate* to be shut at night and other fitting times; (2) that the Moor be laid out for garden purposes; (3) that a common latrine outside the City Wall be removed, and a new one built within the wall upon the foss of the Walbrook, where a "scluys" or "speye" was to be constructed for the purpose of carrying off the filth; (4) that those living on the margin of the Walbrook near the Thames cause the banks of the same to be piled or walled.   *Calendar of Letter-Book I*, p. 137.

A Common Council held on Saturday, 11th. March, 3 Edward IV. (A.D. 1462–3).

That all latrines over the ditch of Walbroke should be abolished.

Also that the owner of land on each side of the said ditch shall clean his portion of the same, and pave and vault it up to its middle line. If the owner should refuse to carry out this order, his land should go to any one who was willing to do so, to hold the same to him and his heirs.

Calendar of Letter-Book L, pp. 21, 22.

A Common Council held 12 July, 17 Edward IV. (A.D. 1477).

Ordinance forbidding the making of "any Priveye or sege" over the

Walbrook or upon any of the town ditches, and ordering the abatement of those already in existence. *Calendar of Letter-Book L*, p. 149.

Stow published the first edition of his *Survey of London* in 1598, and the following are extracts from his writings with reference to the brook. He says it ran "through the midst of the citie unto the river Thames, serving the heart thereof."

And that in the 28. yeare of *Edwarde* the first, it was by inquisition found before the Maior of *London*, that the parish of St. *Stephen* uppon *Walbrooke*, ought of right to scowre the course of the saide Brooke, and therefore the shiriffes were commanded to distraine the sayde Parishioners so to doe: in the yeare 1300. the keepers of those Bridges at that time were *William Jordan* and *John de Beuer*. This water course having diverse Bridges, was afterwards vaulted over with bricke, and paved levell with the Streetes and Lanes where through it passed, and since that also houses have beene builded thereon, so that the course of *Walbroke* is now hidden under ground, and thereby hardly knowne.

Stow's *Survey*, Kingsford, vol. I, p. 14.

Robert Large Mayor, 1439. gave to the new water Conduits then in hand forty markes, and towardes the vaulting over of *Walbrooke* neare to the parish Church of S. *Margaret* in *Lothbery* 200. Markes.

Stow's *Survey*, Kingsford, vol. I, p. 18.

There have beene of olde time also, diverse Bridges in sundrie places over the course of Walbrooke, as before I have partly noted, besides Horshew bridge, by the Church of saint *Iohn Baptist*, now called S. *Iohns* upon Walbrooke. I reade that of olde time every person having lands on either side of the sayd brooke, should clense the same, and repayre the Bridges so farre as their landes extended. More, in the II of *Edward* the third, the inhabitants upon the course of this brooke, were forced to pile and wal the sides thereof. Also that in the third of *Henrie* the fift, this water course had many Bridges, since vaulted over with Bricke, and the streetes where through it passed, so paved, that the same watercourse is now hardly discerned. For order was taken in the second of *Edward* the fourth, that such as had ground on either side of Walbrooke, should vault and pave it over, so farre as his ground extended.

Stow's *Survey*, Kingsford, vol. I, p. 27.

Now from the North to the South, this Citie was of olde time divided not by a large high way or streete, as from East to West, but by a faire Brooke of sweete water, which came from out the North fields through the wall, and midst of the Citie, into the river of Thames, which division is till this day constantly and without change maintained. This water was called (as I have said) Walbrooke, not *Galus* brooke of a Romane captaine, slaine by *Asclepiodatus* and throwne therein, as some have fabuled, but of running through, and from the wall of this Citie. The course whereof, to prosecute it perticularly, was and is from the said wall, to Saint *Margarets* Church in Lothberrie; from thence beneath the lower

part of the Grocers hall, about the East part of their Kitchen, under
Saint *Mildreds* Church, somewhat west from the said Stockes market:
from thence through Buckelsberry, by one great house builded of stone
and timber called the old Bardge, because Barges out of the river of
Thames were rowed up so far into this Brooke on the backside of the
houses in Walbrooke streete (which streete taketh name of the said
Brooke) by the west end of Saint *Iohns* Church upon Walbrooke, under
Horshew Bridge by the west side of Tallow Chandlers hall, and of the
Skinners hall, and so behinde the other houses, to Elbow lane, and by a
part thereof downe Greenewitch lane, into the river of Thames.

This is the course of Walbrooke, which was of old time bridged over
in diverse places, for passage of horses, and men, as neede required: but
since by meanes of encroachment on the banks thereof, the channel being
greatly streightned, and other noyances done thereunto, at length the
same by common consent was arched over with Bricke, and paved with
stone, equall with the ground where through it passed, and is now in
most placed builded upon, that no man may by the eye discerne it, and
therefore the trace thereof is hardly knowne to the common people.

> Stow's *Survey*, Kingsford, vol. 1, pp. 118, 119.

Out of this Royall streete by the South gate of Tower Royall runneth
a small streete, East to S. Iohns upon Walbrooke, which streete is called
Horshew bridge, of such a bridge sometime over the brooke there, which
is now vaulted over.   Stow's *Survey*, Kingsford, vol. 1, p. 239.

Now for the North side of this Lothburie, beginning again at the
East end thereof, uppon the water course of Walbrooke have yee a
proper Parrish Church, called saint *Margaret*.

> Stow's *Survey*, Kingsford, vol. 1, p. 282.

The following extracts are taken from an unpublished
account of the sewers written about 1834:

The London Bridge Sewer was continued along Princes Street in
1834 by the Commissioners of Sewers and carried up to the north side of
Lothbury.

From Mansion Street Northward into London Wall and the land to
the Eastward, beyond the Auction Mart in Throgmorton Street, was
found to consist of indurated Bog Earth to a general average depth of
Nine feet; and in Lothbury about 90 feet of that sewer was tunnelled
between the walls of a very ancient passage, the floor of which was paved
with coarse red tesserae, the whole lying in this layer of bog earth.

The new line intersects the course of the ancient Walbrook which
ran from St. Margaret's Church, Lothbury, across the ground now occupied by the Bank of England, and alongside the south wall of Grocers'
Hall, and under St. Mildred's Church into the Poultry. At the point of
intersection the new sewer was found to be just 16 inches above the deep-
est part of the Channel which the original watercourse had hollowed out
of the stratum of Blue Clay; the new bed being at that point 30 feet
9 inches below the present surface. Masses of Piling with the wall plank-

ing still on the face next the channel were cut through and at the South East Angle of Grocers' Hall, (where the Manhole now is) a bed of very hard concrete pavement, covered with a thin coat of red earth was found at a depth of 17 feet 6 inches.

As the Worshipful Company of Grocers found it necessary to rebuild their Clerk's residence: and, to effect that, wished to destroy so much of the Walbrook Sewer as ran thereby; the Commissioners allowed them so to do; and a private sewer was built by them, which discharges itself into the adjacent manhole in Princes Street.

The following notes are made from an account of sewers written in 1840.

In 1777 Panter was allowed to lay a trunk at the mouth of the sewer of Dowgate Hill to work a water-wheel for some manufacture carried on in his warehouse at Dowgate Dock; upon his paying twenty pounds a year for the use of the water of the sewer. This however grew to be such an annoyance, by impeding the free discharge of the upland waters, that, in 1806, direction was given for its removal.

The use of it however appears to have been persisted in: for, in 1808, it was again ordered to be taken away, but was not finally discontinued until Christmas, 1810.

There was not any sewer throughout Dowgate Hill in early times, but an ancient sewer existed under the footway on the west side of Walbrook, and communicated with the true "Walbrook" or "London Sewer" in Cloak Lane or in Budge Row at the one end, and in Bucklersbury at the upper end.

In 1696 Sir Robert Cotton, on behalf of the General Post Office, was allowed to enlarge a private drain in Bearbinder Lane, which discharged itself into "Walbrook" so as to be 4 feet 6 inches high and 2 feet 6 inches wide; but this would seem not to have been done: as in 1708, a sewer was built, by Sir Robert Cotton, and Sir Thomas Frankland, from Walbrook, through Stocks Market, Bearbinder Lane, Swithin's Lane, and Sherborne Lane up to the General Post Office: and in 1738, when Stocks Market was appropriated for the site of the Mansion House, the City of London built a new sewer from Walbrook, within 7 feet of Walbrook Church, and turned northward to the end of Bearbinder Lane, but the main sewer was carried under the Mansion House and a branch appears at or about the same time to have been formed, which ran northward from this line along the west front of the Mansion House in Charlotte Row; the which branch was destroyed in 1801 from Mansion House Street down to the first drain from that building.

From the west side of this old sewer in Walbrook, a sewer was built by the inhabitants of Barge Yard in 1736, through Bell Alley and under three houses into Barge Yard, which was allowed to be made 3 feet high and 2 feet wide.

In 1765 the Governor and Company of the Bank of England had leave to make a sewer 5 feet high and 3 feet wide, from Cloak Lane along Dowgate Hill up to the south end of Walbrook, and also from the north end of Walbrook through Charlotte Row and across Mansion House Street into Threadneedle Street.

In 1769 Jacomb was allowed to make a sewer from the open part of Dowgate Dock up to the north end of buildings then newly erected by him in Dowgate Dock, between the head of the Dock and Upper Thames Street; and as the "Walbrook" was found to be overcharged with water, it was deemed expedient, in 1770, to extend this sewer up Dowgate Hill to Cloak Lane, and the Bank of England undertook to defray half the cost of this portion of the work.

In consequence of the shallowness and general inefficiency of the sewage of the central part of the city, more especially in 1774 the Commissioners adopted a more extended view of the subject, and commenced a systematic mode of proceeding, by destroying, or disconnecting so much of the old sewer as happened to be in the way, and building an entirely new line at the sole cost of the Commission; and at this time the Dowgate Dock sewer (as an integral work) was begun.

From the mouth, at the head of the open dock, it passed up Dowgate Dock, Dowgate Hill, Walbrook and Charlotte Row, along the Poultry, through the Old Jewry and Coleman Street, into Fore Street: the depth of the whole being considerably greater than any sewer then existing. But notwithstanding this increase of depth even this line of sewer was found to be ineffective, and that portion of the line which extends from Dowgate Dock to the Poultry having been torn to fragments by the enormous pressure of the upland water, a pressure so great as, in the times of heavy floods, to throw up a stream some feet in height from the Gulley Grate at the south end of the Walbrook, in 1819 and onwards to 1823, it was rebuilt and greatly enlarged.

The present dimensions are as follows:

	Depth ft. in.	Height ft. in.	Width ft. in.
In Dowgate Dock			
At the mouth (within side the flange)	9 0		
At Upper Thames Street	12 4	6 6	4 3
In Dowgate Hill			
Between Nos. 22 and 23	10 9		
At College Street	13 6	8 4	4 6
At Chequer Yard	14 4		Do.
At the South end of the narrow part of the Hill			Do.
At Cloak Lane			Do.
At Budge Row	21 6		Do.
In Walbrook			
At Bond Court	18 4	7 10	4 0
At St Stephen's Church	21 0	7 10	4 0
In Charlotte Row			
At Bucklersbury	21 4	7 10	4 0
At Mansion House Street			
At the Circ. Manhole	21 2	7 8	4 0
			3 9

The floor of Dowgate Dock was repaired by the Commissioners in 1778 and 1783.

On the western side of Walbrook portions of the ancient sewer, which lies under the footpath, still remain. They have been connected to the manholes of the lower sewer.

Description of the southern end of the Walbrook.

This natural streamlet which ran through and drained all the centre of the City of London, having been, year after year, encroached upon, arched over, and concealed, and its bed having risen in proportion as the ground surface was raised, is almost entirely unknown, excepting to the officers and workmen of the sewers authorities; and, even to them, it is now more generally known as "The Boundary Sewer."

That it once was a very considerable stream was clearly manifested by the section across its course, which was made in building "The London Bridge Sewer" in Princes Street; its bed lying more than 30 feet beneath the present surface, and the original banks being well defined, while the subsequent

encroachments were clearly marked by a regular and substantial wharfing composed of several tiers of stout piles, capped
with horizontal timbering, and faced with wall-planking. The
banks were still covered, as when they were filled in, with
grass and other vegetation mingled with roots of trees, in
various stages of decay.

The modern rubbish averaged 10 feet 6 inches in thickness.
The black vegetable soil, for 72 feet in width, was 22 feet 3
inches in depth, and thence gradually lessening on either side
as the banks ascended. This section however does not give the
actual width of the rivulet, as it cut through it obliquely.

It can now be only a matter of conjecture, although based
upon facts: but, from the great extent of a layer of black bog
earth, averaging fully 10 feet in thickness on either side of its
course, stretching from south to north, between the south side
of Cornhill and London Wall (exclusive of Moorfields) and
eastward beyond Bartholomew Lane, but of unascertained
width to the westward, coupled with the present existence of
an undoubtedly Roman sewer 18 feet beneath the surface of
Little Moorgate, the mouth of which is cut to the slope of the
trench into which it fell, and the bottom of which, as proved
by the excavation when making the sewer in Blomfield Street,
must have been at least as deep as that of the quagmire in
Lower Moorfields, there seems little or no reason to doubt
that the negligent or intentional obstruction of this natural
watercourse created all the fen land of Finsbury. Whether this
were so or not, the banks of "The Walbrook" can scarcely have
been in earlier times other than a very agreeable spot for residence; for—working from the Thames, northward—the
Friary or Jesus Common, Joiners' Hall, Innholders' Hall,
Dyers' Hall, Skinners' Hall, Tallow Chandlers' Hall, Cutlers'
Hall, the Church of St John upon Walbrook, the original
Church of St Stephen upon Walbrook, the stone building
formerly on the site of Barge Yard, the King's house, called
Comette Stoure, between Bucklersbury and the Poultry, the
Church of St Mildred in Pulletria, the Poultry Compter, the
site of Saint Mildred's Court belonging to the Goldsmiths' and
the Clothworkers' Companies, Grocers' Hall, Founders' Hall,
the property of the Drapers' Company, where now the north-
west part of the Bank stands, Saint Margaret's Church in Loth-

bury, the property belonging to the Leathersellers' Company in London Wall—all of them places still existing or upon record—are and were, near to or upon its banks and accurately define its track. And in addition to these, at a trifling distance on either side were an extensive Royal Palace in the Old Jewry, the remains of a tannery under the site of the Auction Mart in Bartholomew Lane, Drapers' Gardens and Carpenters' Hall. These buildings and possessions, however altered in process of time, may, not improbably, have succeeded the similarly large establishments of British or Roman men of rank; for, super-added to them, the ruined tessellated and other pavements met with in Princes Street, Lothbury and Bartholomew Lane, indicate that at least parts of the banks of this stream were in early days of the city occupied by buildings of no mean cha-racter; while the residences of noblemen and the structures of religious communities, attest that it retained its attractions down to comparatively modern times.

The wreck of the main line of this once useful and agreeable rivulet consists of some detached pieces between the Thames and Grocers' Hall, between Lothbury and London Wall, and northward of Moorfields.

These portions were united until 1774 when the construc-tion of the sewer in the Poultry made the first breach in its course. In 1803, when the north-west quarter of the Bank of England was erected, a further destruction took place, and in 1818, when Finsbury Circus was laid out, all its arms were cut off.

Until about 1774, it was known either as "Walbrook" or as "London Sewer," the epithet "Boundary Sewer" being of modern date. That epithet however is very appropriate, for it almost exactly coincides with the division line of the Wards of Dowgate, Walbrook, and Broad Street, on the east; and Vintry, Cordwainer, Cheap and Coleman Street on the west of its course.

From the mouth under a private wharf on the Thames it crosses Greenwich Street ("Greenwitch Lane," Stow), and pass-ing nearly midway between Friar's Alley and Joiners' Hall Passage (Grantham's Lane, Stow) crosses Upper Thames Street at 38 feet east of Little College Street, then cuts diagonally westward, and passes under College Street at 19 feet 6 inches

west of Little College Street. Thence, its course lies by
Skinners' Hall and Tallow Chandlers' Hall, across Cloak Lane
at 88 feet from Dowgate Hill, under the west end of the Burial
Ground of the parish of St John Baptist at 67 feet from Dowgate Hill, then into and across Budge Row. It is again met
with in Bucklersbury at 71 feet west from the houses in Charlotte Row.

It is there cut off, but from the sewer in Poultry it passed
under the church tower of Saint Mildred's parish, and close
to the east wall of the Poultry Compter Chapel, and that of
part of Grocers' Hall, where it now terminates by receiving part
of the private sewage of that establishment.

Portions of it still remain, as when first covered in, of rubble
work and squared ashlar stone, with which it was repaired by
the Commissioners; but the larger part was either originally
built or at various times rebuilt in brickwork. The arch is
pointed. In 1836 that part which is north of the Poultry having
been severely mutilated by persons cutting into it surrepti-
tiously, and fractured by the weight of buildings erected over it,
a smaller sewer was built within it and pinned tight home to
the old work.

The depth and dimensions are as follows:

	Depth ft. in.	Height ft. in.	Width ft. in.
At the River		8 9	3 0
In Greenwich Street		5 0	3 0
In Upper Thames Street		4 9	3 0
		3 6	2 10
In College Street	10 9	5 5	3 6
			3 10
In Cloak Lane (88 ft. from Dowgate Hill)	10 0	6 9	2 2
		4 3	
In Budge Row (67 ft. from Dowgate Hill)	9 10	5 10	3 0
		3 9	
In Bucklersbury	11 2	5 2	3 0
In the Poultry	14 5	4 6	1 10
		4 0	2 10

We learn from the notes made in 1834, that the bed of the
old Walbrook stream was 30 feet 9 inches plus 1 foot 4 inches
or 32 feet 1 inch below the present street level in Princes Street

at a point about 230 feet from the Royal Exchange frontage
line of the Bank of England. This point is about 2 feet 6 inches
above the level of Bucklersbury. We know the Roman landing
stage level at Bucklersbury was 25 feet below the present level,
allowing 1 foot to water level, or 26 feet in all, we find as follows:

	ft.	in.
Depth of landing stage	25	0
Depth to water level add	1	0
	26	0
Add for rise in ground	2	6
	28	6

Deduct this from 32 feet 1 inch and we get 3 feet 7 inches as
the depth of the stream where it crossed Princes Street. With
regard to the stream near Bucklersbury we can make another
simple calculation.

	ft.	in.
Present level above Ordnance Datum is (say)	42	0
Deduct depth of the Roman roadway	25	0
	17	0
Deduct for level of water below roadway, say 1 ft.	1	0
	16	0
High water is roughly 14 feet above Ordnance Datum	14	0
	2	0

In other words the level of the stream was about 2 feet above
high water mark.

The dimension of 32 feet 1 inch as the depth of the stream
in Princes Street is confirmed by other records. According to
the list in the *Victoria History of London* we read that in the
Poultry a fibula was found at a depth of about 30 feet "on the
banks of the Walbrook," and that vases were found in Queen
Victoria Street at a depth of 32 feet 2 inches (c. 120.122).

As a result I think we can assume that in the neighbourhood
of the Mansion House site the Walbrook was a narrow stream,
about 3 to 4 feet deep.

Plan 66 is the plan of sewers in the neighbourhood of the
Mansion House and shows the course of the old Walbrook. It
was compiled in 1840; it shows the depth of the river along
the old stream was 17 feet 10 inches at Cloak Lane; but no
depth is given north of that point. In Upper Thames Street
the depth of the sewer was 11 feet 3 inches, which was about

the level of the Roman street, consequently I think it fair to assume generally that the old Walbrook sewer was not laid on the bed of the stream. I have indicated by dotted lines the extreme dimensions of the line of elevation near the Mansion House and also near Cloak Lane, as shown on Mr Francis Reader's Plan 63. According to the plan of 1840 the black mud did not extend as far east as Dowgate Hill, but Mr Reader notes an "embankment of piles" east of that hill, but slightly to the south.

I also show a site in Walbrook "which was the Ould Church of St Stephen" from a MS. plan in the Guildhall Library by John Oliver, made the 20th May, 1674. It will be noted that the plan extends about 12 feet beyond the assumed line of the Walbrook, and consequently I think the line of that stream should be slightly further west, because the *Letter-Book C* (p. 71) tells us that the water course was "over against the Chancel wall," and Stow refers to the site as being "ever on the bank[1]," earlier he refers to the obligation of the parishioners to "scoure the course of the saide Brooke[2]."

There is much valuable information in the verbatim report of proceedings before Parliamentary Committees with reference to the Great Northern and City Railway, 1902, and to the Metropolitan Railway Act, 1914. Sir Douglas Fox stated[3] that clay is 32 feet deep in the Poultry, that the Gresham Life Office pumps up 2000 to 3000 gallons of water a day, and that the foundations were taken down 40 feet[4]. Sir M. Fitzmaurice had borings made at the side of the Mansion House at the top of Walbrook and clay was found 30 feet below the street level[5].

At the Gresham Life Assurance Office on the site of St Mildred's Church I was allowed to see the well, it is situated about 48 feet west of St Mildred's Court and near the line of frontage; it is 8 feet in diameter and the bottom is 49 feet below the street level, there are 6-inch pipes projecting into the well, one north, one east and one west; they are about 20 feet higher than the bottom of the well and about 20 feet below street level; the inlet to the west is always running, the others are

---

[1] Kingsford's *Stow*, vol. 1, p. 227.   [2] *Ibid.* vol. 1, p. 14.
[3] *Report*, p. 72, April 11th, 1915.   [4] *Ibid.* p. 112.
[5] *Report*, 16th April, answer number 3250.

usually dry. When the water rises to a height of 16 feet in the well, a pump is automatically set going, and the water is pumped up into the sewer, at about the rate of 2500 gallons a day. The water was analysed and found full of vegetable and animal matter.

When Mr Alfred Conder, F.R.I.B.A., was engaged in the building of the National Safe Deposit premises in 1869, he had to pile along the Walbrook frontage of the building to protect the foundation from water. There is a well on the premises, it is about 45 feet deep from the level of Queen Victoria Street, water rises in it to a height of about 14 feet and is used for the hydraulic lift: sometimes the well runs dry. The water is similar to that below the Gresham Offices. The depth of the foundations of the premises is about 40 feet: the concrete being 6 feet thick. Mr Conder is of opinion the bed of the Walbrook was about 32 feet below street level, and this is further support for the figures given above. From other inquiries in the neighbourhood I learned that there has been less trouble with water from the stream south of Cheapside since the Central London Railway was built.

The engineer to the Metropolitan Railway informed me that peat was found 17 feet below the present level in Blomfield Street, and sand and gravel about 7 to 8 feet below, and that the bed of the river was probably about 20 feet below the present level. At Finsbury Circus the figures were about the same, and 22 feet to the top of the loam or sand. In St Mildred's Court the clay was about 33 feet below the present level. The peat extended from Moorgate Street to Bishopsgate, the bottom of it being about 15 feet above Trinity High Water Mark.

The depth of the paving at the Coal Exchange is interesting, it is about 12 feet below the present street level, which is 20 feet above Ordnance Datum; an average high tide is 14 feet above Ordnance Datum, consequently the paving is about 6 feet below high tide and being near the Roman wall must have been protected from the flooding. The position is in a line with the Roman wall. See Plan 63.

With reference to the width of the stream in Roman times, the evidence of Mr Price is that the roadway stopped at a certain point and after a gap it has continued, the distance between he unfortunately does not mention, but as he refers to the "brook" and the "stream" apparently the width was slight. We learn from the Letter-Books that the stream was narrow in the thirteenth century, and it appears probable that it was narrow in Roman times. As to the so-called "landing stage" there is not much evidence to support it, and there is no reliable evidence that it was used for barges up to the position of the Mansion House. The stream was probably about 3 to 4 feet wide and about the same depth.

PLATE II

INTERIOR OF ST STEPHEN'S CHURCH

The engraving is dedicated to Christopher Wren, Esq., by Samuel Wade

PLATE III

A Prospect of the Inside of S.t Stephen Walbrooke   Ⓢ   Vue de l'Interieur de l'Eglise de S.t Etienne Walbrooke
London   Printed for Rob.t Sayer near Serjants Inn Fleet Street London   a Londre

Chapter II

The Stocks Market

THERE are records of laws for sales and purchases at very early dates. Between 675 and 685 there were the laws of Lothaire and Eadric that a Kent man purchasing goods in London should have three honest men as witnesses or the Reeve of the King's City. In 688 there were the laws of Ina, in 924 the laws of Athelstan, later the laws of Edgar and Cnute, all very similar in effect. Then still later the laws of Edward the Confessor and William the Conqueror, who gave the First Charter to the City of London.

All the quotations in this chapter are published for the first time except the extracts from the *Liber Albus* and *Liber Custumarum*, which have been published in Latin; these are ancient books at the Guildhall. Many references are made to the Letter-Books, which have been published in English up to and including *Letter-Book L*.

In the *Liber Custumarum* there are references to markets as early as 1220.

The following is an abstract from the Charter of 1268 (52 Hen. III):

And that no Merchant or other person shall go out to meet other Merchants coming towards the City by land or by water with their Merchandise and Victuals to buy or sell again, until they arrive at the said City and have there exposed their wares to sale on forfeiture of the thing purchased and pain of imprisonment from whence he shall not escape without a heavy chastisement and that none shall expose his wares to sale which owe Custom before the Duties are levied, on forfeiture of all the goods wherewith it shall happen to be done otherwise. And that no Merchant stranger or other person shall buy or sell any goods which ought to be weighed or troned except according to our trone or beam on forfeiture of the goods aforesaid.

The following is translated from the *Liber Custumarum*, Pt I, 274.

Letters Patent of *Edward I* licencing the Mayor etc. to build.

Edward by God's grace etc. to all to whom the present letters shall

2—2

come greeting. Because on the testimony of our beloved and faithful Ralph de Hengham and William de Brumptone and other creditable persons we have understood that it is not to our damage nor to the hurt of our city of London, if we grant to our beloved Henry le Waleis, Mayor, and the commonalty of the same city, a certain place contiguous to the wall of the church of Wollecherche[1], on the north side of Wollecherche; and a certain other vacant place, contiguous to the wall of St. Paul's churchyard, on the eastern side, between the door of St. Augustine and the street of Westchepe, of which place one half lies in the parish of St. Augustine and the other in the parish of St. Michael le Querne; and a certain other empty place, contiguous to the wall of the foresaid churchyard of St. Paul on the north side, between the great gate of the same churchyard, opposite the aforesaid church of St. Michael, and a certain other gate in the same wall toward the West, opposite the lane of Yvilane —that they may build on them and lease them for the maintenance of London Bridge:—

We have granted for ourselves and our heirs, to the foresaid Henry and Community, that they may build on and lease the foresaid places, as to the convenience of them and of the same city shall seem the better to be expedient, and them thus built upon and let out to rent, hold to themselves and their heirs in perpetuity, for the maintenance of the foresaid Bridge, without dispute or hindrance of us or our heirs whosoever. In witness whereof we have caused these our letter patent to be made.

Witness myself at Hertebire, the 24th day of May in the tenth year of our reign.

The Corporation duly carried out the trust and the building known as the Stocks Market was erected and let to various tenants; later on we get a description of the building, particulars of the rents, etc.

The grant of the land was made in 1282, and the building was quickly erected, and let the following year at £46. 13s. 4d. per ann. and a premium of £40.

The following is from the *Liber Horn*, f. 238, and the *Liber Custumarum*, f. 219 b, and dates about the time of Edward II.

AND because some Buyers and Brokers of Corn purchase Corn in the City of country people who bring it into the City to sell and give upon the purchase a Penny or Halfpenny Earnest money, and tell the country man to take the Corn to their Inns, and there he shall receive his pay; and when he goes and believes he shall quickly have his payment, the Buyer tells him that his Wife has gone out on her business and carried

---

[1] The site of the Mansion House was partly occupied by St Mary Woolchurch, sometimes called St Mary Newechirche or Wolchirchehawe; it is mentioned as early as 1104.

away the key of his Chamber, so that he cannot get at his money; but that if he will depart & return shortly he shall have his pay; and when at another time he returns for his money either the Buyer is not to be found, or, if found, makes some other excuse, by which the Poor Man cannot receive his pay: And sometimes when the Poor Man is waiting for his pay, the Buyer causes the Corn to be mixed; and when he comes to demand his pay, then the poor man agrees to take what the Buyer chooses to assign him or release part of the price; and if he will not do this, that he may take his Corn and carry it away; which he cannot do because it is mixed in another manner than when he sold it: And by such evil delays the poor Men put the moiety of their pay at credit before they are fully paid: IT IS PROVIDED and ordained That he upon whom such deceit shall be practised shall complain to the Mayor, and if they can prove and convict the Buyer before the Mayor of this wrong done to him, the Buyer shall render double the value of the corn and his damages besides, moreover if the Mayor shall find that the value aforesaid shall not be Sufficient for the damages he has sustained then the party offending shall be at the grievous mercy of the King, if he has wherewithal; and if he has not wherewithal to yield the penalty aforesaid, and cannot satisfy the amercement, he shall be put in the Pillory, and there remain one hour of the day at the least: and a Serjeant of the Town being at the side of the Pillory shall with a loud voice declare the cause for which he is placed there.

The following is a translation from the Husting Rolls of Deeds and Wills, 14 (76), and is dated 1283. See also Egerton MS. No. 2885, fol. 39 a.

On the same day and year (On Monday, the morrow of Holy Trinity, 11 Edw: I) a certain writing was read in these words: It was agreed betw: Henry le Waleys, the then Mayor, & the Citizens of London, the Parties demising, on the one part, and Walter Blund Rich: Cnotte, Rob: le Treiere, Stephen Pikeman & John Bandry, Thomas Orpedeman & Geoffry Horne, Fishmongers the Parties receiving on the other part, to wit: That the same Mayor and Citizens have delivered granted & to farm let to the afsd. Walter, Rich: Rob, Stephen, John, Thos: & Geoffry, Fishmongers that House which is constructed for the use of the Butchers and Fishmongers in that plot of ground near *Wolcherchawe*, in the City aforesaid with the Head (*i.e.* of the plot of ground) towards the East without the wall of the same House, which plot of ground also the Illustrious King Edward of England lately gave to the same Mayor and Citizens by his charter, which they have concerning it, for the sustentation of the Bridge of London, as in the same Charter more manifestly appears. To have and to hold to the afsd. Walter, Rich:, Rob:, Stephen, John, Thomas, & Geoffry, Fishmongers All the afsd. House with its appurts. & easements as well below as above, with a competent view on all sides, if necessary, to be made by the afsd. Mayor and Citizens; for the whole life of the Parties before named RENDERING therefore yearly

to the Bridge Masters of London for the time being for the sustentation
of the same Bridge Forty six pounds, thirteen shillings & four pence
sterling, at the four principal terms of the year, to wit, at each term,
eleven pounds thirteen shillings & four pence And which Term the afsd.
Mayor and Commons afsd. will and grant for themselves & their successors that the wardens of the said Bridge shall for ever receive for the
sustentation and amendment of the same Bridge.—And the afsd. Walter,
Rich:, Rob:, Stephen, John, & others for the whole term of their lives
shall have & receive the whole stallage of the Butchers and Fishmongers
there received & to be received so long however as they may conveniently
abide and be placed there with every commodity and profit coming from
the Holders of any places in the same by reason of their stalls aforesaid
And that they may lawfully, during their time, let the House and edifices
which are above to whomsoever they will, and receive the benefit thereof
as they shall think most expedient, And that upon the death of the Butchers and Fishmongers holding places there, they may demise such places
to others for the term of the lives of the Parties taking them as hath been
anciently accustomed to be done by the Baliffs of the City, or if they
prefer, retain them in their own hands for their own benefit during their
lives. Saving nevertheless to the same Mayor and Citizens the Power
and correction to them reserved, if the afsd. Walter, Richard, Rob:,
Stephen, John, Thomas, and Geoffry in demising such places & stalls to
other poor Persons, by virtue of their office, for the year or for term of
life, should be too severe, shameless, or greedy. Also the same Mayor and
Citizens have granted to the sd. Walter, Richd:, Robert, Stephen, John,
Thomas and Geoffry That on whatsoever days the Butchers shall be
there on the West part of the same House towards *the cheap* of London
upon the Pavement the fishmongers may reasonably have stalls to sell
their Fish, on account of Religious or other persons, who on any such
days eat fish and not meat.—Also the same Mayor and Citizens have
granted That they may not permit the stalls of Butchers or Fishmongers
to be elsewhere than in the same House and in the place aforesaid except,
that is to say, *Bridge Street, Eastcheap, Old Fish Street,* and the street of
the Butchers Westward in the Parish of St. Nicholas, and that in their
Houses, as hath been accustomed to be done, And the afsd. Mayor &
Citizens and their successors, The same House with all its appurtenances,
and easements & conditions afsd, will warrant and for ever defend to the
same Walter, Rich:, Rob:, Stephen, John, Thomas and Geoffry, against
all Men for the whole lives of the said Walter, Richard, Rob:, Stephen,
John, Thomas and Geoffry And the same Walter, Rich:, & other their
associates afsd. shall in the meantime sustain the same House at their own
costs & charges so that at the end of their lives The same House may
freely revert to the afsd Mayor and their successors without any deterio-
ration except by long use, and without impediment, and if by misfortune
the said House shall happen to be burnt by foreign fire or otherwise
destroyed by other than by the afsd. Tenants then the Citizens afsd shall
be bound to rebuild the same; And for the observing all these things on
their part the said Walter, Rich:, Rob:, Stephen, John, Thomas, and

Geoffry bind themselves their Heirs & all their goods & Hereditaments moveable and immoveable wheresoever existing And for this demise and grant the afsd Walter, Richard & other their associates have given to the said Mayor & Citizens Forty Pounds of Silver IN TESTIMONY whereof Two writings of the same tenor are made in the form of a chirograph, one of which remains in the possession of the sd Walter Rich: & or their associates sealed with the Common Seal of the City And the other in the possession of the sd Mayor & Citizens sealed with the seals of the sd Walter Richard Rob: Stephen John Thomas & Geoffry, These being witnesses &c.

There are references to "le Stokkes" in *Letter-Book H*, pp. 242, 243.

From the above description it appears that the east wall of the Stocks building was within the boundary of the land, so stalls were erected outside on the vacant land.

The following is a translation from Latin of the Comptroller's Deed No. F. 53, dated 1285.

To all Christ's faithful who shall see or hear the present writing Gregory de Rokeslee Robert de Baring, Nicholas of Winchester Philip the Tailor John de Gysors, Ralph le Blond, John son of Peter, William of Farendon, Robert de Rokeslee, Jocens le Akatour, Martin Box, William le Mazeliner, Robert of Arraz, Anketimus de Beauville, William of Haddestok, Richard Astheroy, John of Northampton, Thomas Box, Aldermen and all the Commonalty of the City of London, everlasting safety in the Lord. The whole of you shall know that whereas our lord the Lord Edward the illustrous king of England has given Henry le Waleys then Mayor of London and the commonalty of the same city in aid of London Bridge those plats of land contiguous to the wall of the church-yard of St. Paul's reaching from the gate of the foresaid churchyard, from opposite the church of St. Michael-le-Quern (S. Michael ad Bladum) towards the east, out unto the lane which is called Ivilane towards the west and from the door of St. Augustine the less towards the south as far as the market of Westchepe towards the North as the charter of our lord the foresaid King to the foresaid Mayor and Commonalty purports and witnesses. And the same our lord Edward King of England aforesaid afterwards the foresaid plats, specially gave and granted by charter to the said Henry le Waleys and his heirs as in the charter of the said lord King made concerning this to the same Henry is contained: We the foresaid Aldermen and all the Commonalty of the City aforesaid for us our heirs and successors the same grant of our lord the King aforesaid made to the same Henry his heirs and assigns accepting with unanimous assent and will remitt and quit-claim to the same Henry his heirs and assigns all right and claim which we had or could have in the foresaid plats of ground built or to be built upon as they lie with their appurtenances from us our heirs and successors forever, so that, to wit, that neither we nor the fore-said Aldermen nor the Commonalty of the City aforesaid nor any others who by us or for us any right or claim in the said plats of ground with the appurtenances by reason of the gift of our foresaid Lord the King in aid of the foresaid Bridge made to the said mayor and commonalty or by any other right, may exact or claim in the future. In witness whereof we have put the seal of the Commonalty of London to the presents. These being witnesses Sir Ralph de Sanndwich then warden of London, Walter le Blound and John Wade holding place of Sheriffs, Sir John de Kirkely, Master William de Luda, Hugh de Kendal, John de Beauquelle and others Dated at London in full Hustings Tuesday next after feast of St. Edward, the King, 13 Edward I (1285).

In December, 1299, we find a record of the names of certain butchers at "le Stocke"[1].

The following is an extract from the *Liber Horn*, fol. 314, 1305, 34 Edw. I:

On Thursday next after the Feast of the Conversion of St. Paul in the 34th. year of King Edward by Masters John le Blund, the Mayor of London, John de Wengrave, Thomas Romeyn, Walter de Fynchingfeld, Richard de Resham, Adam de Fulham, Richard de Gloucester, Richard de Whlehale and Thomas Sely, Aldermen It was commended to the Fishmongers of Bridge Street and of old Fish Street, then present That they should, under grevious penalty, permit the Freemen of the City, Fishmongers, standing at the stalls, to trade with them, and freely obtain their portions of the Merchandizes, as is fitting and just, and as the liberty of the City requires.

The following is from the *Liber Horn*, fol. 320 b, the date is 1311. It also appears in another form in *Letter-Book D*, p. 281:

Be it Remembered That on the Wednesday next after the feast of St. Gregory the Pope in the fifth year of the Reign of King Edward the son of King Edward, before John de Gisors, Mayor, Nicholas de Farndon, John de Wyndesore, William Trente, Roger de Trowyk, Nicholas Pickot, and Henry de Gloucester, Aldermen, an assembly was held by the good Men of the commonalty to ordain and treat concerning the state of the Butchers and Fishmongers holding Places at the Stocks, on which day it was agreed, by the said Commonalty, That all those who have taken their places, by demise, of John le Bevere and of the six other good Men to whom Henry le Galeys formerly the Mayor, and the whole commonalty granted and demised the same Places to wit "All that House which is called the Stocks" for the term of life of the said John le Bevere and of his companions, for a certain sum of money which they annually yielded to the Bridge of London; So that the said John and the others might demise those Places to Butchers and Fishmongers, according to that which is more fully contained in a certain writing indented, made between the afsd Henry, the Mayor and the commonalty of the one Part and the said John le Bevere and his companions, on the demise afsd and

[1] *Letter-Book C*, p. 55.

enrolled in the Hustings; may have and hold their Places which they have taken of the afsd. John or of any of his companions, provided it can be shown here in Court before the Mayor, that they took such places of the same John or any of his companions and that for term of their life, etc. And it is in like manner agreed that other Butchers who have hitherto taken places by demise of the Bridge Masters, and have paid fine thereof, to hold for the term of their life, and the same can make appear, may have and hold the same. And that from henceforth those places which are not held in form afsd shall be taken into the hands of the City, and demised by the present Masters, To be held yearly, for the best sum at which they can be leased And it was agreed that no Masters from henceforth shall have power to demise any places for term of life, without the assent and will of the Mayor and Aldermen and Commonalty for the time being. (1311.)

On March 12th, 1311–2, an assembly was held to consider the status of butchers and fishmongers tenanting the house called "le Stokkes"[1].

The following is from the *Liber Horn*, 1312, 6 Edw. II:

THE KING to the Mayor & Sheriffs of London, Greeting.

WE have received information by the grievous complaint of John de Brahyng, Fishmonger, before us laid, on behalf of himself and others exercising that trade in the same City; That William de Ware, Stock-fishmongers, exercising such trade there, hath frequently committed, and ceases not from day to day to commit Forestallings and Brockages and other trespasses and wrongs, to the reproach and manifest dishonour of all persons exercising the trade of selling stockfish, onions, garlick, walnuts, and other such victuals,—and also against the approved custom amongst those who have exercised that trade there; To the great damage & loss of us & our community afsd and of all Persons resorting to the said City & selling such victuals there; We willing to prevent such injuries & frauds, Command you, That having called before you the afsd John and William, & heard the reasons, as well of the sd John, for himself and others exercising such business in the sd City; as the afsd, William, in the premises, and having fully examined into the truth thereof; you cause to be amended, in the manner, what you shall have found to have been unjustly attempted by the said William; and if he shall be found guilty thereupon, That you chastise the said William accordingly to his desert, that that chastisement may make others afraid of offending in like manner; that we may hear no more clamour thereupon, whereby we ought to put our hand to this in another way. WITNESS ourself at Windsor the 13th. day of February in the sixth year of our reign.

On November 1st, 1319, reference is made to the shambles called "les Stokkes." A man had brought bad meat to sell at

---

[1] *Letter-Book D*, p. 281.

the shambles, and he was sentenced to be set on the pillory and the carcasses burnt beneath him[1]. In 1320 the meat of three alleged foreigners (*i.e.* non-freemen) was seized because it was offered for sale by candle-light at les Stokkes, after curfew was rung at St Martins le Grand, one man proved he was a free man and his meat was returned to him, but the remainder of the meat was forfeited to the use of the Sheriffs[2].

On April 25th, 1323, a complaint was made that certain people had erected shops and stalls outside the Stocks Market building, to sell fish; they pleaded guilty and promised not to offend again[3].

On February 14th, 1323–4, certain men were prosecuted for selling fish contrary to the ordinance made for the common good[4].

On the same day it was confirmed that the rents should be devoted to the maintenance of London Bridge[5].

The following is a translation of the Egerton MS. No. 2885, fol. 40. It is also referred to in *Letter-Book E*, p. 189, and is dated 7th July, 1324.

Afterwards on Thursday next before the feast of the Translation of St. Thomas the Martye, 7th. July, in the 17th. year of the reign of King Edward son of King Edward (1324) Hamon de Chikewell, Mayor, Adam de Salesbury and John of Oxford sheriffs & the Aldermen went to the foresaid house called the Stokkes and caused to come before them the fishmongers standing there and had read before them the King's confirmation that from henceforth outside the said house they should not expose their fish for sale on fish-days neither in shops nor upon stalls under forfeiture of the things exposed for sale and the loss of the liberty of the City. If a second time they transgressed or contravened the ancient ordinance contained in the said confirmation etc.

And afterwards on Friday next following came John Sterre and Roger alte Vienge wardens of the bridge and gave it to be understood to the Mayor Sheriffs and Aldermen that notwithstanding the warning given to the said fishmongers about the premises, Benedict de Shorne fishmonger exposed his fish to sale within his shop and outside of his shop upon stalls Wherefore Peter de Hungrie Serjeant of the Chamber was bidden to attach all the fish which he should find exposed to sale there outside the house called the Stokkes and bring it before the Mayor Sheriffs and Aldermen at the Guildhall. Which very Peter went to the said house and because he found the said Benedict selling his fish within

---

[1] *Letter-Book E*, p. 110.
[2] Riley's *Memorials*, p. 141.
[3] *Letter-Book E*, p. 179.
[4] *Ibid.* p. 184.
[5] *Ibid.* p. 186.

his shop and upon stalls outside the said shop and not within the said
house called the Stokkes he attached there of the said Benedict's fish, to
wit, white salted herrings, and three salt fish called "lenges" and brought
them to Guildhall before the said Mayor Sheriffs and Aldermen, and
bade the said Benedict on behalf of the Mayor and Commonalty come to
the said Guildhall before the said Mayor Sheriffs & Aldermen to answer
wherefore outside the said house called the Stokkes his said fish, against
the Ordinance and grant of the lord King he has exposed to sale within
his shop and upon stalls. Which Benedict indeed came and because he
could not affirm but that he exposed his fish to sale outside the said house
called the Stokkes after the prohibition made to him and theother fishmongers it was considered that the said herring and fishes forfeited should
remain to the use of the sheriffs etc.

Benedict de Shorne, fishmonger, was found guilty of the
above offence and his fish was seized[1]. On May 6th, 1325,
reference is made to the fact that the Mayor and Commonalty
of the City had built a certain place adjacent to the wall of the
churchyard of the church of Wolcherchehaghe and let it out
for rents for the maintenance of London Bridge, and that the
house was called "les Stokkes" for the sale of meat and fish
which were not to be sold elsewhere except in places of old
prescribed, certain men had offended and pleaded guilty[2].

The following is a translation of the Egerton MS. No.
2885, fol. 41. It is also referred to in the Chartulary in the
Comptroller's office fol. 48, and *Letter-Book E*, p. 200.

On the Monday next after the feast of St. John before the Latin
Gate (6th May) in the 18th. year of the reign of King Edward son of
King Edward (1325) Robert atte Folde, Benedict Shorne John Thur-
good, Robert Hore, Stephen de Hodesdone, Stephen atte Steples, Elias
atte Folde and Thomas Swetynge fishmongers at the Stokkes were
attacked to answer the Community of the City concerning the plea that
whereas the lord Edward of famous memory King of England father of
the lord King now granted for himself and his heirs to Henry le Waleys
then Mayor and the commonalty of the City aforesaid that they might
build upon & let to rent a certain plat contiguous to the wall of the
church-yard of Woolchurchehawe on the north-side in the parish of the
same church for the maintenance of the bridge and the said plat thus
built upon and let to rent might hold to themselves & heirs for the maintenance of the foresaid bridge forever: And the foresaid Henry the Mayor
and commonalty aforesaid caused a house to be built upon that foresaid
plat and to be called the Stokkes and appointed it for the selling of flesh
and fish there and the rent issuing from the stalls there to be for the
maintenance of the said bridge: and likewise granted and appointed that

---

[1] *Letter-Book E*, fol. 190.   [2] *Ibid.* p. 200.

elsewhere in the foresaid City than in that house & place aforesaid stalls of butchers or fishmongers should not be permitted except in the places as anciently accustomed, from which time the butchers and fishmongers the rent proceeding from those stalls have returned to the wardens of the Bridge for the time being in support of the same bridge, and our lord Edward King of England the foresaid ordinance composition and grant by his charter for himself & his heirs has granted and confirmed; the said Robert and other etc. witholding the foresaid rent, other stalls for the selling of fish in the King's high street and in all the other places contiguous and neighbouring outside the foresaid house upon their own authority have now newly made against the foresaid ordinance by which the rent of the said house which is the greatest part of the (maintenance) of the foresaid Bridge is withheld yearly to the value of £20. because the stalls are not placed in the same house (and) because thus they sell their fish outside the foresaid house to the damage of the whole community 100^{11}. And thus they are ready to prove by so much etc.

And the foresaid Robert and the others have come and cannot affirm but that they have sold their fish against the foresaid ordinance as they are charged and they place themselves in the grace of the Mayor and Commonalty and ask licence etc and they have etc.

And the agreement is such viz: that the said Robert and the others and each of them for himself have granted that from henceforth they shall not against the foresaid ordinance sell their fish outside the foresaid house. And if it happen, which be it far from them, that any of them by himself or by his people on any fish day sell or cause to be sold his fish against the ordinance that every day any of them who thus against the foresaid ordinance has or have sold his fish by himself or by his men each of them for himself (ought) to pay and return to the wardens of the foresaid bridge for the time being in the name of the commonalty aforesaid for each day on which he has thus sold his fish by half a mark sterling. And nevertheless that there shall run upon them the forfeiture of the fish thus exposed to sale against the ordinance as has been accustomed to be done. And to pay the half mark each of them all his goods at the discretion of the Mayor for the time being, shall oblige and bind.

The following is a résumé of a "Charter of divers liberties," dated 6th March, 1327.

CHARTER, assented to in Parliament, referring to the Privilege of London, confirmed by Magna Charta; & inter alia, provides & grants:

That the Market Steward or *Clerk of the Market* of our Household, may not from henceforth, sit within the Liberty of the aforesaid City, nor exercise any office there, nor any way draw any Citizen of the said City to plead without the Liberties of the said City, of any thing to happen within the Liberties of the same.

AND that the Sheriffs of the same City (which shall be toward the aid of the farm of the said City) may lawfully have the forfeiture of victuals & other things & merchandises, according to the tenor of the

Charter thereof made to the Citizens, & shall not be debarred thereof hereafter contrary to the tenor of the same Charters.

AND That no Surveyor & Taker, officer & other Minister of us & our heirs, or of any other, shall make any Prizes in the said City or without, of the goods of the Citizens of the said City, contrary to their Will & pleasure, unless immediately they make one payment for the same, or else they have respite thereof with the good will of the seller.

AND That No Market shall be henceforth granted by us or our Heirs to any within seven Miles in circuit of the said City.

In 1331 the butchers at the Stokkes petitioned that no butcher who has failed once or twice in his payment should sell his wares there until he has paid off his arrears, that no foreigner should sell there by retail, that no butcher shall take another's man until he has paid up arrears to his master, that all butchers must dwell in the city[1].

On 22nd July, 1336, it was decided that all rents appertaining to London Bridge in the place called "les Stokkes" should be levied by the two Wardens of the Bridge[2].

The following is a full translation of *Letter-Book E*, pp. 298–9, an abstract only of which has hitherto been published.

Ordinance for the plats at the Stokkes

Memorandum that on Monday the Feast of St. Mary Magdalen in the 10th year of the reign of King Edward the Third after the conquest it was ordained by Reginald de Conduit (de Conductu) Mayor, John de Grantham, John de Preston, John de Oxford, John Hamond, Richard le Later (and twelve others named) aldermen, William Hannsard etc. (thirty others named) and other Commoners of the City for the common will of the same city and the safety of the custody of London Bridge that all rents belonging to the said Bridge in the place called the Stokkes shall be wholly levied by Walter Neel and Alan Gille wardens of the same, any demise thereof made to any one by former wardens notwithstanding, as appears by a certain letter signed with the common seal and to the said Walter Neel and Alan Gille by the said Mayor and Aldermen delivered, in these words:—

May it appear to all by the presents that we, Reginald de Conduit, Mayor, the Aldermen and Community of the City of London, have granted and given full power to Walter Neel and Alan Gille Wardens of the Bridge of the City aforesaid to collect, and to the use of the same Bridge wholly for the future to levy the whole rent issuing from all the plats as well of the butchers as of the fishmongers in the place called the

[1] Riley's *Memorials*, p. 179.   [2] *Letter-Book E*, p. 299.

Stokkes, any demise made thereof by former wardens to any one notwithstanding. In witness whereof the common seal is appended to the
presents. Given in the chamber of "Gildaule," London, Monday next
after the feast of St. James the Apostle in the tenth year of the reign of
King Edward the Third after the Conquest.

On 22nd May, 1345, an ordinance was made prescribing
the days and places for butchers, poulterers and fishmongers,
to sell their goods so as to avoid overcrowding the street between the "Stokkes" and the Conduit in Cheap Ward[1]. These
regulations are printed in *Memorials* by Riley, p. 222, etc., and
reference is made to penthouses adjoining the Stocks building.

On 20th July, 1345, it was agreed that fishmongers wash-
ing their fish at "les Stokkes" should be punished[2].

On June 29th, 1346, the Mayor and Commonalty granted
to the Church of St Mary de Wolchirchehawe in perpetuity a
plot of land extending from the house of "les Stokkes" up to
the gate of the churchyard and situate at the east end of the
church, being 7½ feet long on the north side and 4½ feet on the
south[3].

The following is a translation from *Letter-Book F* of the
memorandum recording this grant.

Concerning a certain plat granted to the Church of
St. Mary of Wolchircherchehawe (*sic*)

Memorandum that on Wednesday the Vigil of SS Peter and Paul in
the twentieth year of the reign of King Edward the Third from the
Conquest, Richard Later, Mayor of the City of London, by the common
assent of all the Aldermen and the whole community of the same city
has granted to God and the church of St. Mary of Wolchirchehawe of
the said City a certain empty plat of ground at the eastern end of the same
church lying lengthwise by the foresaid church from the House called
les Stokkes as far as the gate of the churchyard of the same church, and
similarly lengthwise by the highway from the corner of the same house
called the Stokkes as far as the said gate. And it contains in breadth at
the northern end by the Stokkes 7½ feet and at the southern end at the
said gate 4½ feet. To have and to hold all the said plat of land with the
appurtenances to God and the foresaid church forever.

In 1351 a man sold a putrid capon and was sentenced to
the pillory, the capon being carried before him to the pillory,

---

[1] *Letter-Book F*, p. 123.   [2] *Ibid.* p. 128.   [3] *Ibid.* p. 157.

and a proclamation made to the people giving the reason for the sentence[1].

On March 4th, 1360–1, the butchers claimed to sell their meat at the Stocks on fast days, this was disputed by the fishmongers. The Wardens of London Bridge produce the deed dated 14th February, 1323–4[2].

In 1360–1 it was ordained that the butchers should sell their meat at a reasonable price, viz.: the best carcass of a sheep for 2s., the best "loygne" of beef for 5d., the best "pestel" or hand of pork for 3d., the best "loygne" of pork for 4d. etc.[3]

The following is translated from the Egerton MS. No. 2885, fol. 41, and is identical with the Chartulary at the Guildhall, fol. 82. There is also an account of this in *Letter-Book G*, pp. 127–8.

Memorandum that on the 4th. day of the month of March in the 35th. year of the reign of Edward III after the conquest (1360–1) the butchers standing in a certain place called the Stockes grievously complaining to John Wroth then Mayor and the Aldermen of the City of London have shown that the butchers standing in the foresaid place ought to sell their flesh there on the flesh days and further they said that they ought to stand there and sell their flesh on the vigils of Christmas and Easter, and that such custom they and their predecessors, butchers standing in the foresaid place were wont to use and enjoy without hindrance of anyone. But on the eve of Christmas in the 34th. year of the reign of the foresaid King Edward the fishmongers standing in the foresaid place moved the foresaid butchers from their stalls in the place so that they could not expose their flesh there for sale to the grave damage of them the butchers and against the ancient custom aforesaid. Whereof they beg the Mayor and Aldermen that they give them a remedy and justice concerning the premises. And because the Mayor and Aldermen desire to be more fully informed concerning the premises, the forementioned butchers are told to await their day for this before the foresaid Mayor and Aldermen, Tuesday next before the feast of St. Gregory the Pope next coming. And if they have, concerning such a custom as they claim any special deed to declare the truth of the premises, let them have it there on the same day.

And William de Grenyngham Serjeant of the Chamber is bidden that he warn the fishmongers standing in the foresaid place to be there on the same day to answer concerning the premises. And also that he warn Richard Bacon and John de Hatfelde chaundeler, wardens of London Bridge, that they be there the same day, and if they have in their

---

[1] Riley's *Memorials*, p. 266.   [2] *Letter-Book G*, p. 127.   [3] *Ibid.* p. 139.

possession in their custody any ordinances or compositions touching the men of the foresaid misteries that they have them there on the same day to declare the truth of the premises.

On which Tuesday the foresaid butchers have come and the fish-mongers standing in the foresaid place and the foresaid wardens of London Bridge likewise have come. And the complaint of the foresaid butchers being recited before the foresaid Mayor and Aldermen in the presence of the foresaid parties the forementioned butchers are asked if they have any special deed for having such a custom as they formerly claimed to have as above. Who say that they have not thereof any special deed, but they say that they and their predecessors butchers have enjoyed such custom and they request that that may be allowed them: And upon this the foresaid Wardens of London Bridge produce here in court special deed sealed with the common seal of the foresaid City, which was made in the time of Hamon de Chykewell then Mayor of the same City touching the compositions between the men of the foresaid misteries in these words:

"To all Christ's faithful to whom the present letters shall come Hamon de Chikewell Mayor, the Aldermen and all the commonalty of the City of London Greeting."

In which deed here in full court read and heard is contained that the fishmongers may sell their fish in the foresaid place on fish-days and the butchers on flesh-days but no mention is made concerning the foresaid two days, viz: the eves of Christmas and Easter that the foresaid butchers ought to stand there to sell their flesh, but only that the foresaid fish-mongers may sell their fish in the foresaid place on fish-days and the butchers flesh on flesh-days.

Therefore it is granted by the Mayor and Aldermen that the fish-mongers may have their stalls in the foresaid place for selling their fish on fish-days and the butchers may have their stalls there for selling their flesh on flesh-days as is contained in the foresaid deed. And if it happen that the foresaid butchers can afterwards find any special deed or other memorandum which are of record that they ought to stand in the foresaid place on the foresaid two days, viz. Christmas Eve and Easter Eve, as they claim above, then it shall expressly be allowed them without contra-diction of anyone, notwithstanding judgement thereof returned to the contrary, etc.

The following is a translation of Egerton MS. No. 2885, ff. 32–3.

Here begin the Ancient Statutes of the Fishmongers of London

The men of the fishmongers halmote say that they ought to have two law-motes in the year, to wit one against the feast of St Martin and the other against Lent and all the fishmongers and they who are of the

PLATE IV

Stocks Market near Cornhill

VIEW OF THE STOCKS MARKET. LOOKING EAST

PLATE V

VIEW OF THE STOCKS MARKET, LOOKING EAST

halmote ought to be there, and he who shall be wanting, because he is not there falls into the mercy of 21.*d.*

Further they ought to forbid in that halmote that any fishmonger sell fresh fish before mass is celebrated at the chapel on the bridge or at the Church of St Magnus.

They say also that the said fishmongers ought to sell fresh fish after the foresaid mass and salted fish after prime.

They say also that no one of the foresaid fishmongers ought to go towards the fish beyond the appointed bounds: these are the bounds, the chapel on the bridge, Baynard's Castle, and Jordan's Quay, unless that fish be lying for sale as at Berkynge, Northflete, Derteford or other more remote market.

No one may buy fish in any vessel afloat unless the ropes be placed to the shore.

No one ought to avow any fish, unless it be his chattel, upon the fish itself to gain or lose.

The men of the said office give to the bailiff two marks by the year, to wit, one mark against Christmas and one mark against Easter, to wit, by farthings halfpence and pence as the collectors can collect. And therefore they give those two marks, because if anyone of the halmote be impleaded in the Hustings the bailiff conducts him out of the Hustings to the halmote in Bridge Street. The Monks of St Albans give to the bailiff yearly a mark, but the bailiff ought to go, or to send for it.

The spindelerbot which brings fresh mulwel or ray, out of 26 mulwels and 26 rays shall give to the ship one mulwel and one ray, and if it has not one kind of fish shall give two fishes[1]. And if it has a merlynge and another fish, he shall give the half of one sort and the other half of the other sort; and if the whole (is) of merlyngs he shall give 26 merlyngs and as to the boat a halfpenny. A Hocschip of Flanders gives the same custom as to fish, and as to the ship 11*d.* if it happen in the soke of Bridge Street. A mangbot gives the same custom as to (fish)[2]. And he who brings sprats shall give a tandle of sprats except those who are of the city of London who shall not give custom, and as to the ship a farthing.

The ship which brings mackerel shall give 26 mackerel, to wit that which owes full custom.

The ship which brings fish in dossers, the serjeant (*seruiens*) shall take out of each dosser one fish, except these fishes, Mulwel, Ray, congre, dory, turbot, "bars," shads, and red mullet. In the same way out of dossers which come by land and by horsecarriage a halfpenny, those which owe custom.

A Welk-boat out of 5 tandles, shall give at least one tandle with a plack[3] and if it has more than five tandles it shall not give more, and as to the boat a halfpenny.

A boat which carries dabs shall give out of a hundred 26 dabs and

---

[1] Apparently two fishes of different kinds are meant.
[2] Word lost because of hole in parchment.
[3] ?Whether this is plaice (or placo, a coin).

although it have more it shall not give more. And if it come in dossers it shall give out of every dosser one.

A Merfwyn (? mereswyne = dolphin) shall give a penny, and if the heart is taken out[1] the bailiff shall have the inward part with the tail and fins in the town.

A congre which comes to the water the bailiff shall have one of the best and another, next best for his money as shall happen in the buying. And if it sails with tholes[2] shall give a halfpenny, and if it sails in "Or-lokes"[3] shall give a penny. And if it is of the Cinque Ports it shall not give money.

An oyster boat which sails with tholes shall give a halfpenny and if with "Orlokes" a penny.

A ship of Scotland which brings salmon, 2 salmons: if salmon and mulwel, a salmon and a mulwel; if salmon and haddock, one salmon and 13 haddocks: if all haddocks, 26 haddocks: if all herrings 100 herrings except red herrings, and the ship shall give 11d.

The first boat which comes from Gernemuth (Yarmouth) with herring which owes full custom shall give 200 herrings, which come...[4] which owe custom shall give 100 herrings.

From the cart which brings salmon the bailiff shall take 1 salmon according to the best or second best and from the cart 2d. And if it bring mackerel it shall give 5 mackerel; and if it bring merling it shall give 5 merlings: and if it bring herrings it shall give 5 herrings, and the cart 2d: and if it bring eels, nothing of the fish, but from the cart 2d.

From the cart which comes to the market, the bailiff of the fish-mongers shall have a fish but no money, except in Bridge Street and in the fishmarket[5] towards the west.

A ship with a scaltre[6] which stays[7] shall give 2d. and a ship with "beilis" (? = bills or beak) which stays[7] shall give 1d. And if they do not stay shall give nothing.

He who brings land fish after supper may well be allowed to house his fish and on the morrow to sell it in the due place.

Whoever finds anyone of the halmote selling fish without the stated bounds, may well be allowed to take the fish thus bought although for-feited and he shall have the half of the fish and the bailiff the other half.

No stockfishmonger or apprentice or other carrier ought to enter a ship to buy fish before they are called.

No stranger ought to buy of a stranger.

No stranger ought to enter any Welk-boat unless called, and the sailor or he to whom the Welks belong ought to measure them.

No one ought to sell fish retail upon the Quay.

No one may carry welks cooked to sell in the streets without losing his welks and under pain of a heavy amercement.

---

[1] *Sicardatur* suggests the cleaning and cutting up of the fish.
[2] Thole pins.
[3] Rowlocks.
[4] Word lost.
[5] *piscenaria.*
[6] A pole used for oar or rudder.
[7] *que sedet.*

In 1363 different traders made a present of money to the king. The butchers at the Stokkes contributed £6[1].

The following is a translation from *Letter-Book G*, f. 158 b. A reference is published in *Letter-Book G*, p. 194. The letter is without date, but others on the same page are of 39 Edward III (1365).

The King to the parson of Wolchirchhawe.

The King to Richard parson of the Church of St. Mary of Wol-chirchhawe greeting. We have received a complaint from the Wardens of our Bridge of London, containing that although cognizance of pleas of the lay fee in our kingdom especially belong to our crown and dignity: and that you claiming that the stalls and benches at the Stokkes in the City of London whose issues and rents from ancient times are annexed to the repair and maintenance of the foresaid Bridge ought to belong to you and to your church, on your own authority without process of any law have intruded yourself into the same: and because the said Wardens have demised to farm to certain men the stalls and benches which from ancient time have remained annexed to the same Bridge and at the dis-posal of the same Wardens have fulminated and intend to fulminate sentence of excommunication against them and the foresaid farmers to the injury of our crown and dignity and the grave damage of the same wardens and farmers and against the law and custom of our kingdom. And because we do not will that cognizance of pleas of the lay fee in our said kingdom by the fulmination of such sentences shall in any way be lessened we forbid you under the penalty which is incumbent that you attempt anything which may tend to our prejudice or to the hurt of our crown and royal dignity or presume to attempt in any way, recalling without delay the sentence if any for this reason by you or by your com-mand has been fulminated; for we shall be ready to show you in our court full and swift justice concerning the premises. Witness etc.

Several of the meetings of the Court of Common Council were held in the Upper Chamber of the Guildhall and are men-tioned during the 14th century, the building referred to is the old Guildhall; the present building was not completed until 1422. This subject was dealt with by the author in a lecture reported in the *Journal of the Royal Society of Arts*, June 3rd, 1910.

On July 25th, 1370, a man was condemned to stand in the pillory for three hours for cutting off the purse or hanging bag of a woman at "les Stokkes"[2].

On July 25th, 1374, the course of the Walbrook was leased for seven years to a "brewere," of the Moor on

---

[1] Riley's *Memorials*, p. 314.   [2] *Ibid.* p. 264.

condition that he kept the course clean[1]. Rent nil, he taking for every latrine built upon the course 12 pence yearly, he to keep anything of value he might find in the course[2].

The following is translated from the French original, it is dated 31st October, 1380, there is a note only in *Letter-Book H*, p. 156.

BECAUSE the Streets about the City of London are broken and impaired to the great damage and Nuisance of People, Horses & Carts passing such ways, the which necessarily require to be amended; We charge and command that you levy or cause to be levied from one day to another, commencing from the day of making these (Presents) unto the end of one year next following, fully to be completed. The Underwritten customs, of things coming or going through the gate where you are dwelling, and the suburbs thereof, to wit, of every Horse load with any manner of vendible thing, one Farthing. Of any cart load with any vendible thing, one penny. Of every cart load with loam, gravel or sand for every twelfth time, one penny. Of every cart bringing dung or rubbish out of the said Franchise every week, Four pence. Of every Man or Woman's Package beyond the value of five shillings, one Farthing, wool skits and wool fells always excepted. Of every Horse, Heifer, Ox and Cow vendible, one farthing. And to cause the money thence arising to be delivered to the Chamberlain at London under the seal of the office of Mayoralty the last day of October in the fourth year of the Reign of our Lord the King Richard the second.

On July 20th, 1382, a petition was made that strangers who brought fish to the city might stand at "les Stokkes" as of old accustomed[3].

On 15th August, 1382, there was a petition to the Mayor, Aldermen and Common Council assembled in the Upper Chamber of the Guildhall by the commoners of the said Common Council that Adam Carlelle, late alderman, had abused the strange fishmongers whilst selling their fish at the Stokkes, and praying that he might be debarred from holding any public office in the city and from wearing a livery. The prayer was granted[4]. This is more fully set out in Riley's *Memorials*, p. 468, etc.; it is stated that "Adam in a haughty and spiteful manner, cursed the said strangers." Later on Adam Carlelle caused the whole sentence to be null and void.

On October 30th, 1382, the servant of a "stok fisshmongere" was found standing among foreigners (*i.e.* men who were not freemen of the city) selling herrings at six for a penny like

---

[1] *Letter-Book G*, p. 324.   [2] Riley's *Memorials*, p. 379.
[3] *Letter-Book H*, ff. 193–4.   [4] *Ibid.* p. 197.

a foreigner, although he had bought them the day before at Billyngesgate at 22 for a penny. His master confessed the man did it according to his orders, consequently the master was sent to prison for forty days, and further condemned to stand in the pillory at Cornhulle for an hour with some of the herrings hanging from his neck[1].

On May 6th, 1383, it was decided that the Aldermen of the Wards of Colemanstret, Bradstret, Shepe, Walbrok, Vintry, and Douegate, should take steps to prevent the watercourse of the Walbrok from becoming stopped by refuse, etc.[2]

On June 24th, 1384, it was decided to consider whether the Wardens of the Bridge should receive help with regard to the building "les Stokkes," which yearly paid £60 and more for the maintenance of the bridge, being occupied by foreigners, who paid nothing towards the Bridge or to anything else[3].

In July, 1384, the oath of those elected to the Common Council was considered, the grant to Henry Waleys is referred to, and the building called "le Stokkes," and the letters patent of May 4th, 1282, the rental being devoted to the maintenance of London Bridge, and it was decided to continue the custom[4].

March 1st, 1386–7, a proclamation was made appointing the places for foreign drapers to sell cloth, and mentioning the Stokkes[5].

On October 28th, 1407, a proclamation was made forbidding the sale of fish or flesh by retail except at Le Stokkes and four other markets[6].

On February 27th, 1408–9, a proclamation was made forbidding the sale of certain fish except at "lez estokkes" and two other markets[7].

On December 9th, 1409, a proclamation was made forbidding the sale of certain fish except at "lestokkes" and four other markets[8].

On February 26th, 1434–5, there was a grant of an annual rent of £50 charged on the great tenement called "les Stokkes" and other property assigned to the use of London Bridge[9].

[1] *Letter-Book H*, pp. 202–3. [2] *Ibid.* p. 216.
[3] *Ibid.* p. 234. [4] *Ibid.* pp. 242–3.
[5] *Ibid.* p. 301. [6] *Letter-Book I*, p. 61.
[7] *Ibid.* p. 71. [8] *Ibid.* p. 82.
[9] *Letter-Book K*, p. 180.

The following is extremely interesting as it is an early reference to the easement of right to light, it is referred to in *Letter-Book K*, p. 267. The original is in Latin.

Common Council Monday 5 March 20 Henry VI [1441–2]

It is considered that the Mayor shall takine to him 4 Aldermen and 4 commoners whom he thinks best, to treat with the Rector and parishioners of the Church of Wolchurche lest in building their church they hinder[1] the lights of the City's house called the Stokkys and to compensate somewhat the said rector and parishioners in their work for the cause aforesaid as shall seem expedient to them.

18 April 20 Henry VI [1442]

Bridgemasters to receive of the Chamberlain £20 of money in his custody to be paid to the Rector of Woolchurch for having a space of 15 feet between the Church and the Stocks (*Journal* 3, f. 90 b).

On 19th April, 1442, a deed printed below was signed stating the two Masters of London Bridge should contribute to the rebuilding of the Church on condition that the vestry adjoining the Stokkes at the east end of the Church should be pulled down, and a new north wall erected 15 feet away from the Stokkes Market building, so as not to obstruct the lights of the market, they further grant an easement of a footway from the east end of the Stokkes and thence under the parsonage to the "Pultrie[2]."

> A Composition between the parson and Wardens of Saint Mary Wolchurch and the Wardens of the Brigge for the saving of the lightes of the stokkes in the byldyng of the seyd Church and vestiare of the same.

To alle People these present lettres endented seyng or heryng John Skipton Parson of the Churche of oure Lady of Woolchurch beside the Stokkes of London John Bracy Chaundeler and Thomas Cook the yonger draper Citezeins of London Wardens od the Workes and godes of the same Churche, John Sturgeon Mercer John Humbre Brewer, Henri Brai, draper, Richard Hakedye Grocer and John Frost Mercer Citezeins of London and parisshens of the same Churche sende gretung in oure lorde. For so moche as the saide oure Churche beyng now old and feble and stondyng nye the Walle of the Courne Market place of the said Citie called the Stokkes afore said stoppyng gretely the lightis therof We purposyng the Churche to do drawe doune and of newe to edifie and make agene in hasty tyme had ordeyned to have do sette the walle of the same newe edifying more utter toward the Northe as ferre as oure

[1] *Offendant.*   [2] *Letter-Book K*, p. 272.

Churchawe grounde ther streccheth joynyng even to the forseid walle of
the seid market place called the Stokkes en enlargyng of oure Churche
and savynge of more grounde of oure Churche hawe of the southside of
oure said Churche. Whiche byldyng should have be cause of more stoppyng of the lightes of the same marketplace. Nevirtheles We the said
Parson Wardens and parishens of the said Churche beyng entreted by
the worshipfull persones Maire Aldermen and Commoners of London
to favour and save the lightes of the same Marketplace to the beteryng
of the same place in yelding and arreysing therof more availe and revennes
yerely to the beter sustentacion of the Brigge of London. To the whiche
the same place called the Stokkes and revennes therof bilongen and
yerely perteynen. And for a certenne competent somme of money by
Thomas Cook the elder Draper and John Herst Skynner Citezenes of
London now maisters of the said brigge of London by avise and assent of
the said Maire and Aldermen and Commoners of London to us the said
Person Wardens and parisshenis of the seid church toward the newe edifying and makyng of the same aforhande the day of makyng herof yoven and
paied have granted and these oure present lettres by comune assent of all
people of the saide parisshe herto gadered and aggreed for us and oure
successours have confermed to Robert Clopton nowe Maire of London
and to the Comunalte of the same Citee to the use of the seid brigg for
the encresyng kepyng and savyng of the lightes of the seid place called the
Stokkes, that is for to say that we the seid parson Wardeyns and parisshens
shall before the Fast of Pentecost which shall be in the yere of our Lord
mccccxliijth do drawe doune the vestiarie of our saide Churche the whiche
vestiarye late was of newe made and ther stondeth now atte the Est end
of oure saide Church joynyng to the wall of the Stokkes and that we
shall byfore ye saide Fest of Pentecost do arrase vy the North walle of
oure saide chirche there of newe to be made within the saide oure olde
Churche above the grounde in height of a fote in lengthe from the Est
end of the same Chirche doune to the parsonage of the same in the West
lxxij fote of assise Which new Northewalle so to be arreised shall be sette
from the seid Walle of the Stokkes xv fote in space of brede bytwne the
said walle of the said Stokkes and the same newe walle strecchyng all the
lengthe of lxxij fote aforesaid countyng the same space of xv fete betwene
bothe the said walles above the Water Tables of the same Walles. So
that afterward whan the same newe North Wall of our said Chirche is
full arreised and made up we shall do throwe doune to the grounde the
seid old North Walls of our said Chirche now ther stondyng so nye the
seid Walle of the said Stokkes. And ther we shall leve the said space of xv
fote of brede bytwene the said Wall of the Stokkes and oure saide newe
Walle in all the said lengthe perpetually in savyng of the seid lightes above
and bynethe of the seid place called the Stokkes all the said lengthe of
lxxii fete duryng To have and to holde and to rejoyse the easementes of
all maner lightes shewyng and comyng in atte all maner wyndowes made
and to be made above and bynethe in the seid Wall of the said Stokkyes
yoynyng to the said Churchawe duryng the lengthe aforsaide in maner
and fourme above declared to the forseid Maire and Comunalte and to her

successours to the use aforsaid for evirmore withoute eny lettyng or en-
pechement of us the said Parson Wardens and parisshens or eny of vs or
of oure successours and with oute eny maner thing there to be sett vp
and edified by us or eny of vs or for vs or eny of oure successours within
the seid bred of xv fete bytwene the said walles above or bynethe duryng
the seid lengthe in stoppyng or appeiryng of the seid lightes or eny part
therof in eny tyme comyng. Also we have graunted for vs and oure successours that there shall be a comune fote way perpetuelly by daylight to
go be and thorgh as oute of the Strete at the Estend of the said Stokkys
and the seid owre Churche of nowe to be made and edified ledyng vnto
the ground under the seid parsonage and so under the same parsonage
into the strete called the Pultrie ther by the way and posterne now vsede
vnder the same parsonage in recompense of that foteway which heretofore hath be vsed and zit it on the Southeside of the said olde Chirche
bytwene the Chirchehawe and the same Chirche and that way on the
south side of the said Chirche and to be shette vy and closed therfore and
the seid foteway bytwene the seid Chirche and Stokkes to serve and to be
occupied in the stede of the same by dailight onely ans on myghtes tyme
to be shote like as the seid other way on ye Southeside is nowe and hathe
be vsed heretofore In witnesse of the whiche thyng to the on partie of
thes lettres endented toward the seid now Maire and Comunalte of
London remaynyng We the said Parson Wardens and parisshens of the
seid Chirche have sette ourseal and to that other part of these lettres endented to vs bylenyng the forseide Maire and Comunalte have do sette
the comune seal of the saide Citee of London. Wreten at London the
xix day of April the yere of the Regne of Kyng Henry the sixt after the
conquest the xx^{the}.

On July 22nd, 1444, a petition was presented to the Common Council complaining that people passing by the "pultrie"
and the "stokkes" and the main streets found the smell of
"Swannes gees heronsewes," etc., kept in the houses a great
nuisance, and suggesting they might be kept in "oute weyes
niggh London Wall" and elsewhere[1].

On November 6th, 1450, there was a grant of £20 for a
term of five years made to a late warden of London Bridge,
charged on "le stokkes," etc.[2]

The Church of St Stephen Walbrook is on the south side
of the Mansion House, divided from it by a narrow footway,
and the following extract is from Guildhall MS. No. 1056.

Indenture made—October 1484: between Richard Leesqwyer
patron of the parish Church of St. Stephen in Walbrook of London, and
Mayster John Sutton parson of the same and Roger Grove and John
Mason churchwardens of the same of the one party and William Bufford

[1] *Letter-Book K*, p. 289. [2] *Ibid.* p. 332.

citizen and mercer of London dwelling in a tenement in Berebynder Lane in the parish of our Lady of Wolchirche of London: "the said tenement abutting upon the Churchyard of St. Stephen's aforesaid on the north side," of the other party: witnessing that the said patron parson and churchwardens licence the repair of a stone wall $15\frac{1}{2}$ foot in length and 3 ft. thick, at the south end of his tenement abutting on St. Stephen's churchyard, and when newly built to have two windows in it to let light into W. Bufford's tenement.

The following is translated from Latin. It is referred to in *Letter-Book L*, p. 239.

Common Council Thursday 1st February
2 Henry VII (1486–7).

At this council it was agreed by Sir Henry Colet mayor etc. that Master John Archer rector of the Parish Church of B. Mary of Wolchirch and his successors shall have and receive yearly the sum of 4 marcs forever from the commonalty of the City of London by the hands of the custodians of the Bridges of London for the *lower part* of the Stocks where the fishmongers and butchers sell their victuals and that there shall be made thereof a real composition and that Master William shall be proctor of the City in the same cause and that he shall have authority under the common seal.

The following are from the Guildhall *Repertories*.

4 July 21 Henry VII (1506).

It is agreed by Mayor and Aldermen that every inhabitant within the Stocks occupying stalls to sell flesh shall pay towards the
marc   parcel of vii marks late granted to the king 40.*s.* Provided always that this act shall be (no?) preceded hereafter to bind future inhabitants and occupiers nor the Bridge master. *Repert.* I, f. 171.

22 Feb: 13 Henry VII (1497–8).

Mr. Colet etc Aldermen Robert Wiston and other "comeners" appointed to see where the Sesperall shall be made for the water that now runneth at the Stocks. *Repert.* I, f. 34 b.

14 May 1 Henry VIII (1509).

Whereas Robert Coke butcher for many years hath occupied stalls and standings in the Stockkes and hath well and truly paid for the same until now of late he hath withdrawn himself and his flesh and selleth the same in the suburbs without the liberty of the City and in the country, and occupieth no stall or standing in the Stokkes whereby the same stand "in manner desolate to the common hurte of this Cite" it is agreed that he shall either keep a *standing* and a *room* at the Stockkes or else be disenfranchised at the next common council. *Repert.* II, f. 89 b.

The following note with reference to St Stephen Walbrook is from Guildhall Library MS. No. 1056.

The will of Thomas Reede, citizen and Paynter steyner of London dated 6 January 1508.

I bequethe etc....my body to be buryede in the Aley of the Church-yerde of the Parish Church of Seint Stephyn in Walbroke of London without the Est Dore of the precession way of the same church....

This procession way was probably entered from Bearbinder Lane.

The following are further extracts from the Guildhall *Repertories*.

9 August 4 Henry VIII [1512]

At this Court it is decreed that no butchers shall keep open shop to sell flesh after Thursday next coming without the old bounds of the "Shamells of East Chepe" and St Nicholas Shambles and that no Butcher occupy any board within the Stockkes after Thursday next without licence from the lord Mayor upon pain of imprisonment. *Repert.* II, f. 138 b.

21 Sept. viz. St. Mathew's day 4 Henry VIII [1512]

Whereas variances have lately been depending between Water Maykyn Draper and James Apot grocer dwellyng togedir ayenst the Stocks in the parish of St Marie Wolchurch in Bradstrete ward for laying their wares such as cloth and other merchandise upon their several stalls next the streets' ends it is awarded by this court that the said Water shall hereafter lay his cloth and ware upon his stall as high as the bar of iron fastened at the overend upon the post set between the parties aforesaid and the said James Apot to lay his wares upon his stall in like wise and of like height. *Repert.* II, f. 141.

31 July 1 Henry VIII [1509]

Mr. Copynger and Mr. Monnox aldermen and the Chamberlain of this City with the plumber are appointed to view both the waste water running from the Great Conduit in Cheap and that from the Stokkys and to report to this court to what place of this city it should be thought most convenient fot the common weal of the same for the same waste water to be conveyed. *Repert.* II, f. 71 b.

Monday 5 May (1520)

It is agreed by this court that the Pageant devised by Rastall to stand at the Litill Conduit by the Stokkes shall go forth and take effect. So always that the charges thereof exceed not xv*l*. *Repert.* v, f. 285.

4 June 16 Henry VIII [1524]

At this Court came Hertwell and Emery two of the inhabitants of the ward of Cornhill and exhibited a bill concerning the corner tenament that Bulkeley now dwelleth in by the Stokkys and they say that the said tenement is "nowe altreate[1] and transposyd than yt was" at the tyme of

---

[1] Altered.

the decree thereof made in the time of Mr. Acheley Mayor 4 July 4 Henry VIII, and they desire that the king's inquest may inquire upon the premises. Whereupon it is agreed that the said inquest shall see the decree and receive such evidence as Hertwell and Emery shall produce. *Repert.* VI, f. 105 b.

Tuesday 12 December (1524)

John Hyggins, John Dyngley and Andrew Austen butchers to have all the house of the Stokkys which has been used for butchers from the feast of Easter next for the term of 7 years paying the old rent yearly, "viz, 16.*s.* 1*d.* weke[1]" provided that if they "leve their sayd lees" during the term, they give the Bridge master a year's warning. *Repert.* VII, f. 73.

Tuesday 22 January (1525)

At this Court J. Hyggins, Dyngley and Austen butchers (as above) came, the bridge-master having complained of them for their rent of the Stocks being behind. Hyggins and Dyngley would have then given warning "to leve the same and Andrew Austen would not And so they have respyte till Shroftyde to know their myndes." *Repert.* VII, f. 263 b.

Tuesday 24 Oct. (1525)

At this court came Stephen Warde "wexer" and John Clerke Draper desiring aid of the Court for the mending of the little Conduit at the Stokkes for water to be had there. The chamberlain is commanded to view and report on the same to the Court. *Repert.* VII, f. 65.

7 April 1527.

At this courte it is agreed that the Bridge master and the Renter of the Bridge shall assess every borde what the bochers shall pay for every borde in the Stokkes and that they shall provide for viii persons to take all the xvi bordes there and that they shall lett the same to them by endenture. *Repert.* VII, f. 254 b.

As the Letter-Books are only published as far as *L*, I give the following extract from *Letter-Book O*, dated 1527:

Spencer Maior

VII° die Aprilis[2]

Item at this daye it is agreed that the Brigge master and the renter of the Bridge shall assesse everyborde what the bochers shall paye for every borde in the Stokkes And that they shall provide for VIII persons to take all the XVI bordes there and that they shall lett the same to them by indenture.

---

[1] ?Whether weekly intended.
[2] The year not given otherwise than by name of the Mayor.

The following are extracts from the *Repertories*:

Monday[1]   of July 26 Henry VIII [1534]

At this court it is agreed that for the oversight of the markets for selling of flesh according to the statue provided that 2 upper wardens of the drapers calling to them five of their own company 2 of them to be at the Stokkis, 2 at St. Nicholas Fleshambles, two at East-Chepe and own at Ledynhall and divers officers to wait on them (*sic* unfinished). *Repert.* IX, f. 64.

Lune vi. die Julii aº xxvi. Hen. viii. (1534)

AT thys Coʳte for the oversight of the mkett for sellyng of flesshe accordyng to the estatuyt yn that case ordeignyd & prvyded It ys agreed that twoo upper Wardeyns of the Draps callyng to theym fyve other of theyre owne company twoo of theym to be at the Stokks twoo at Saynt Nycholas flesshambles twoo at estchepe & one at Ledynhall there to remayne betwene fyve & six of the clokke in the mornyng and there to contynue for the tyme folowyng that ys for to say upon Mondayes & Wednesdays from six of the clokke afore noone of the same dayes tyll ix of the clokke then next folowyng upon Tuysdayes & Thursdayes from six of clokke on the mornyng tyll ix of the clokke then next ensuyng and at after noone of the same dayes from three of the clokke tyll fyve of the clokke than next folowyng and upon Saturdayes from vi of the clokke afore noone of the same dayes tyll ix of the clokke than next folowynge and after noone from iiii of the clokke tyll vii than next folowyng and this order to be obs'vyd yᵉ next weke by the me'cers yᵉ iiiᵈᵉ weke by yᵉ grocers & yᵉ iiii weeke by the Goldsmythes And twoo officers of my lorde the Mayer three officers of the one Shryeff & three officers of the other Shryeff to awayt upon the sayd coïers at the Stokks ii of the Shryeffs officers at Saynt Nicholas flesshambles ii of the Shryeffs officers at Est-chepe and twoo other of the Shryeffs officers at Ledynhall ev'y officer to have a whyte rodde yn hys hande conteignyng yn lenght twoo yardes the sayd officers to awayte upon the sayd coïers by the space of one hole moneth next ensuyng and the sayd coïers to awayt at the place above appoynted by the space of one hole weeke nowe next folowyng And the said Coïers to be chaungyd ev'ry weeke And the sayd officers to be chaungyd ev'ry moneth The sayd Coïers to have full power & authorytie to see the ma'ket well & truely kept and the transgressors & offenders punysshed yn lyke manᵉʳ case and condicon as my lorde mayer & my maisters the Shryeffs were there present after the discrecon of the sayd Coïers And it is further ordered that the Wardeyns of the Me'cers the next corte here to be holden shall certifye thys corts yn wrytynge of the names of suche of theyre company as shall survey the m'rkett aforesayd the next weeke ensuyng And yn lyke mannᵉʳ the second weeke next

---

[1] Blank in MS.

ensuyng the Wardeyns of the Grocers and after theym the Wardeyns of the Goldsmythes and soo weekely the other craft after theyre degress yn order tyll an other order be takyn yn by half. *Repert.* IX, f. 64 b.

Thursday 9 July 26 Henry VIII [1534]

Item that Master Wardens of the Mercers have certified this court the names of certain of their company that shall survey the markets this next week ensuing that is to say:—

Nicholas Lewson			Robert Pakyngton	
Thomas Burnell	Mercers		William Gresham	Mercers
Robert Palmer			William Robyns	
William Lokke				

Repert. IX, f. 65 b.

23 July 26th year.

Item the Wardens of the Grocers have certified this Court the names of certain of their company that shall survey the markets of this City for this next week ensuing that is to say:

Thomas Bowyer	John Lane	
William Laxton	Roger Pynchester	Grocers
William Bodeley	William May	
Richard Osborne		

Repert. IX, f. 68 b.

Thursday 11 March 26 Henry VIII [1534–5]

Item that the wardens of grocers upon Easter Eve next coming shall oversee the markets for selling of flesh for one whole week then next following.

Item that all foreign butchers and that other that bring flesh to London to be sold shall from time to time "bringe the talowgh with the Karkeys of the same." *Repert.* IX, f. 99.

Tuesday 23 January 28 Henry VIII [1536–7]

Item at the instance of Mr. William Forman Alderman who made request that Edward Typpyng citizen and haberdasher of London whall have a lease of the Stocks after the lease of Robert Smyth fishmonger expired, which is dated 14 Sept. 19 Henry VIII, it is agreed that Typpyng shall have the same for 10 years in like manner as R. Smyth now holdeth paying £20 yearly: for which grant Typpyng has promised to pay £5 for an income toward the reparations of the Bridge. *Repert.* IX, f. 237 b.

Tuesday 16 April 28 Henry VIII [1537]

Item to the letters of Lord Beauchamp for a lease of the fisshe market of the Stokkes "in the favour of Robert Smyth his servant it is answered that it is granted already which if it had not been granted the same should have been granted afore this time" at the contemplation of the Duke of Norfolk but the same was past afore." *Repert.* IX, f. 247.

Thursday 19 April 28 Henry VIII [1537]

Item it was fully agreed by this Court by their whole assents and consents at the instance of Mr. Forman alderman that Edward Typpyng haberdasher shall have a lease to him made by the Bridgemasters of London or otherwise for his more surety for term of ten years to begin immediately after the lease expired of Robert Smyth fishmonger, which lease is made of the Stocks in the parish of St. Mary Wolchurche dated 14 Sept. 19 Henry VIII and of all that pertaineth to the Stocke, Typpyng to have the same in the same manner as R. Smyth occupieth, paying yearly to the said Bridge masters, their attorney or successors £20. For which grant Typpyng has promised to pay £5 sterling for an income towards the repairs of the Bridge, of his benevolence; which the Bridge-masters acknowledge themselves to have received. *Repert.* ix, f. 248.

Tuesday 6 June 34 Henry VIII [1542]

It is agreed that the inhabitants of the Parish of our Ladye of Wool-churche shall pay wholly of themselves for this present time the XVth due from that parish and that the butchers and fishmongers standing in the Stokkys within the said parish shall be utterly discharged thereof unless the said inhabitants can hereafter prove that the said butchers and fishmongers of right ought to pay any part thereof than such part shall be truly repaid to them to the inhabitants by order of this Court. *Repert.* x, f. 260.

The following is from *Letter-Book O*, f. 71 b, and is quoted by Stow (vol. 1, p. 226, Kingsford's edition):

At this time there were in the Stocks Markets for Fishmongers 25 Boards or Stalls rented yearly to £34. 13. 4. There were for Butchers 18 Boards or Stalls, rented at £41: 16: 4. and there were also Chambers above, rented at £5: 13: 4. In all £82: 3: –.

The following are extracts from the *Repertories*, and un-published Letter-Books.

Thursday 1 February 34 Henry VIII [1542–3]

At this court Sir Rowland Hyll knight and Alderman made his report in writing concerning the certainty of the rent of the Stocks and chambers in the Stocks as hereafter ensueth:—

Item Imprimus in the Fysshe Stokkys xxv boides paying wekelye xiij.*s.* iiij*d.* sum the hole yere   xxxiiij.*li.* xiij.*s.* iiij*d.*

Item the flesshe stokkys xviij bordes xvj.*s.* j.*d* a weke sum the yere   xlj.*li.* xvi.*s.* iiij.*d.*

Item XV chambers   v.*li.* xiij.*s.* iiij.*d.*

Item it is this day ordered by the court here that the Brigemasters and the assessors of the XVth within the parish of Our Lady Wool-churche shall for this present year assess the whole inhabitants, and occupyers of the Stokkys as indifferently as they can by their discretions towards the payment of the XVth with the inhabitants of the said parish, so that they rate not them in the whole above xl.*s.* Further that the inhabitants and occupiers of the Stokkys shall at all times here after be contributory with the inhabitants of the ward of Walbroke towards the payment of every xvth at any time hereafter within the City to be levied gathered and paid at for and with the payment of 40.*s.* and not above. *Repert.* x, f. 306 b. *Vide* also *Letter-Book Q,* f. 71 b.

Thursday 15 May 36 Henry VIII [1544]

Item forasmuch as the Butchers of the City "blynded in averyce and syngular geyne and lucre" have now of late enhanced the prices of all kinds of victuals that they meddle withal and put to sale, that not only the commons of the City and others repairing to the same have been greatly grieved thereby, but also the complaint thereof hath come to the King's most honourable council "to the no lytyll displaisure of the Lord Mayer and Aldermen" of the City. And the Wardens of the said Fellowship have not at any time hitherto seen the reasonable prices set by the Lord Mayor upon the said victuals observed and kept. It is therefore now enacted that John Rouse George Elyott (and six others named) mercers severyng themselves by the number of two into four companies shall give attendance upon Saturday next coming from 6 o'clock in the morning until 11 o'clock in the forenoon, and from 1 o'clock to 5 o'clock in the afternoon of the same day, in every of the flesh markets hereafter mentioned, that is to say St. Nicholas Shambles the Stocks, Leadenhall and Eastcheap, and that they and every of them give like attendance in every of the same several markets according to their division and allotment upon Monday Tuesday Wednesday and Thursday then next ensuing in every of the forenoons of the same days, diligently surveying and foreseeing that no person or persons within any of the said markets transgress or break at any time the prices of the flesh there to be sold, hereafter rated: that is, the pound of beef from Christmas to Midsummer for $\frac{3}{4}d.$: the pound of mutton 1*d.*: the pound of veal $\frac{3}{4}d.$ and half a farthing; and from Midsummer the pound of beef for a halfpenny and $\frac{1}{2}$ farthing. Mutton for 1*d.* the pound of veal for 1*d.* the best lamb for 2.*s.*; the second lamb for 20.*d.* and the meanest for 16*d.* and the half of any such lamb and also the quarters after the same rate at all times of the year; and pork at all time of the year for $\frac{1}{2}d. \frac{1}{2}$ farthing the pound. And John Lane, William Butler etc. (six others named) grocers are likewise here nominated by the court to give like attendance upon Saturday then next ensuing in every of the said Markets and also upon every of the other four days afore reherse then next ensuing in like manner and semblable entent in every point as the said John Rouse and his companions are assigned to do. *Repert.* xi, f. 70.

Thursday 9 Sept 38 Henry VIII [1546]

It is agreed that the act made in the Mayoralty of Sir John Cotes concerning the payment of 40*s.* by the tenants farmers and inhabitants of the Stocks towards every XVth paid by the parishioners of St. Mary Woolchurche shall be void, and the said sum of 40*s.* from henceforth shall towards every XVth to be levied be paid by the Bridgemasters of the City and not by the farmers and occupiers of the Stocks. *Repert.* XI, f. 283. (See also *Letter-Book Q*, f. 185 b.)

Item it is this day enacted by the Court that no manner of butcher or butchers either free of the City of foreign, shall from henceforth utter or sell any kind of flesh either in Newgate Market, Chepside, Graschurch market or in the open street at Leadenhall, but only in the common market places of the City of ancient time appointed, viz. St. Nicholas Shambles, in the Stocks in Eastcheap and in no other places in the City. And that all and every foreign butcher or butchers or other persons, being foreign, desiring to bring any maner of beef mutton veal pork or lamb to the City to be sold shall from henceforth sell the same at certain stalls and places appointed for them in Leadenhall and that only on Wednesdays and Saturdays in the forenoon and not after 12 o'clock of either day, the market bell being rung and in no other places upon pain of forfeiture of the flesh so sold or put to sale contrary to this act either by freeman or foreigner. Provided always that it shall be lawful for all women and market folks and victuallers not being butchers repairing to this City with butter cheese fruit and other victuals to be put to sale in Newgate market Cheapside and Grasechurch market veale pork bacon "sowse" and such things as in time past hath been accustomed notwithstanding this present Act. *Repert.* XI, f. 283 (see also *Letter-Book Q*, f. 186, f. 208).

Thursday 15 Sept 1 Edward VI [1547]

Item the Wardens of the butchers have day over until the next Court here to make a direct answer whether they and their fellowship will take the whole flesshe market place at the Stokkes in ferm of the City or not. And they were also enjoined straitly to admonish all their fellowship to order the entrails of beasts which they usually cast into the River of Thames better than they now do "and not to anoye the same Ryver therewyth eny more" upon the peril that may ensue according to the law. *Repert.* XI, f. 347.

Monday 9 Sept 3 Edward VI [1549]

Item for certeyn urgent considerations and causes movying this courte yt is this day orderyd and agreed that lyke survey shalbe wekely had and made over the bochers put any fleshe to sell within the IIII common markett places appoynted within this cytie for the same by VIII substantyal sad and discrete commoners of the XII most chiefest companyes of this Cytie to be appoynted wekelye by the several wardeyns of the same companyes as was had and except in Maye in the last tyme of the Mayoraltye of Sir Rauf Waren knight to surveye and see that they truely obey and observe all such pryces from tyme to tyme as the lord Mayor for the tyme being shall sett upon their fleshe. And that the felowship of the Fyshemongers shall upon Wednysday nexte comynge begynne to make the said survey. And that daye seven night VIII of the Company of the Mercers to do the lyke And so furthe orderlye lyke number of the rest of the said XII companes to do lyke servyce and attendannce there

PLATE VI

VIEW OF THE STOCKS MARKET, ST STEPHEN'S CHURCH, ETC.

Drawn by Nichols, engraved by Fletcher, published by T. Boydell, 1753

PLATE VII

VIEW OF THE STOCKS MARKET, LOOKING SOUTH
By kind permission of the Governors of the Bank of England

as their tourne shall come. And it is also orderes that they shall wekelye upon the frydaye give lyke attendannce in the III common fysshe markets for lyke intent and purpose and so to contynewe the same servyce untyll they shalbe thereof dyscharged by this courte. And that precept be made further to the Wardenns of the said companyes for the execution thereof. *Letter-Book R*, f. 32 b.

Friday 3 April 5 Edward VI [1551]

At this Court it was ordered that twelve sad and discreet commoners of every of the twelve chief companies of the City shall weekly by turn take pains to survey the four several flesh markets of the city viz. St. Nicholas Shambles Eastcheap the Stokks and Leadenhall, and there take order with the butchers and other persons putting flesh there to sell, that the buyers thereof may have as reasonable pennyworths thereof, and be as indifferently handled therein as they the surveyors "by their sad discretion and consciences" think that the sellers may afford the same. And for due execution of this order the Court presently appointed Barnard Jenyns etc. (twelve names) Skynners to be the said surveyors viz. two of them for the Stocks, four for Leadenhall and three to each of the other markets, there to give their attendance for the intent aforesaid from 6 o'clock in the morning daily (Sundays excepted) until 11 o'clock in the forenoon and from 1 o'clock to five o'clock in the afternoon from Saturday next coming in the morning until Thursday at night then next following, every one of them having in his hand a white rod of two foot long. And then the next Saturday in the morning like number of the company of the mercers to be named by the wardens to execute the said order. And from thenceforth like number of the rest as their turn shall come and of many of the said xij companies to be thereunto appointed as aforesaid by their wardens orderly to do the like as their turn shall come. And that this survey shall thus be continued till this court shall be otherwise advised. *Repert.* XII, pt. 2, f. 318.

Wednesday 20 January 5 Edward VI [1551-2]

Ordered that certain sad persons of every of the twelve chief companies of this City shall survey the flesh markets of this city in such course as they lately did until Shrovetide next and to see that the butchers there sell their meat at the appointed prices And the Fellowship of the Skinners shall begin the same survey on Saturday next in the morning. *Repert.* XII, pt. 2, f. 239.

Thursday 7 June 1 Mary [1554]

Item the ordering and letting of the house at the Stocks late in the occupation of "parson Johns" belonging to the Bridgehouse was solely referred to my Masters the Aldermen being surveyors of the same house. *Repert.* XIII, f. 168.

Thursday 24 March 4 & 5 Philip and Mary [1557-8]

Item it was granted this day that John Nycolls girdler shall have the flesh and fish market places commonly called the Stokes with all the chambers over the same by lease for 21 years next after the feast of the Nativity of St. John the Baptist next coming for the yearly rent of £61. 4s. 8d. and that the Bridge house shall at the City's charges bear all manner of reparation of the premisses during the said term. *Repert.* XIV, f. 18 b.

Friday 15 March 2 Elizabeth [1559–60]

At this court it was ordered that albeit the Company of Sadlers have in their hall lately made an order that no man in their company "should sett upon their stalles any wares to the shewe," yet it shall at all times be lawful for any of the said company of Sadlers without punishment to set out their ware on stalls "to the shewe" as in times past; and whereas the same company ordered that no person being free of the Company of Sadlers and not of the livery of the company should have more than one apprentice at once, this court orders that it shall be lawful for such person to have one other apprentice besides, after the first apprentice has served 4 years and not before. Item it was agreed that my lord Mayor with the Aldermen at 2 o'clock in the afternoon meet at the Grey Friars church and so proceed to view the most convenient places within the City for the Markets to be kept for "pultrye wares" as well for freemen as for foreigners and that there shall be a court of Aldermen holden on Monday next to consider the "pulters" and the prices of "pultrey wares."

Monday 19 March 2 Eliz.

At this court the bill concerning "pulters" and "pultrye wares" and other victuallers was agreed upon in every point and decreed to be put in speedy execution, the tenor whereof is entered in the journal of the lord Mayor. Abstract, *Repert.* XIV, f. 311–311 b.

Saturday 28 Sept. 2 Elizabeth [1560]

At this court after reading the Queen's letter to the lord Mayor to take order for the observance in the City of her Proclamation yesterday concerning the abatement of the valuation of "the base moneys comenly called testones and two pences"; it was agreed that Mr. Avenon and Mr. Baskerfeld Aldermen should forthwith repair to the Shambles in Eastcheap and assisted by two discreet persons of the Ironmongers' Company and two others of the Goldsmiths' Company whom the wardens of the two several companies were charged to send thither and view the said market this forenoon in such wise that the Butchers should honestly use themselves both in taking of the said money according to the valuation appointed by the proclamation and also in selling reasonable pennyworths of their victuals, or "ekee to committ them to ward."

And the like survey by 2 other aldermen and 2 persons out of two other companies of St. Nicholas Shambles and Leadenhall. And Mr. Cowper and Mr. Bankes were assigned to make a like survey forthwith of the market place at the Stockes and the wardens of the Grocers, vintners and Skinners to be here tomorrow for the like survey. Abstract, *Repert.* XIV, f. 383.

Tuesday 1st. Oct. 2 Elizabeth [1560]

Item it was ordered that like precepts shall be made out to the 12 head companies of the City to make like survey over the butchers in the four several flesh market places of this city and also the flesh markets as they were appointed to make in the second mayoralty of Mayor, Warren and in the mayoralty of Henry Amcotts knt. for uttering their victuals at reasonable prices. And that 2 of the company of Goldsmiths shall continually and daily assist the said surveyors in Every of the four markets "to take away such doutes contencion and stryfe as shall fortune to arise in any of the said markettes by reason of the vncertentye of eny coynes that shall ther fortune to be offered to be payed for eny of the said vytells." *Repert*. f. 384 b.

30 June 1569

It was ordered that the peace men shall every day in the weke except hollie dayes bringe there peace to be sold into Chepe side Newgate Markett Leaden hall and Grace Churche and the same to contynne vntill the Xth Auguste there to be sold and in no other place. *Repert*. xvi, f. 482 b.

Tuesday 18 June 19 Elizabeth [1576]

It was ordered that Sir Thomas Offeley etc. Aldermen shall confer with William Heynes Fishmonger concerning the request made by the Queen by her letters directed to this Court in the favour of the said William Heynes for a lease to him to be granted of "the Stockes in the powltry" and that they consider and peruse the lease heretofore made by this City unto one [1] Whyte. *Repert*. xix, f. 212.

Thursday 11 July 19 Elizabeth [1576]

Item it was granted by this Court that William Heynes fishmonger shall have a lease to him made of the City's house called the Stockes and of all the Chambers over the same for the term of 21 years and for the yearly rent of £56 4s. 8d. to be paid to the use of the Commonalty of this City, the same term to begin after the death of the widow of Raffe Whyte. And the said Wm. Heynes to covenant with the City not to put out any of the now tenants or occupiers, nor raise the rents of the now tenants "nor permytt or suffer any person to water any kynde of fysshe there" and at his proper costs to bear the reparations of the same premisses during the said term. *Repert*. xix, f. 220.

Tuesday 4 April 23 Elizabeth [1581]

Iten yt was orderyd that preceptes shalbe forthe wyth made and dyrected to thaldremen of the severall wardes of Langborne and Walbrooke to cawse all the Stalles in Lumberd Streete on bothe syde of the waye, betwzt St. Mary Wolchurche and the Stockes to be presentlye reformed in suche maner and forme as the stalles lately weare uppon London brydge and in Thamystreete. *Repert*. xx, f. 185.

---

[1] Blank in MS.

Tuesday 30 January 24 Elizabeth [1581-2]

Item yt was orderyd that M. Chamberleyn of thys Cyttye shall yearelye from henceforthe durynge the pleasure of thys courte paye vnto Symon Hearyng Goldsmith that ryngeth the Markett bell in Cheape Syde the somme of vj.*s.* viij.*d.* by the yeare at the fower tearmes or feastes of the yeare most vsuall vz. the feast of thannuncoacion of our Ladye, the feast of St John Baptyste St, Mychell Tharchangell and the byrthe of our Lord God by equall porcions, the fyrst payment to begynne at the feast of thannunciation of our Ladye next insuinge. *Repert.* xx, f. 283.

Tuesday XIX April 1586

Item Mr. Barne etc (3 others) aldermen are appointed by this court "to take paynes" to end the matter between Richard Wystone barber-surgeon and Mr. Robert Aske one of the Bridgemasters of this City touching the Greene yarde or else to make report. Abstract, *Repert.* xxi, f. 286

Thursday 28 April 28 Elizabeth [1586]

Item at this court Mr. Barne etc appointed (as above) make their report in writing the tenor whereof ensues: Whereas heretofore question hath grown between Robert Aske citizen and goldsmith of London and Richard Wystowe Barber-surgeon, keeper of Leadenhall, touching the Green Yard adjoining Leadenhall on the Eastside and the profits of the stalls hanging and standing in the Green yard. Robery Aske claiming the latter and profit of the Stalls hanging and standing thereon by grant of the Lord Mayor and this Court, as an entire thing distinct from the office and keepership of Leadenhall and Richard Wystowe claiming the same and the benefit of the stalls thereon as a member of Leadenhall and incident to the office of the keepership of that Hall; and whereas the Lord High Treasurer of England hath directed his letters to the court in behalf of Richard Wystowe, by occasion whereof and "for the great regard that this court hath of soe honorable a patron and favourer of the good estate of this Cyttye" they thought it good to make agreement between the parties by way of mediation rather than examine the rights of the grant of the keepership and the Green Yard to Aske, and therefore committed the ending of the matter to Mr. Barne etc., who make report that the parties are willing to submit themselves to the order of the court. Whereupon the court after long deliberation have decreed that Robert Aske and Richard Wistowe shall during their lives jointly and Richard Wistowe if he survive R. Aske during his life alone, shall occupy the office of keepership of Leadenhall and the Green-yard and shall take to their own use the profits of all stalls hanging and standing in the said Hall and Greenyard without any account to the Chamber of the City of London as here tofore accustomed, paying yearly to the chamber of London to the City's use for Leaden Hall three score and sixteen pounds 13.*s.* 4.*d.* in equal portions at the feasts of St. Michael and the Annunciation. But if Robert Aske survive R. Wistowe, as owing to grants in reversion of the keepership of Leadenhall, he cannot enjoy that office, it is ordered that he enjoy the keepership of the Green yard with the profits of all the stalls thereon without account during his life, and shall receive to his own use at the hands of him or them who have the Keepership of Leadenhall the profits of all stalls hanging or standing in the Hall in such sort as they have been and are paid to the Chamber of London in consideration whereof Aske shall continue to pay the said rent of 3 score and sixteen pounds thirteen shillings and fourpence. And after the decease of both the parties the Greenyard and the stalls thereof shall be distinct as heretofore from Leadenhall and the office of keepership thereof and the reversioners of the said several offices of keeperships of Leadenhall and Green Yard shall render account of the profits from the stalls in either place to the Chamber of London heretofore. And during the life of Robert Aske and Richard Wistowe and of the survivor of them the letting of the stalls shall be at their or his direction not displacing any man now in possession of any stall without informing this court. And further it is ordered that no butcher shall keep a stall hanging or standing for meat in the street adjoining Leadenhall, but all butchers which resort to that market shall keep their stalls within Leadenhall or in the Green Yard, if there be sufficient room for the same.

"Whiche report being read vnto the same Courte was very well liked," and ordered to be entered in the "Reportarie" and observed in all points. *Repert.* XXI, f. 292 b.

Tuesday 18 July 1592

"Where a markett for herbes fruyte and such lyke hath of late yeres been suffred to be kept within the street of Cheapside betwene the Cross there and thould change whiche in anncient tymes was free from any markett, and is at this daye so pestred with herbwyves Fruterers and such like as by means thereof the whole gouldsmythes rowe is so forestalled as that her Ma^tis subiectes can verye hardelye passe that waye and the parisioners and inhabitanntes thereaboutes greatlye burthened with the charge of the carryinge awaye and clensing of the streete of the soyle made by reason of the said markett and where also the said markett is vsually kepte vppon the sabaothe dayes to the great dishonor of Almightye God, and everye other daye from morninge untill IX of the clocke at night and sometymes with candell light verye dangerous for fyer and manye other inconveniences are there suffred contrary to the anncyent custome of this Cytie. For reformation whereof it is ordeyned and enacted that from hensforth the usurped markett in the place aforesayd betwene the Crosse and the olde Change shall be ether utterlye removed for ever or elsyf that any herbwyves fruterers or such like shall hereafter stand there with their herbes frutes or other thinges to be soulde that every such person shall stand tenne fotes distance at the lest from any stall or dore in Cheapsyde, and noe Markett be kepte or anythinge there soulde at all uppon the Sabaothe dayes and the marketts there every workedaye to begynne and ende at dewe and lawfull howers according to the laudable vsage and custome of this Cytye." Also persons standing there to sell herbs, fruit etc shall from time to time pay a reasonable contribution towards the cleansing and carrying away of the soil and filth left there. And that John Hoare shall take care to see this order performed and to collect the said contribution, accounting thereof to the parishioners of the several parishes of St. Peter, St. Matthew and St Foster in West Cheape as often as required, this order to have continuance at the pleasure of this court. *Repert.* XXII, f. 408 b.

The following are abstracts from an Act of Parliament re-lating to Markets 1599, 42 Eliz., and is taken from the *Guildhall Journals*, f. 150 b. Dated 1559, 42 Elizabeth.

That all laws heretofore made being yet in force for the good govern-ment & reformation of the great abuses of the Markets of the sd City shall be & continue in full force & effect.

That if any persons shall from & after the last day of Febr. forestall regrate or engross any victuals Fruit or other market wares coming to be sold &c. the same shall be seized and forfeited to the uses aftwds ex-pressed.

That four sufficient persons, and one other Person being a Freeman to be appointed by the Mayor & Aldermen, be added to the former num-ber which are already appointed, and called Overseers of all the Markets, which four or any of them shall walk & in continue in the Markets all the Market time, & cause the Market Bell to be rung at the hour of twelve, that the Market people may take Notice & presently avoid the Market. And take offenders before the Mayor or any other Justice of the Peace to be punished at their discretion.

That all those officers formerly appointed or hereafter to be appointed other than the four last appointed overseers shall weekly preserve to the Lord Mayor an account in writing of defects in their several circuits touching the abuses afsd. And that the said four overseers now appointed or hereafter &c. shall, once in every week, set down in a Register, which shall be in the custody of the Alderman or his Deputy of their Market circuits, all such Market defects & offences, with the Names of those taken before the Lord Mayor & their several faults; to the end that an abstract may be drawn out every 3 months under the hand of the Alder-man or Deputy and delivered by such overseers to the Lord. Mayor for the time being.

That if any Market folks bringing victuals fruit or other market wares, and in such sort covering or shadowing the same as not to show it; Then the overseers shall cause every Basket to be opened, & there to sell it at such price as they shall think fit with the consent of the owner: And upon refusal they shall enjoin the owner to carry a sample before the Lord Mayor that he may set the price, which when prised shall be forthwith sold in the said Market, if the said Market will bear it.

Punishment of overseers negligent in their duty.

Lord Mayor to appoint new overseers on the death of any of the four overseers newly appointed.

That all such forfeitures or seizures as shall become one by way of forfeiture or seizure, shall be to the uses following: i.e. One half to the Chamberlain for the use of the City; & the other half to the use of the said officers.

Clerks of Mayors Court to give information of any forfeiture.

Penalty of officers making unjust charges.

Thursday 9 Oct, 1600

Item yt is ordered that Mr. Chamberlen shall but and provide two payre of scales and waightes for the service of the new Markett howse within Bisshopsgate. *Repert.* xxv, f. 159 b.

10th April 1601.

The order and determination made and taken by Sir Stephen Soame knight and alderman of London with the consent of Mr. Lowe and Mr. Rowe aldermen of London committees appointed by the right ho: William Rider nowe Lo: Maior of the Citty of London and other his worshipfull brethren aldermen of the same for the ending of the causes and matters betweeene the Inhabitantes and Tenantes of the whole Markett place called the Stockes in the parishe of St. Marye Wollchurche Hawe London on thone partye and John Catcher of London esquire leassee of the said whole markett place on thother partye whereupon the said aldermen committee this tenth day of Aprill 1601 annoyne regin domine nostre Regine Elizabeth xliij°. have concluded and agreed as followeth vizt.

1. Furste in consideration that the said John Catcher by his lease is charged with the repayring upholding and manteyning of the Leades and whole howse nowe in divers places thereof verye ruynous and decayed and with payment of all fifteenes to be ymposed upon the said place and with payment of the tithes to the person of the said parish churche and sondry other charges within and about the saide place which the Leassee of the saide place heretofore hathe not bene charged with, but hath been discharged by the Bridgemasters, and nowe altogether ymposed upon the said John Catcher: that nowe therefore the Tenanntes Fishmongers in the Fish Markett of the said place and every of them (except only Ethelbright Stanner Fishmonger and one of the nowe tenants there) shall hold and enjoye those severall shoppes which they now severally occupye And shall yerely from the feaste of Thannunciation of the blessed virgin Mary last past before the date herof forthwardes pay three half pence every weeke in money for every foote of assize in length of every shoppe as rent for the same to the said John Catcher his executors or assignes by the week by the moneth by the quarter of the yare, as yt shall please the said John Catcher to demaund the same. And that they shall so holde the same shopps every one but during his naturall lief for his owne proper use. And shall not lett sett alienate exchange nor otherwyse do the same shoppes nor any of them without the consent of the said John Catcher or his Assignes.

2. Where there hath been grete controversye betweene the above named Ethelbright Stanner and the said John Catcher for and about fower of the shoppes in the said Markett place that now are or late were in the occupation of the said Ethelbright or his assignes, wherunto he had not nor hath any maner of right other than of sufferance whereby grete debate hathe arrysen betweene him and the said John Catcher: the said Committee with one consente for the pacifying thereof doe order and determyne That the said John Catcher shall henceforth for ever remytt and clierly release the said Ethelbright Stanner his executors and assignes all and every suche some and somes of money as the said Ethelbright dothe owe and is behinde for rent of the said fower choppes in arrerage at the feaste of the Annunciation of the blessed Virgin Marye last past before the date of theis presentes amountyng to the some of xxs. at the least. And that the said Ethelbright Stanner in consideration thereof shall forthwith surrender into the handes and disposition of the said John Catcher two of the said fower shoppes And that the said Ethelbright shall holde and enjoye the other two of the said fower shoppes for his owne proper use for and during his naturall lief. And shall from the said Feast of Thannunciation of the blessed Virgin Marye forthwards answeare and paie to the said John Catcher his executors and assign yerely three halfe pence every weeke for every foote of assize in lengthe for either or everye of the same two shoppes by the weeke monethe or quarter of the yere as the said John Catcher shall demand the same as rent for the same two shoppes. And that the said Ethelbright Stanner shall not lett alyenate exchange nor otherwise do away the same shopps or either of them without the specyall assent and consent of the same John Catcher or his assignes and also that eyther of the saide Ethelbright Stanner or John Catcher shall forthwith seale and delyver to other a generall release to other of all manner of actions and demaundes from the beginning of the worlde untill the xxvth day of Marche now last past.

3. Item the said committees do order and determyne That all and every the Butchers now Tenanntes in the Flesh Market of the Stokes aforesaid shall holde and occupye their severall shoppes which they do now use and enjoy as they now holde the same And that every of the same Butchers shall paye for every shoppe yerely to the said John Catcher his executors or assigns three halfpence in money every weeke for every foote of assize in length of every such shoppe by the weeke monethe or quarter of the yere as the said John Catcher shall demaund the same. And that none of the same Butchers shall have or enjoy the same shoppes longer than for term of his naturall lief, and shall not lett sett alyenate exchange or otherwise do away any of the same shoppes without the specyall assent and consent of the said John Catcher or his assignes.

4. Item that all and every person and persons now tenantes and occupiers of the severall Chambers lying over the said whole Markett place shall have and enjoye during their naturall lifes the same chambers which they now occupye so long as he shall keepe himselfe sole and vn-maryed and do paye for every such Chamber to the said John Catcher

or his assignes xiij*s*. iiij*d*, of lawfull money of England at fower usual feaste daies in the yere by even portions. And also that William Massye Painter shall holde and enjoye all such roomes as he now occupieth over the said Markett place during his naturall lief, paying to the said John Catcher or his assignes from the Annunciation of the Virgin Mary nowe last past double the rent that he nowe answeareth for the same roomes at fower usuall Feast daies by even procions. And that none of the Tenanntes of the saide Chambers or roomes shall lett sett alyenate exchange or otherwise do away the same roomes or chambers or any of them without the specyall assent and consent of the saide John Catcher or his assignes.

5. And it is further ordered concluded and agreed by the Committees above named That if at any tyme hereafter any tenant or tenantes in the said Fleshe or Fishe Markett shall refuse and denye to do pay and performe as in the contentes of the said Order and determynation is mentioned meant and declared, that then and so often yt shall and may be lawfull to the said John Catcher his executore or assignes (with the specyall consent and agreement of the Lo: Maior and Court of Aldermen or of us the said Committees or two od us authorized in that behalfe by the said Courte first had and obteyned) to pull and take downe the stall and stalls borde and bordes shoppe and shoppes of all and every such tenant Butcher or Fishmonger as shall refuse to accomplishe paie and performe the said order and determynacion and untill he and they shall have refourmed him and thenselfes and fully agreed to accomplishe and performe the same without any further suite or matter in lawe to be attempted in that behalfe.

STEPHEN SOAME
HENRY ROWE.

Which Report being read in this Court was by the same ordered to be entered into the Reportarye. *Repert.* xxv, f. 264 b *seq.*

Tuesday 15 September 1601

Item yt is ordered that Mr. Bridgemasters shall shewe the counterparte of Mr. John Ketcher's lease of the Stockes to some of the Cittyes Councell and to take advice thereof concernyng covenauntes to be performed on the parte of the tenantes and thereof to enforme this Courte. *Repert.* xxv, f. 275 b.

Thursday 24 September 1601

Item yt is ordered that Mr. John Catcher and Edward Catcher his sonne shall upon Thursdaie next make a sufficient answeare in wryting upon their severall othes. vnto the Englishe Bill exhibited against then in this Courte by the Fishmongers Butchers and others the occupyers of the shoppes standinges or stalles and chambers at the Stockes otherwise he or they making default for his or their contempte to be committed to one of the compters of this Cittye there to remayne during the pleasure of this Courte. *Repert.* xxv, f. 278.

Thursday 10 November 1601

Item the cause depending in this Courte by Englishe Bill and answeare between the Fishmongers Butchers and others tenants or occupiers of the shoppes standinges stalles and Chambers within the great stone house called the Stockes, plaintiffs, against John Catcher thelder and Edward Catcher his sonne defendts. is referred to ye hearing and examination of Sir Stephen Soame knight Mr. Rowe Mr. Lowe Mr. Bennett Mr. Godard Aldermen and Mr. Commen Sergeant and they or any three or more of them after examination thereof to make their reportes in wryting to this courte. And in the meane tyme all suites in lawe betweene the said defendts or ether of them against the plaintiffs or any of them shall cesse and be no further proceeded in. And Nicholas Ambrose to warne them etc. *Repert.* xxv, f. 302.

Thursday 12 November 1601

Item it is ordered that Mr. Hollidaye Mr. Cambell Aldermen shall joyne with the Committees formerly appointed to heare and examyne the cause complayned on to this Courte by ye occupyers of the stalles and shoppes within the Stockes against John Catcher and Edward Catcher his sonne, and they or any fower or more of them to meete togeather and to enter into further examynacion of the saied cause and to ende or to make reporte thereof to this Courte within one moneth which if they shall not performe then the said Mr. Catcher to proceed in his suite in lawe against them without further delaye. And John Stubbes to warne them. etc. *Repert.* xxv, f. 303 b.

Tuesday 8 December 1601

Item further daie is given by this Courte vntill the next Courte here to be holden after the Feast of the Epiphanie next vnto the Committee appointed for the examination of the cause betweene the occupiers of the shoppes and stalles within the Stockes and John Catcher Pewterer and Edward his sonne for the hearing and ending of the said cause. *Repert.* xxv, f. 313 b.

Tuesday 12 January 44 Elizabeth [1601–2]

Item it is ordered that the suyte depending in the utter Courte betweene Edward Catcher playnetiff and Ethelbright Stanner deft shalbe stayed during the pleasure of this Courte. And that the former Commyttees according to a late order sett downe in this courte or any fower or more of them shall heare and ende a cause depending in this Courte by Englishe Bill betweene the Butchers and Fishmongers tenantes or occupiers of the Stockes playnetiffes against John and Edward Catcher defts or else to make report unto this courte of their doinges therein. And that in the mean tyme John Catcher the father be enjoyned that the said Edward Catcher do not proceed in his suite in the kinges bench against David Jones and John Haver Butchers untill the Commyttes have made Reporte. And John Stubbes to warn them etc. *Repert.* xxv, f. 324.

Tuesday 14 December 1602.

Item this daie the certificat of Mr. Stephen Soame knight and others towching certen orders agreed upon by them the fowerth daie of August last between John and Edward Catcher on the one partie and the inhabitantes tenantes and occupiers of the Stockes was here read liked and allowed of The tenor whereof hereafter enseweth vizt.

Quarto die Auguste 1602 annoque xliiii°
domine nostra Elizabeth Regine, etc.

The certificate of us whose names are subscribed towching certen orders agreed vpon by vs betweene John and Edward Catcher on the one partie and the inhabitantes tenantes and occupiers which now are or hereafter shalbe of the whole Markett place called the Stockes in the parish of St. Mary Wollchurch Hawe Londom of the shoppes stalles and chambers belonging to the same to be performed as well on the parte and behalf of the said tenantes or occupiers as on the parte and behalf of the said John and Edward Catcher.

First it is ordered that every person or persons exercizing the arte or mistery of Butcher or selling of flesh within the said place called the Stockes shall pay to the said John or Edward Catcher or their assigne or assignes weekely and for every weeke in the yere three halfe pence for every foote in length conteyned in the shoppe soe occupied by any such Butcher or Butchers and that none of the said Butchers shall occupie above one shoppe at one shoppe at one tyme and that only for his own proper use and no otherwise (*sic*).

Item that every fishmonger tenante or occupier of aney shoppe stall or standing within the place aforesaid shall paye likewise three half pence weekly and for everi weeke in the yere for every foote in length of the said shoppe stall or standing and that none of the said fishmonger shall occupie above two shoppes at one tyme and that for his owne proper use and not otherwise.

Item that every person or persons butchers and not others being lodged in anie room or chamber over the said place called Stockes shall pay for the said chamber or room yerely the rent of x.*s*. to be paid quarterly and that yf anie of those persons which nowe inhabit the chambers shall dye departe away or marry that then he or they which shall after that come into the same chambers shall paie the same yerely rent of x.*s*. and xxvj.*s*. viij.*d*. for a fyne vnto the said John Catcher and Edward Catcher or their assignes, and soe from tyme to tyme as anie such chaunce shall happen.

Item that every of the said Butchers and Fishmongers which nowe occupie the said shoppes or stalles or any of them shall enjoye anie of their shoppes or stalles during their naturall lyves and that after the death of anie of them being maryed his wief shall enjoye the same shoppe or stall during her sydowhood only and that yt shalbe lawful for anie of the said Butchers or Fishmongers to assigne over his interest and estate for his own lief and his wives during her widowhood to any butcher or fishmonger being a freeman and upon every such alienation or assignement of estate the new tenante to paie by waie of fyne or attornement unto the said John Catcher or Edward Catcher or their assignes the somme of xx.s. at his first entrance therevnto. And that none of the said Butchers fishmongers or other persons which soe shall use occupie or enjoye the said shoppes stalles or chambers or any of them shall at any tyme or tymes hereafter doe or committe anie annoyance or other acte or thinge contrary to anye of the covenantes or articles mencioned or comprized in the indenture of lease thereof made or to be made by the Maior Commonalty and Cittizens of the Citte of London unto the said John Catcher and Edward Catcher.

And finallie that of anie of the occupiers of the sayd shoppes or chambers shall wilfully refuse to obey theis orders that then the said John Catcher and Edward Catcher and their assignes shall or maie take their due remedye by lawe against every such offender without staye to be made by this Courte

Stephen Soame.   Thomas Bennett,   Leonard Halliday.   Henry Rowe

Whereupon it is ordered that the lease formerlie drawen ingrossed and assented vnto by the Committees for leasing of the Citties Landes to be made to the said John Catcher and his sonne Edward of the said Stockes and Markett shalbe made to the said Edward Catcher in sorte as yt sholde have bene to them both Saving that one yere is added to the newe lease by the said Committee to make up the same one and thirty yeres from Mydsomer laste. *Repert.* xxvi, pt. 1, f. 65 *seq.*

Court of Great Ward mote

Monday 10 January 45 Elizabeth [1602–3]

At this Courte it is ordered that Edward Catcher gent. shall have a lease of the Stockes sealed with the common seale of this City in sorte as is already agreed upon by the Committees saving their wordes to be added and inserted into the said lease videlicet that the Butchers shall paie noe rent at all hereafter vnto the said Edward Catcher his executors or assignes during the tyme conteyned in his lease for the first six weekes in every Lent during that time.

Item it is ordered that the Bridgemasters shall presently viewe the defectes and wantes of lead lately taken away by John Catcher pewterer deceased from the Stockes as this Courte is informed and to make report thereof to this courte. *Repert.* xxvi, pt. 1, f. 78 b.

Tuesday 25 January 1602–3

Whereas there was a former lease granted unto John Catcher in his lief tyme lately deceased and to Edward Catcher his sonne nowe surviving of the whole Stonehouse and markett place called the Stockes for the term of XXX yeres, it is this daie ordered that forasmuch as the said Edward Catcher is to covenant with this Citty in his lease to performe such orders as were sett down and agreed upon by the Committees appointed for the hearing and appeasing of the controversyes between ye said John Catcher in his lief tyme and the said Edward Catcher and the nowe tenantes and occupiers of the said Stonehouse as appeareth in the Reportory that he shall have a lease of the same stone house called the Stockes for the term of XXXI yeres to beginne at midsomer last for such rente and under such conditions as were formerly agreed on by the said committees. *Repert.* XXVI, pt. 1, f. 86.

Thursday 27 January

It is ordered that a lease of the Stockes lately granted by the Committees for letting of the City's lands to Edward Catcher gent. shall not be sealed nor delyvered to the said Catcher before this Court be first made acquainted therewith. *Repert.* XXVI, pt. 1, f. 91 b.

11 February 4 James I [1606–7]

Item whereas complainte is made that suche as keepe kitchins under yᵉ buildings of yᵉ royall exchange doe annoy the streates there by casting of all theire fowle and stinkinge water into the said¹ (street?) For reformation whereof it is ordered that a sewer shalbe made vnder yᵉ grounde for convayance of the said water unto yᵉ Stockes at yᵉ equal chardges of the Maior and Commonaltie and of the companie of Mercers. *Letter-Book CC*, f. 198.

Thursday 9 Nov. 1613

Item whereas complaint hath byn made that there is demanded and received of the country victualer and others for their standing in the Marketts of this Citty extra ordinary and under fees to the greivance of the people and that the Freemen Butchers and Haysters doe gretly pester the said Marketts and hinder the standing of the country victualer. It is thought fitt and soe ordered by this Court that Sir John Gayre knight and alderman Mr. Alderman Atkins and Mr Alderman Gibbs or any two of them calling unto them whom they shall thinke fitt shall heare the said complaints and duly examine what duties have byn received and what of right ought to be paid for standing in the said Markett as aforesaid it being now informed that there is only due a penny for pickage and consider what is fitt to be done for reformation of abuses in the said Marketts and for the well ordering of the same according to former actes and orders of this court. And the said committees to certify unto the Court in writing under their hands how they find the same and their opinions. And William Piddocke to warn and attend them. *Repert.* LVII, f. 5.

Thursday 12 June 1623

Item this day upon reading of a petition exhibited to this Court, by the inhabitants of Cheapside London for reformation of the annoyances and abuses in the Markett kept in the said street of Cheapside, it is ordered by this court that Sir John Leman (and seven other aldermen named) or any four of them, Mr. Greene (and eight other persons named) or any six of them shall hear and consider the grievances of the said inhabitants,

¹ Word omitted in MS.

for redress of the said abuses, and consider all former orders and acts made in that behalf, and certify the court what they conceive fit to be done therein, and the serjeant and yeoman of the chamber to warn and attend them. *Repert.* xxxvii, f. 184.

Tuesday 8 June 1630

Item this day upon reading of a petition exhibited unto this court under the handwriting of many of the inhabitants in Cheapside London "for redresse of a great abuse and wronge offered vnto them by divers bakers, hearbwomen and others that stand and keepe market before their dores in Cheapeside aforesaid to the Petitioners great annoyance and hinderance," it is ordered by this court that the petitioners confer with Mr. Mosse and inform themselves what laws within the City are in force for reformation of the abuse, and advise with him and Mr. Stone what is further necessary to be done therein, and accordingly to prepare the draught of an act for the approval of this court, that the latter may refer it to the next common council to be enacted. *Repert.* xliv, f. 268 b.

Tuesday 11 October 7 Charles I [1631]

Item this day upon the humble petition of the freemen Bakers resorting heretofore to the Market in Cheapside with their bread and of the poor "hearbewomen" sitting in the same market, restrained from selling their wares there by a late act of Common Council, it is thought fit that the right hon^ble the Lord Mayor shall at his discretion appoint the Bakers to sell their bread in Cornhill on the South side of the Street, and the herb-women to sell their herbes in Broad street until other order to taken by this Court at the Common Council. *Repert.* xlv, f. 529 b (abridged).

Saturday 1 June 1633.

Item this day the draught of an Act of Common Council tendered to this court "for restreyning as well the forreynor as the Freeman to sell flesh in the marketts of Cheapside and Newgate and in the streets of Leaden hall" is by this court referred to the consideration of Mr. Recorder Sr Hugh Hamersley Sr James Cambell knights and aldermen and aldermen Parkhurst Clitherow and Stone or any four of them, to alter or add thereunto according to their discretions and to certify their doings to the court in writing under their hands. *Repert.* xlvii, f. 251.

Tuesday 5 June 1638

Item it is ordered by this court that Mr. Marshe the City's solicitor shall at the City's charge take care to defend the suit prosecuted in the Court of Star Chamber by Mr. Wardens and Society of Gardiners against John Fisher yeoman of the Channell for disturbing and removing such of the gardiners as sit in Cheapside Market with their herbs. *Repert.* lii, f. 184

Thursday 16 November 1643

Item this day upon the humble petition of the M^r. and Wardens and Commonalty of Butchers, London it is ordered by this court that Sir

John Gayre knight and Alderman M^r. Alderman Atkyns and Mr. Alderman Gibbs Mr. Serjeant Phesant and Mr. Serjeant Greene and Mr. Mosse or any three or more of them calling unto them whome they shall thinke fitt shall heare and consider of the matters in difference between the said petitioners and Jasper Dartnoll Farmer of the Flesh Markett in Leaden hall and concerning all abuses in all other Marketts within this Citty. And they to certify unto this court in writing under their hands how they find the same and their opinions. And John Bancroft to warne and attend them. *Repert.* LVII, f. 10 b.

Thursday 18 September 1645

Item this day upon reading a petition to the Court from the Company of Butchers London for the due and speedy execution of the ordinances and acts heretofore made for the reformation of abuses in the markets of the City, it is ordered by the Court that Sir John Gayre knight and alderman, Mr. Alderman Fookes Mr Sheriff Gibbs Mr. Sergeant Green Mr. Common Sergeant and Mr. Mosse comptroller of the Chamber or any four of them calling before them the Mr and Warden of the said company of Butchers and whom else they think fitt shall forthwith hear the grievances expressed in the petition and what else can be alleged for the well ordering of the Markets and consider the acts of Common Council and the orders of this Court in that behalf and what in them in the present times is fit to be altered or added thereunto. And to certify the court in writing under their hands how they find the same and "their deemings and opinions herein." And it is ordered that Mr. Chamberlain shall not from henceforth make any composition for any arrest or suit commenced in any of the Courts within this City upon any penal act of Common Council or information whatsoever. And Barnard Clapshowe to warn and attend them. *Repert.* LVII, f. 217 b (abridged).

The following deed is at the Record Office, Guildhall:

11 August 1645

To ALL CHRISTIAN PEOPLE to whome this pr'nte writing shall come Edward Dichfeild Cittizein and Salter of London SENDETH GREETING in our Lord God everlasting WHEREAS the Maior and Cominalty and Cittizeins of the Citty of London by their Indenture of Lease under the Com̄on Seale of the said Cittie for the severall considerac̄ons therein menc̄oed Did lease betake and to ferme lett unto the said Edward Dichfeild, ALL THAT their greate Stonehouse com̄only called or knowne by the name of the Stocks, with all and Singular th apptenãcs, situate & being w̄thin the parish of St. Mary Woolchurch hawe of the said Citty of London together with the flesh and ffish marketts thereunto belonging, and all the roomes and chambers over the same, and the roomes or Stalls situate on each side of the West doore of the said ffish markett, with all such blocks stalles boards quarters Ironhooks and other necessaries whatsoever, as to the same or any of them did belong or app̄rtaine, and specified in a Schedule thereunto annexed, That is to say all such stalles blocks

and boards as in the flesh markett then remained meete and necessary
for the sale of flesh, and all such stalls blocks and boards as in the ffish
markett then remaining meete and necessary for the sale of ffish: Which
foresaid greate stone house; called the Stocks was covered w̄th lead,
haveing thereunto gutters and pipes of Lead for the conveyance of water
thence; To Have and to Hold the foresaid Stonehouse called the
Stocks and all & Singular other the premises with every their appr̄tenanc̄s,
unto the said Edward Dichfeild his executors administrators and assigneis,
ffrom the feast day of the Annunciacon of Our Lady St. Mary the virgin
then next coming after the day of the date of the said Indentr̄ of Lease,
unto the end & terme of one & ffifty years from thence next ensuing and
fully to be compleate & endid, Whereupon the yearely rent of ffifty and
six pounds fower shillings and eight pence of lawfull money of England
paieable on fower feast dayes or termes in the yeare therein specified is
reserved, As by the said Indenture of Lease bearing date the Twoo &
twentith day of January No. Dni 1633 And in the Nineth yeare of the
reigne of our now Sov'aigne Lord King Charles over England, contayning
divers other covenants grants articles and agreem̄ts more att large doth
and may appr̄e; Since then sealling of w̄ch said recited Indentr̄e of Lease
the Wardeins of London bridge and Clerke of the Bridge House by their
lycense indorsed on the back of the said Indentr̄e bearing date the Nineth
day of this instant August, they have lycensed the said Edward Dichfeild
to assign and sett over the said Lease & pr̄mises thereby demised & terme
of yeares therein to come unto Robert Osbolston Cittizein and habdasher
of London As by the said Indorsed lycense subscribed unto by ffrancis
Kirby and Henry Allen Wardeins of London bridge, and Wm. Mongre
Clerke of the Bridghouse, appr̄eth Now Know Ye therefore that I the
said Edward Dichfeild for and in consideracon of a certaine competent
sume of good and lawfull money of England to mee in hand att or before
th'ensealling and deliv'y hereof by the said Robert Osbolston well and
truely paid, the receipt whereof I doo hereby acknowlidge, and to be
therewith fully sattisfied & contented, and of the same sume and every
part thereof I doe cleerely acquit and discharge the said Robert Osbolston
his executors administrators and assigneis and every of them forever by
theis pr̄nts Have granted bargained sold aliened assigned and sett over,
and by this my present writeing, doe fully freely cleerely and absolutely
grant bargaine sell alien assigne sett over and confirme unto the said
Robert Osbolston, As well the said recited Indenture of Lease, and
Stonehouse called the Stocks w̄th the appr̄tenancs and all other the premises thereby demised, As also all my whole estate right tytle interest
property use possession revercon, terme of yeares to come claime & demand whatsoever w̄ch I have, or any other prsone or prsons whatsoever,
to or for my use hath or have, or may or can claime to have, to come and
to be expired of in or unto the Stonehouse and other the pr̄mises with
their appr̄tenanc̄s in and by the said recited Indentr̄e of Lease demised
By force vertue or meanes of the said recited Indenture of Lease or
other wise by any waies or meanes whatsoever To Have and to Hold
the said Stonehouse and all and Singular other the premises with their

and every of their apprtenancs in and by the said recited Indenture of
Lease demised, together with the said Indenture of Lease, and all and
every other the said bargained premises in and by theis p̅rnts ment mencoed
or intended to be assigned and sett over, and every p̅rt and parcell thereof,
unto the said Robert Osbolston his executors administrators and assigneis
ffrom the day of the date hereof forthwards for and dureing soe long time
such residue and so many yeares as and yet to come and unexpired of the
said terme of ffifty and one yeares in and by the said Indent̅re of Lease
granted AND I THE SAID Edward Dichfeild doe covenant and grant for
my Self myne executors and ad̅mistratr̅s, to and with the said Robert
Osbolston his executors admistratr̅s and assigneis and every of them by
theis p̅rnts in manner & fourme following that is to say, That the said
recited Indenture of Lease and premises thereby demised, and all other
the said granted premises in and by theis p̅rnts ment men̅co̅ed or intended
to be assigned & sett over, on the day of the date hereof are & be and soe
att all times from hensforth for and dureing all the rest and residue yet
to come & unexpired of the said terms of ffifty and one yeares, shall continue remaine and be unto the said Robert Osbolston his executors ad-
mi̅strators and assigneis free and cleere and thereby acquitted exonerated
and discharged, or from tyme to tyme, sufficiently saved and kept harme-
less, by mee the said Edward Dichfeild myne executors admistrators and
assigneis of and from all and almanner of former and other bargaines
sales quitts grants leasses estates fines forfeitures Surrenders extinguish-
ments rents arrearages of Rent, reentries Judgm̅ts execucons Extents
Debts of record, Statute merchant and of the Staple, Recognizanc̅s, and
of and from all other tythes costs charges incumbrancs whatsoever had
made omitted don or suffered by mee the said Edward Dichfeild att any
time before then Sealling hereof, (The said yearely rent of ffifty and six
pounds fower shillings and eight pence, and other the covenants grants
articles condic̅ons and agreem̅ts in the said recited Indentre of Lease
reserved and contayned, on the Tenants or Leassees p̅rt and behalf from
henceforth to be paid prformed & kept alwaies) AND further That hee
the said Robert Osbolston his executors admi'strators and assigneis,
payeing the said yearely rent, and prforming fulfilling and keeping all
such other covenants grantes articles reprc̅ons condic̅ōns & agreem̅ts in
the said recited Lease reserved and contayned on the Tenants or Leasses
p̅rt and behalf to be paid kept & prformed according to the effort and true
maning of the said Lease, shall and may lawfully peaceably and quietly
have hold occupie possesse and enioy the said Stonehouse and other the
premises with their apprtenanc̅s in & by the said recited Lease demised
according to the 'ffort & true meaning of the said recited Indenture for
and dureing all the rest and residue of the said terme of ffifty and one
yeares, wt̅hout the lett suite trouble deniall molestacon eviccon or inter-
rupcon of or by mee the said Edward Dichfeild myne executors admi'strators or assigneis, or of or by any other prsone or prsons whatsoever
by myne or their meanes act consent right tytle interest or procurem̅t
IN WITNESS whereof to this my present writeing I the said Edward
Dichfeild have put my hand and seale, Dated the Eleaventh day of

August N⁰ Dni 1645 And in the One & twentith yeare of the reigne of our Souv'aigne Lord Charles by the grace of God King of England Scotland ffrance and Ireland Defender of the faith.

Edwd. Dichfeild.

The following are further extracts from the *Repertories*:

Tuesday 2 June 1657

This day was presented unto the Court by the Goldsmithes and others inhabiting Cheapside between Woodstreet end and Paules Gate an humble petition complaining of the great annoyance and damage they dayly sustaine and ye greate danngers themselves and passengers are exposed unto by the standing of Men women and their children and servants with hearbes plantes rootes fruite and other like commodities there soe filling and pestering the said streete with a multitude of Basketts vessalls and other things that the common passage is thereby exceedingly streightened and stopped and noe way left to and from the Petitioner's howses besides the further annoyance thence arising from the vnwholsome smells and stenches of the parings and refuse of roots plants and other filth there left and lying scattered perishing and corrupting; whereas by severall Lawes and provisions that part of the said street ought to be kept free and cleere and none of the comodities aforesaid to be there uttered or put to sale. And hereupon this court seriously advising of some more effectual way of redresse of the said evills than is yet provided, did after much debate and consideration herof had resolve and order, That such fruite hearbey cabages Hartichikes and other plants and garden commodities before mentioned as upon further consideration shall be thought fit to be removed from Cheapside shall have place to be set and sould in Paul's churchyard and for that purpose Sir Thomas Vyner, Sir John Dethick knights and Aldermen, Mr. Alderman Ireton, Mr. Alderman Underwood Mr. Alderman Thomson and Mr. Sheriffs or any three or more of them are hereby appointed to call before them the said inhabitants or any others they think fitt and to advise and consider of the particular commodities needful and convenient to be soe removed And certify unto this Court in writing under their hands on this day seaven night how they find the same and their opinions And David Powell to warne and attend them. *Rep.* LXV, f. 119.

Tuesday 9 June 1657

Whereas against direct lawes orders and provisions greate numbers of men and weomen and their children and servants doe dayly on the worke dayes all the day long sit in the high streete of Cheape with multitudes of Basketts Tubbs and other vesells of fruite Rootes hearbes plants flowers and other garden commodities to sell and utter, and doe thereby soe fill pester and streigten the said streete that not only the Inhabitants are much hindered and damnifyed in their trades and estates but they and all people travailing and passing through the same streete exposed to manifold hazards and dangers and many hurts and mischeifs have happened besides the further annoyance thence arising from the vnwholesome smells and stenches and refuse of roots plants and other filth continually left and lying scattered and corrupting in that principall streete and passage of the Citie: Now this Court having well advised of reforming the said evills and abuses doth therefore thincke fitt and order that from and after the 6th day of August next coming noe person or persons shall stand or be permitted to stand and abide at any time with any goods or commodities, (excepting bread) to sell or put to sale in that part of the said street of Cheap side lying between Bread Streete and Paulschurchyard (the same having never bene appointed a markett place for any comodities whatsoever) nor shall stand or be permitted to stand or abide with carts horses or otherwise in any other place or part of the said streete of Cheape or Cheapeside on any day or time of the week with any fruite rootes hearbes plants flowers or garden comodities (excepting Peascods) to sell or put the same to sale but that every one who shalbe found doeing the contrary shalbe taken and for his offence be indicted and punished according to lawe. And that noe annoyance may ensewe by the permitting of Peascodds to be still sould as formerly in the said streete the shells are to be constantly swept up and conveyed away that they may not by remaining and corrupting produce any noysome or offensive smells. And that there be not wanting a knowne and convenient place Whither all may resort for buying and selling the said commodities It is further ordered by this court that the country people and gardiners shall have place or may stand with the said fruite Rootes hearbes plantes flowers and other garden commodities (excepting Peascods) in all parts of the voyd place on the north side of Paules within the channells and in noe wise beyond or without the said Channells And maye soe sitt and abide with their comodities as they may or ought to doe in other publique Marketts of this Citie Provided that none shall bring any carts or horses within the place aforesaid nor any to sit or have with them there at one tyme above such number of Tubbs or Basketts and of such Bignes as from time to time shall be limited and appointed by the Lord Mayor of this citie for the time being And for the better execution of this order the Serjeant and yeoman of the Channell and the Beadles of the Wards respectively where the said streete or any the places aforesaid are scituate or being and all others whome it shall concerne are charged and commanded by this Court to be intent and diligent in and about the cleering of the street of Cheape in manner before expressed and from the comodities aforesaid and setling the country people and gardiners (whoe sell the same) in the place aforesaid and to take upon them theis service and performe the same effectually at their utmost perills. [*Repertories*, LXX, f. 128.]

It is ordered by this Court that the decayes of the common sewers in the Powltry and Walbrooke shall bee forthwith repaired And that the workemen take notice and certifie vnto this Court the names of all persons whoe have made privies vnto the same or within other the Common sewers that speedy course may be taken against them for the said offence. *Repert.* LXIX, f. 363.

The following document is in the Guildhall Library:

TICHBORNE MAIOR.

Tuesday the ninth day of June 1657.

WHEREAS against divers Lawes, Orders and provisions, great numbers of Men and Women and their Children and Servants doe daily on the weeke daies, all the day long, sit in the high-street of Cheape, with multitudes of Baskets, Tubbs and other vessels of Fruit, Roots, hearbs, plants, flowers and other Garden Commodoties to sell, utter, and doe thereby to fill, pester and streighten the said Street, that not only the Inhabitants are much hindred and damnified in their trades and estates, but they and all people travailing and passing through the same street, exposed to manifold hazards and dangers, and many hurts and mischiefs have hapned, besides the further annoyance thence arising from the unwholsome smells and stenches of the pavings and refuse of Roots, Plants and other filth continually left and lying scattered and corrupting, in that principall Street and passage of the City: Now THIS COURT having well advised of reforming the said evils and abuses, doth therefore thinke fit and Order, that from and after the sixth day of August next coming, no person or persons whatsoever shall stand or be permitted to stand or abide, at any time, with any goods or commodities (excepting Bread) to sell or put to sale in that part of the said street of Cheape or Cheapeside lying between Bread-street end and Pauls Church-yard (the same having never been appointed a Market place for any commodities whatsoever) Nor shall stand or be permitted to stand or abide with Carts, horses, or otherwise in any other place, or part of the said Street of Cheap or Cheapside, on any day or time of the Weeke with any Fruit, Roots, Hearbs, Plants, Flowers, or Garden Commodities (excepting Peascods) to sell or put the same to sale, but that every one, who shall be found doing the contrary, shall be taken, and for his offence be indicted and punished according to Law. And that no annoyance may ensue by the permitting of peas-cods to be still sold as formerly in the said street, the shells are to be constantly sweept up and conveyed away, that they may not by remaining and corrupting, produce any noisome or offensive smells: And that there be not wanting a knowne and convenient place whither all may resort for buying and selling the said commodities: IT IS FURTHER ORDERED BY THIS COURT, that the Countrey people and Gardiners shall have place or may stand with their said Fruit, Roots, Hearbs, Plants, Flowers and other Garden commodities excepting peas-cods, in all parts of the voyd place on the North-side of Pauls within the Channells, and in no wise beyond or without the said Channells, And may so sit and abide with their Commodities as they may or ought to doe in other publique Markets of this City, Provided that none shall bring any Carts or horses within the place aforesaid, nor any to sit or have with them there at one time above such number of Tubs or Baskets, and of such bignesse as from time to time shall be limited and appointed by the Lord Maior of this City for the time being: And for the better execution of this Order, the Serjeant and Yeoman of the Channell, and the Beadles of the Wards respectively where the said Street, or any the places aforesaid are situate or being, and all others whom it shall concerne, are charged and commanded by this Court to be intent and diligent in and about the clearing of the Street of Cheape in manner before expressed, and from the commodities aforesaid, and setling the Country people and Gardiners, (who sell the same) in the place aforesaid, and to take upon them this service, and performe the same effectually at their utmost perills.

The above extracts, etc., deal with the history of the Stocks Market up to the time of the great fire of London. The rentals are mentioned but are more fully dealt with in the next chapter.

The following are a few notes upon the Walbrook during the same period referred to at greater length in Chapter I.

In 1277–8 it was ordered that the course of the Walbrook should be freed[1].

On October 28th, 1277, it was agreed that the course of the Walbrook should be entirely freed from rotten matter and other obstruction and nuisances, and that gratings be replaced at each tenement on the course[2].

In 1288 it was determined that the course of the Walbrook should be made free from dung and other nuisances, and that the rakes should be put back again upon every tenement from the Moor to the Thames[3].

On July 20th, 1291, an inquisition was made as to who were bound to repair the bridge over the Walbrook near the Bucklersbury, and it was decided that the owners of four tenements were to do so[4]. It seems probable that the four tenements adjoined the bridge, two on each side of the stream.

On July 11th, 1300, there was an inquisition as to who were bound to repair the covering over the water course of the Walbrook, over against the chancel wall of St Stephen de Walebroc, and the parishioners were held liable[5].

On April 23rd, 1345, nine men were sworn to see that the water-course of the Walbrook was not impeded[6].

On July 2nd, 1415, it was decided to build a latrine within the city wall upon the foss of the Walbrook, and that those

---

[1] *Letter-Book A*, p. 217.   [2] *Ibid.* p. 212.
[3] Riley's *Memorials*, p. 23.   [4] *Letter-Book A*, p. 177.
[5] *Letter-Book C*, p. 71.   [6] *Letter-Book F*, p. 120.

living on the margin of the stream should cause the banks to be piled or walled[1].

On March 11th, 1462–3, it was decided that all latrines over the ditch of Walbroke should be abolished, and that each owner of land on each side of the ditch should clean out his portion of the same and pave and vault it up to the middle line[2].

On July 12th, 1477, an ordinance was made forbidding the making of "any priveye or serge" over the Walbrook, and ordering the abatement of those already in existence, and no rubbish or filth was to be thrown into it[3].

[1] *Letter-Book I*, p. 137.
[2] *Letter-Book L*, pp. 21–2.
[3] *Letter-Book L*, p. 149.

PLATE VIII

THE STATUE OF KING CHARLES II

PLATE IX

THE STATUE OF KING CHARLES II

Chapter III

Market Rents and Tenants

IN the last chapter the history of the Stocks Market was dealt with, but the rental was only incidentally referred to; it is now proposed to give a few facts with regard to the payments made by the tenants and also to describe the building.

The following are extracts from the MSS. at the Guildhall:

Rental ordered by Richard Bacom and John de Hatfeld, Wardens of the Bridge and written by John de Caulfeld chaplain. 32 Edward III [1357–8].

Rental of Tenements belonging to the Bridge of London in London Southwark Hatchesham Camerwell Lewesham and Stratford as they are situated in diverse parishes.

[Original in Latin.]

In the Parish of St. Stephen Walebrok

In the same parish are two shops under one building sometime John Pecok's of which Walter Page holds one and the heir of Thomas of Somersete holds the other: and they are situated between a tenement of the said Walter Page on the northern side, and a tenement of John de Bedeford formerly Peter de Bosenham's on the southern side and the highway called Walebroke on the western side. And it owes yearly to the Bridge of London 2*s.* (*i.e.* the whole building apparently).

In the parish of St. Mary Wolnoth

In the said parish is a tenement of Hamo Lumbard's in the corner of St. Swithin's Lane situated between the tenement of John Osekyn on the western side and the tenement of Walter Garlek on the eastern side, and the lane called Berebynder's Lane on the southern side. And it owes to London Bridge yearly 13*s.* 4*d.*

Item in the same parish is a tenement of John Fyssch in the corner of Shetebourne Lane and it is situated between the tenement of Nicholas Hotot formerly Warin Menge's on the west and south. And it owes yearly to London Bridge 2*s.*

Sum 15*s.* 4*d.*

At the Stockes

Next the church of St. Mary of Wolcherchehawe is a certain fold[1] called the Stockes appointed for the butchers and fishmongers selling flesh and fish there, whose rent is uncertain because sometimes it is worth more and sometimes worth less, according to how the plats are occupied with the butcher on flesh days and with the fishmongers on fish days.

Upon which *Falda* called the Stockes are three dwellings and a room for placing pledges[2] in, of which one dwelling is there at the eastern end towards Cornhille, which Thomas Draper now holds. And he returns thence yearly 30s.

Item there is there at the western end towards the conduit another dwelling which John Lovekyn junior now holds and he returns thence yearly to the Bridge 20s.

Item there is there another small dwelling which a certain "Huxster" holds, who is called Thomas Worteman, in the middle of the house upon the Stockes on the north side. And he returns thence yearly 10s.

Item there is there on the Stockes on the south side a chamber which is given to the Collector of rent to put his pledges in. And he returns nothing thence[3].

Within the Stockes

And it is to be known that in the foresaid enclosure called the Stockes are 71 plats, measured by the table of the fishmongers, viz. in length $4\frac{1}{2}$ feet 2 thumbs of the feet called "Paulisfet" of which each plat occupied by the butchers on flesh days is worth 4d. the week.

And each plat occupied with a fishmonger on fishdays is worth weekly 3d.

Of which plats on the southern side next the church there are nineteen. And on the north side there are eighteen.

Item in the middle of the house on the southern side in a row there are fifteen. And in another row in the middle of the house towards the north are fourteen.

Item at the eastern end of the same house are 3 plats and at the western end there are two.

But the rent coming thence cannot be summed up for certain, because the said plats are sometimes occupied and sometimes not. And thus sometimes they are worth more sometimes less as appears in the rolls of account of the wardens of the Bridge aforesaid through divers weeks and divers years.

Outside the Stockes

Item it is to be known that at the Western end outside the Stockes are 5 plats for fishmongers selling fish there on fish days of which each plat when occupied is worth weekly 3d.

[1] Falda = fold, but perhaps it should be here translated enclosure.
[2] Or securities, probably goods pledged as securities to the Bridgemasters.
[3] These entries have been crossed out, probably because the rooms were held at a later date by other tenants.

Item outside the Stockes there are 22½ plats under the walls of the house appointed for the butchers there selling flesh on fish days, whereof 18 plats are under the wall on the North side and 4½ plats are under the wall at the Eastern end, of which each plat when occupied is worth weekly 2d. But they are never fully occupied and therefore they cannot be summed up for certain.

The reference to the foot of St Paul is somewhat rare and refers to the standard measure marked in the Cathedral, in a similar way to the standard measures now marked in Trafalgar Square and in the Guildhall. Other references are mentioned in the *Gentleman's Magazine*, 1852, pp. 57 and 276.

Roll of Account of the Warden of London Bridge from the 29 September the Feast of St. Michael the Archangel to Richard II to the same Feast 6 Richard II [1381–1382].

Sum total of receipts 255L. 19s. 6d. Out of this the accountants ask allowance (among other items) for the vacation of 25 cupboards above the Stockes for 52 weeks brey weekly 4d. 21£ 13s. 4d.

Receipts from the Stockes

On Saturday next after the feast of St. Michael (Sept. 29)			
From the Fishmongers standing within and without		19s.	0d.
From the Butchers standing there	£1	7	4
On Saturday next before the feast of the Apostles Simon and Jude (Oct. 28)			
From the fishmongers standing within and without		19	0
From the butchers standing there	1	7	4
(And so weekly until Lent)			
On Saturday the first of March from the Stockes			
From the fishmongers standing within and without		19	0
From the butchers nothing because it is Lent			
(And so for 6 weeks)			
On Saturday next before the feast of St. George the Martyr (Apr. 23)			
From the Fishmongers standing within and without		19	0
From the Butchers standing there	1	9	0
On Saturday next after the feast of S. Mark Evangelist (Apr. 25)			
From the fishmongers standing within and without		19	0
From the butchers standing there	1	9	0
(And so until Mid-summer)			

On Saturday before the Feast of the Nativity of St. John
 the Baptist (June 24)

From the fishmongers standing within and without		19	0
From the butchers standing there	1	4	5

 (And so until Aug. 9).

On Saturday the vigil of St. Laurence (Aug. 10)

From the fishmongers standing within and without		12	1¼
From the butchers standing there	1	4	5

On Saturday next before the Feast of the Assumption of B.
 Mary (Aug. 15)

From the fishmongers standing there within and without		19	9
From the butchers standing there	1	2	5

On Saturday the Vigil of St. Bartholomew the Apostle
 (Aug. 24)

From the fishmongers standing within and without		6	7½
From the butchers standing there	1	2	5

On Saturday after the feast of the Decollation of St. John
 the Baptist (Aug. 29)

From the fishmongers (as above)		8	9
From the butchers	1	2	5

On Saturday next before the feast of the Nativity of the B.
 Mary (Sept. 8)

From the fishmongers standing within and without		7	3
From the butchers standing there	1	2	5

 (And so for the next three weeks until Michaelmas
 6 Richard II).

Account of the Wardens of London Bridge from Michaelmas 19
Richard II to Michaelmas 20 *Richard II* [1395–6].

  Item the same answer for £90 3s. 7d. received from the fishmongers
and butchers standing at the Stocks.

  Item they answer for £10 10s. 9d. received from the foreign clothiers
standing above the Stockes throughout the said year selling cloth.

Received from the Stockes

On Saturday next before feast of St. Michael viz. 25th Sept.

From the fishmongers standing within and without	10s.
From the butchers standing there	10s.

 (And so every week until Lent)

On Saturday 26 February

From the fishmongers standing within and without	11s. 10d.
From the butchers nothing because Lent	

On Saturday 4 March
From the fishmongers as above   14   3
From the butchers nothing because Lent

On Saturday 11 March
From the fishmongers   13   4
From the butchers nothing because Lent

In the following weeks until Easter from the fishmongers the receipts are: 14. 6, 15s., 15s., and 14s.

After Lent the receipts are as follows weekly:

	Fishmongers		Butchers	
	s.	d.	s.	d.
Saturday 15 April	12	6	10	6
Saturday 22 ,,	11	0	10	6
,, 29 ,,	14	0	10	6
,, 6 May	12	0	10	6
,, 13 ,,	14	0	10	2
Saturday Eve of Pentecost 22 May	13	0	11	10
,, 27 May	13	8	10	4
,, 3 June	12	3	11	6
,, 10 ,,	12	6	12	0
,, 17 ,,	12	4	11	0
,, 24 ,,	14	4	4	0
,, 1 July	13	3	14	6
,, 8 ,,	13	2	11	0
,, 15 ,,	11	2	10	2
,, 22 ,,	15	1	13	6
,, 29 ,,	13	7	11	10
,, 5 August	11	10	11	4
,, 12 ,,	12	6	11	3
,, 19 ,,	11	2	11	9
,, 26 ,,	11	4	13	2
,, 2 Sept.	10	2	12	6
,, 9 ,,	9	3	12	6
,, 16 ,,	9	11	12	6
,, 23 ,,	14	2	12	6

In the *Chronicles of London Bridge* by Richard Thomson, an antiquary (p. 268), there is a translation of a copy of a deed borrowed from the Corporation in 1653; it is in the Harleian Collection at the British Museum, No. 6016, folios 82–97. It is lucky the copy was made as the original is lost. At the end the copyist wrote "Finis 11 March 1653." There is no date to the list of properties, which is in Latin, but it is evidently later than the document printed above which was made in 32

Edward III (1357–8), and is now at the Guildhall; this is proved by the fact that tenements are sometimes referred to as some time or formerly belonging to the tenants mentioned in the existing Guildhall documents. As an instance, in the Harleian MS. we read of a corner tenement in the Parish of St Mary Woolnoth which was "sometime of Hamo Lumbard." In the Guildhall Rental the tenant mentioned is Hamo Lumbard. Again in the Guildhall document one tenant on the first floor of the Stocks building was "John Lovekyn junior." In the Harleian MS. the tenant of the same room was "John Lovekyn." This man is referred to in the Calendar of Wills, Court of Husting. He was trustee for Adam de la Pole "stockfishmonger," who died in 1349. He was Sheriff in 1342, was afterwards four times Mayor and died in 1368. It is true he had a nephew of the same name, to whom he left certain property, not at the market, but it is doubtful if the nephew would be alive 68 years later, or 1436, the date in the *Chronicles of London Bridge*; and William Walleworth was Lovekyn's "servant."

The translation from the Harleian Collection gives a description of the Stocks Building which is of great interest, but is difficult to understand because it contains the following words (p. 269, lines 1 and 2): "Upon this Cattle stall are three mansions, and one slaughter house built above it," and again line 11: "Also on the South part of the Stocks is a slaughter house, for which rent is not paid." The idea of a slaughterhouse on the first floor of a building was rather startling, and a comparison of the *Chronicles of London Bridge* with the Harleian MS. proved that the translation, which was published in 1825, is a very bad one. When the following corrections are made it will be found that the document at the British Museum practically agrees with the original document of 1357–8 at the Guildhall, which is printed above.

P. 268, line 6 from the bottom of the page, "Cattle-Fold" should be simply "Fold."

P. 269, line 1, "Upon this Cattle stall are three mansions, and one slaughter house built above it" should read "Upon this fold are three mansions (*i.e.* dwelling houses) and a chamber for putting pledges in, whereof one dwelling house is there at the Eastern end towards Cornhill." Line 11, "Also on the

South part of the Stocks is a slaughter house, for which rent is not paid" should read "There is there upon the Stocks on the south side a room which is delivered to the Collector of rent to put pledges in." Line 13 "places measured for the Fishmongers' tables" should be "places measured by the Fishmongers' tables," *i.e.* the table was used to measure the spaces, all the tables being the same size.

Line 15, "Poulisset" should be "Paulisfet," *i.e.* Paul's feet.

The date assigned to the document in the *Chronicles of London Bridge* is 1436, but from the above facts it was probably a few years later than the Guildhall rental of 1357–8.

From two ancient deeds at the Public Record Office we gain further information, as follows:

C. 1675. Indenture witnessing that John Madley bailiff of the manor of Carleton of Sir Thomas Findern, knight has delivered to Harry Bray, draper, dwelling at the Stokkys, London, nine hundred five score and ten fleeces. Feast of St. Bartholomew. 23 Henry VI [1445].

B. 2125. Demise by John Prior of the Charterhouse to Isabella Bremen, widow, of London, of tenements in the parish of St. Mary Wolchirche, near by Stokkes for ten years. 24 October 5 Edward IV [1465].

From the Bridgemasters' Accounts:

Robert Colbroc ⎱ Masters.
William Trymnell ⎰

2 Henry VI [1424]

24th June. The fishmongers for their station at the Stockes by the rent collector[1] collecting this week	16s. 1d.
The butchers for their station there by the same rent collector this week collected	16s
1 July. The fishmongers for their station at the Stockes this week by the rent collector together with 5s. of the debt for the station of Agnes Barbour long in arrears	21s. 7d.
The butchers for their station there this week by the same rent collector collected	15s. 2d.
8 July. The fishmongers for their station at the Stockes by the rent collector this week	16s. 8d.
The Butchers for their station there by the same rent collector this week	15s. 6d.

[1] reddituarius.

15 July. The fishmongers for their station at the Stockes this
    week by the rent collector   15s. 2d.
        The butchers for their station there by the same rent
    collector   15s. 4d.

Bridgemasters' Accounts 1460–1484

Rental of proper Rents of London Bridge renewed at the Feast of
St. Michael the Archangel 39 Henry VI [1460].

The Stokkes

From John Pychard pelterer[1] for	40s.
From John Hay gentilman	28s.
From William Pycard tailor for 1 room	7s.
From Robert Alwent tailor for a room	6s. 8d.
From John Steyndrope for a room	6s.
From Henry Worle Barber for a room	6s. 8d.
From William Gladwyn for a room	10s.

Sum 104s. 4d.

The above refer to the rooms on the 1st floor.

*Account of Peter Aldfold and Peter Caldecote Wardens of the
Bridge of London from Michaelmas 39 Henry VI to Michaelmas
1 Edward IV [1460–1461]*

Farm of the Stokkes. (They render account) of £40 received of the
wardens of the craft of Butchers for the farm of half of the Stokkes of
London on the north side there selling flesh this year, thus by Nicholas
Wyfold late mayor of the City of London and the aldermen of the same
city and Thomas Cooke and Thomas Davy late wardens of the foresaid
Bridge to Richard Fremet and John Bowle then wardens of the same
craft of Butchers in the name of the Society of the foresaid craft demised,
to expose their flesh to sale there as in the composition between the same
Mayor aldermen and wardens of the bridge on the one party and the said
Richard Fremet and John Bowle in the name of the foresaid Society on
the other party thereof made, is fully contained; to be paid yearly to the
foresaid wardens of the Bridge and their successors or their certain
attorney every week of those 46 weeks falling outside Lent 17s. 4½d.
and more in addition[2] on Saturday the eve of Quinquagesima the Saturdays 9d. on the vigils of Quinquagesima and Eastereve being reckoned
within the said 46 weeks.

And of £28. 14s. 7d. received from Edmund Newman, Henry Smyth
and William Laurens citizens and stock fishmongers of London for the
southern side of the Market called the Stokkes called the Fishmarket
thus to them demised by Peter Aldfold and Peter Caldecote wardens of
the said Bridge to have and hold the said southern side or market to the
foresaid Edmund Henry and William from the 27th day of February in
the 38th year of the reign of the lord Henry VI late, in fact but not by

---

¹ pellipar.   ² Plus in toto.

right, King of England to the end of ten years then next following and fully to be completed: returning thence yearly to the said wardens and his successors or their certain attorney £27. 14s. 8d. to be paid every week thereof 10s. 8d. as in a certain indenture between the said wardens of the one party and the foresaid Edmund Henry and William of the other party thereof made fully contains.

Sum—£67. 14s. 8d.

1 *Edward IV.* (1461)
  Rental

11 Tenants	£5.	6.	4.

  Account

Farm of Butchers & Fishmongers	£67.	14.	8.

4 *Edward IV.* (1464)
  Rental. St Mary Woolchurch

2 tenants	£4.	13.	4.
Stocks			
11 tenants	4.	13.	0

  Account

Farm. William Stalon & John Rooke, Butchers	£40.	5.	9
John Cotyngham & Thomas Cotyngham, Fishmongers	£28.	3.	4.
	£68.	9.	1

8 *Edward IV.* (1468)
  Rental Stocks

14 Tenants	£10.	4.	4.

  Account

Farm of Stalon & Rooke. Butchers	£41.	3.	3.
„ „ Thomas Cotyngham Fish	28.	14.	2.
Boards		3.	4.
	£70.	0.	9.

12 *Edward IV.* (1472)
  Rental. St Mary Woolchurch

19 Tenants	£10.	8.	4.

  Account

Farm Stalon & Rooke, Butchers	£40.	5.	9.
William Postlothe, Fishmonger	28.	3.	4.

16 *Edward IV.* (1476)
  Rental. St Mary Woolchurch

16 Tenants	£10.	4.	4.

  Account

Farm of Stalon & Rooke Butchers	£40.	5.	9.
„ „ Fishmongers	28.	3.	4.
	£68.	9.	1.

17 *Edward IV.* (1477)
  Rental
    Stocks
      14 Tenants   £10.   4.   4
  Account
      Farm of Stalon & Rooke Butchers   £40.   5.   9.
      „   „   Fishmongers   27. 15.   2.
                                                           ――――――――――――
                                                             £68.   0. 11.

18 *Edward IV.* (1478)
  Rental
    Stocks
      14 Tenants   £10.   4.   4.
  Account
      Farm of Stalon & Rooke Butchers   £40.   5.   9.
      „   „   Fishmongers   28.   4.   3.
                                                           ――――――――――――
                                                             £68. 10.   0.
  Rental
      1479 16 Tenants.   1480 18 Tenants.   1481 & 1482 16
         Tenants each year £10.   4.   4.
  Account
      1479, 1480, 1481, 1482. Farm of the Butchers
         (no names given)   £40.   5.   9.
      1479. Farm Fishmongers   £18.   5. 10.
      1480.   „   „   21.   7.   8.
      1481.   „   „   22. 17.   0.
      1482.   „   „   21. 11.   8.

1 *Richard III.* (1483)
  Rental
      16 Tenants. Stocks   £10.   4.   4.
      (Note among them John Waleys)
  Account.
      "They be charged w^t xxxviij^{li} xj^s ix^d receyved of divers Bochers
for the fferme of that parte of the Stokks called the ffleshemarket
paing therefore every weke oute of lenten from Mighelmas unto
Shrovetide xvij^s vj^d and every weke from Erstereven unto Mighelmas w^t in the tyme of this accompte ev'y weke xvj^s j^d The whiche
parte of the Stokks called the ffleshemarket was wonte to be lete
before the tyme of this accompte for xvij^s vj^d wekely oute of lenten
And it is so nowe graunted by my lorde the Meyre and the Courte
for certeyn considerations moving them for xvj^s j^d wekely out of
the tyme of lenten. And with xx^{li} xviij^s ij^d receyved of divers ffysshe-
mongers sellying ffysshe at Stokks on the partie called the ffysshe-
market so lenten this yere by aprowment
                    S$\bar{m}$ lix^{li} ix^s xi^d"

2 *Richard III* (1484)
  Rental
      Atte Stokks.

Robert Marler for a teñᵗ late John Rose	v^{li}
Sir John Cherbery	x^s
John ffreman	viij^s
Thomas Johnson	vj^s viij^d
John Semon	x^s
Richard Parson	v^s
Humfrey Watson	v^s
Thomas Bradshawe	x^s
Robert May	vj^s viij^d
Richard Bonde	vj^s viij^d
Roger Walsale	vj^s viij^d
Willm̃ Esses	vj^s viij^d
William Barbo^r	vj^s viij^d
Thomas Bradshawe	vj^s viij^d
John Batte	vj^s viij^d
Thomas Downe	vj^s viij^d
James Long	vj^s viij^d
Robert Adams	v^s viij^d

                    Sm̄ xj^{li} iiij^d

  Account

Farm of Butchers of part of the Stokks called Fleshmarket	£38. 12. 0.	
Fishmongers	20. 15. 7.	£59. 7. 7.

1 *Henry VII* (1485)
  Rental

Stocks	£11. 0. 4.

  Account

Farm of Fishmongers & Butchers	£57. 5. 6.

The same sum appears in the Rental for the years 1486, 1490, 1493, and the Farm is variously given as £58. 8s. 7d., £59. os. 4d., £54. 19s. 8d.

The Rental is missing from 1495 to 1501, but the Account is recorded.

The Account for 14 Hen. VII (1498) gives the following:

Ferm of the fishemongers sellyng fisshe at the Stokks on that p̃ty called the fishem̃ket nowe leten to ferme to Willim̃ Barker for a terme of yeris paying therfore ev̾y weke duryng that t̾me vij^s vj^d and moreov̾ at ⸺ q^{r}ter of the yere x^s Sm̄ xx^{li}. And Bochers sellyng fleshe on that other p̃ty called the fleshemarket paying therfore ev̾y weke out of lenten xvj^s j^d. Sm̄ xxxvj^{li} xix^s x^d.

                    Sm̄ to gider lvj^{li} xix^s x^d.

(Barker's name appears down to and including 1504.)

17 *Henry VII* (1504)
  Rental

East end of the Stocks	
8 Tenants	£7. 4. 8.
West end of the Stocks	
11 Tenants	£3. 15. 8.
	£11. 0. 4.

  Account

Farm of the Fishmongers	£20.	
„ „ „ Butchers	£36. 19. 10.	£56. 19. 10.

23 *Henry VII* (1507)

Similar entries to the above except that Gerard Chauncey appears as the Farmer.

M 1505 Jawes Chauncey is given as farmer
1506 Gerard Chauncey „ „

10 *Henry VIII* (1518)
  Rental

East end of Stocks	£7. 14. 8.
West „ „ „	£3. 16. 8.
	£11. 11. 4.

  Account

Farm of Fishmongers let to		
Gerard Chauncey	£20.	
Butchers	£36. 19. 10.	£56. 19. 10.

11 *Henry VIII* (1519)
  Rental

East end of the Stocks	
8 Tenants	£7. 14. 8.
West end of the Stocks	
11 Tenants	£3. 16. 8.

  Account

Ferm of fishmongers at the Stocks for selling fish at part of Stocks called Fish market let to Robert Smyth	£20. 0. 0.	
And Butchers etc.	36. 19. 10.	

This entry occurs down to 28 Henry VIII, 1536.

29 *Henry VIII* (1537)
  Rental

East end of the Stocks	
8 Tenants	£7. 14. 8.
West end of the Stocks	3. 16. 8.

Account

Ferm of Fishmongers for selling fish at the part of the Stocks called Fish market let to ferm to Robert Typping[1]	£20.	0.	0.
And Butchers for selling flesh at part of the Stocks called Flesh market	£36.	19.	10.
	£56.	19.	10.

37 *Henry VIII* (1545)
Rental

East end of the Stocks			
8 Tenants	£7.	14.	8.
West end of the Stocks	£3.	16.	8.
	£11.	11.	4.

Account

Money received for selling Fish (as above) let to Edward Tipping	£20.	0.	0.
And Butchers (as above)	36.	19.	10.
	£56.	19.	10

Stocks Market   1st February 1542.   Cotes, Mayor.

Att this Court, Rowland Gyll, Knight & Alderman made his Report in writing, concerning the certainty of the Rentes of the Stokkes & Chambers as herafter ensueth—

Item. In the fish Stokkes 25 boards, 13/4*d* a weke—
Sum the hole yere £34. 13. 4.
Item. In the fleshe Stokkes 18 boards, 16/1*d* a weeke—
Sum the yere £41. 16. 4.

Item. 16 Chambers, Total £5. 13. 4.

Letter-Book Q, fo. 71 b.

9th September 1546.

Item. For Certain, good & reasonable considerations moving the Courte, it is this day agreed, enacted, and decreed by the same, that the Acte here made by the sayd Courte for and concerning the payinge of 40/- by the Tenants, Fermers, and Inhabitants of the Stokkes towards the payment of every Fifteenth, to be payed by the Inhabitants of the Parishe his service of our ladye of Woolcherche shall utterly cease, lose, & be void, and that the sayde sum of 40/- shall as well at the present tyme as it all and every tyme & tymes from henceforward be answered

[1] *Robert* Typping is evidently a mistake. The following appears in the proceedings of the Court of Aldermen. 23 January 28 Henry VIII (1536–7); Edward Typping, haberdasher to have lease of the Stokkes for 10 years, after the lease of Robert Smyth expires which is dated 14 Sept. 19 Hen. VIII (1527), paying £20 per annum for which Typping promised to pay £5 for an income towards the reparation of the Bridge. *Rep.* IX, fo. 237 b. On the 19th April, 1537, the Court decided that Typping should have a lease of the Bridgemasters for his more security. *Rep.* IX, fo. 248.

and payed towards the payment of Fifteenth thereafter, to be levyed and payed by the Brydgemasters of this Cytie for the tyme beinge, and not by the sayde Fermers and occupyers of the sayd Stokkes or any of them any thinge in the sayd former Acte contained to be contrary notwithstanding.   *Q*, fo. 185 b.

2 *Edward VI* (1548)
    Rental

East end of the Stocks			
8 Tenants	£7.	14.	8.
West end of the Stocks			
Richard Mauncell for 11 chambers	£3.	16.	8.
	11.	11.	4.

    Account

With the rent of the flesh and fish market	£50.	0.	0.

(A similar entry to the above occurs down to 1555.)

2 & 3 *Philip & Mary.* 1555.
    Rental

East end of the Stocks			
William Bitmanson	£3.	6.	8.
John Crouchman	£2.	0.	0.
Richard Mauncell for 6 Chambers	£2.	8.	0.
West end of the Stocks			
Richard Mauncell for 11 Chambers	£3.	16.	8.
	£11.	11.	4.

    Account

Received for flesh and fish market	£50.	0.	0.

1562.
    Rental

St Mary Woolchurch			
W. Bitmanson	£3.	6.	8.
J. Crouchman	£2.	0.	0.
The Stocks			
Rauffe White for 5 Chambers in the East end & 12 Chambers in the West end, with the flesh & fish markets these all in the lease for the rent by the year	£56.	4.	8.

Similar entries occur down to 1571.

1572.   Joan White appears in place of R. White & continues down to 1579.

1580[1].   William Heynes had the lease from Midsummer down to 1598.

   [1] *Rep.* xix, fo. 220. William Heynes fishmonger to have a lease of the City's house called the Stocks for 21 years at rent of £46. 4. 8. to be paid for the use of the Commonalty the same to begin at the death of the widow of Raffe Whyte—Court of Aldermen. 11 July 19 Eliz. 1576. Heynes obtained this Lease by request of Queen Elizabeth. See *Rep.* xix, fo. 212.

1599. John Catcher had Lease.
       (He died Jan. 1602–3.)
1602–3. Edward Catcher had Lease.
       (1617) Sub let to John Male.
       (1625) „ „ „ George Pollon.
1633. Edward Ditchfield had Lease.
1668. Robert Osbaston as Sub tenant to Ditchfield.
1669. Osbaston appears in Arrears List.
1670. The Property disappears from the Rental.
       (Note. The entries under St *Mary* Woolchurch occur with
       varying rents long after the Mansion House was built.)

From the many references to the first market building in
the foregoing pages, and elsewhere, we can get a very good idea
of it; we learn that the site was on the north side of the Church
of St Mary Woolchurch Haw, that the grant of land was made
by Letters Patent in 1282 according to the Husting Roll of
1283, that the building was let in 1283, and that it consisted
of two floors. The building is frequently referred to as "Le
Stocke," "Le Stokkes," "Les Stokkes," "Lez estokkes," "Lestokkes," there were stalls and benches in the building. Corn
was sold at the building (see pages 38 and 92).

According to Stow the site of the Stocks Market was on
the north side of the Church called "Woole Church where
sometime (the way being very large and broade) had stood a
payre of Stocks, for punishment of offenders, this building
tooke name of these Stockes," he states that the rent was
£46. 13s. 4d. p.a.[1] No doubt Stow obtained his information at
the Guildhall and the document he had access to for his information is the Husting Roll of 1283 printed above, chapter
II, p. 21.

The building was detached, for it had "a competent view
on all sides," there were "edifices on the first floor," there was
provision for the sale of fish or flesh "on the Western part of
the same house towards the Cheap of London." Cloth was sold
on the upper floor[2]. In 1345 there is a reference to pent houses
adjoining the building[3].

In the rent roll of 1381–2 we hear of "25 cupboards
above the Stocks." In 1386 cloth could be sold at the Stocks[4],
and for the year 1395–6 the sum of £10. 10s. 9d. was

---

[1] Stow, Kingsford's editon, vol. I. p. 226.   [2] See *Letter-Book H*, p. 301.
[3] Riley's *Memorials*, p. 223.   [4] *Letter-Book H*, p. 301.

"received from the foreign clothiers standing above the Stockes."

In 1357–8 in the rental of tenements we read of seven dwellings or rooms on the first floor, one dwelling let at £1. 10s. p.a., one £1 p.a., one 10s. p.a.; a total of £3 p.a. for three out of seven rooms: but in 1381 the 25 cupboards produced the large sum of £21. 13s. 4d. p.a.

Although we do not know how the market building of 1282 was constructed (it was possibly of wood) the information in the Guildhall deed of 1357 is so clear that it is possible to prepare a plan of the building which may be regarded as fairly accurate. The following are the data:

There were 71 plats each about 4 feet 6 inches long, and the positions of them are given. There were nineteen on the south side, and nineteen times 4 feet 6 inches gives 85 feet 6 inches as the inside length of the building; on the north side there were only 18, this would mean 4 feet 6 inches less in length and no doubt allowed for the entrance door. Then there were two middle rows, one 4 feet 6 inches × 15 = 67 feet 6 inches in length and the other 4 feet 6 inches × 14, here again the missing 4 feet 6 inches was doubtless for a passage space. At the eastern end there were three lengths of 4 feet 6 inches or 13 feet 6 inches, and at the western end only two, here again we get allowance for the doorway. Plan 2 shows the arrangements. On the assumption that there were no divisions between the plats the internal length was 85 feet 6 inches, and allowing a reasonable space between the rows the width was 27 feet. If we allow 12 inches as thickness of the walls, we get external dimensions of 87 feet 6 inches by 29 feet. If we refer to Leake's distorted plan (Plan 7) the dimensions average about 86 feet by 30 feet which corroborates the above plan. No stairway is shown inside the building, the market building of 1410 had stair ladders outside. In the illustration walls 3 feet thick are shown, making the total length of the building 91 feet 6 inches, and the width 33 feet[1].

Let us now consider the second building, erected 127 years after the first structure. In *Chronicle of London, 1089–1483*, edited by Nicolas, it is stated[2]: "Also in this yere (1410) the

---

[1] Leake's Plan shows the second building which was of stone, and had apparently about the same floor area as the earlier structure.   [2] P. 93.

stokkes between the Cornhull and the Poultrye was begone to make, and in the yere next folwnge it was full complet and made."

We learn from information printed above that there were windows on the south side of the building on both floors; that when the Vestry of St Mary Woolchurch Haw was rebuilt about 1442 adjoining the Stocks building, and blocking up the light, it was pulled down; that the Church, which was 72 feet long from east to west, and previously near the wall of the Stocks building, was re-erected 15 feet away. There was a public footway between the Church and the Stocks building, and this passed under the parsonage which was at the west end of the passage and built over it; the footway to be used only during the day-time. Water was laid on to or near the building, and there are references to this in the years 1509, 1520 and 1525. In 1527 there were 16 boards in the building. In 1542 we learn there were "15 chambers" in the building, 25 boards for butchers, and 17 boards for fishmongers. In 1554 there is a reference to the house or chamber occupied by "Parson Johns." In 1601 and 1645 we learn that the building was covered with lead, that men could occupy the rooms or chambers as long as they remained bachelors, but if they married the tenancy terminated. In 1645 the building is referred to as "that great stone house" and there are several references to the "Stone House." It was covered with lead[1].

In the Registers of St Mary Woolnoth and St Mary Woolchurch Haw, by Brooke and Hallen, under the entry for 1601–2 we find there were stocks in the parish and that the approach to the chambers on the upper floor was by ladders, evidently on the north side of the building as they interfered with the public way.

Stow refers to the second building as follows:

This Stockes market was again begunne to bee builded in the yere 1410 in the 11 of Henry the fourth, and was finished the yere following. In the yeare 1507 the same was rented 56 pound, 19 shillings ten pence. And in the yeare 1543, John Cotes being Mayor, there was in this Stockes Market for Fishmongers 25 boards or stalles rented yearely to thirty four pound thirteene shillings foure pence, there was for Butchers 18 boardes or stalles, rented at one and forty pound, sixteene shillings

[1] Plan 2 shows the internal arrangements of the 13th century building and the stone walls and surroundings of the 1410 building.

foure pence, and there were also chambers above, sixteen rented at five pounds, thirteene shillings foure pence, in all £82. 3. 0.

Stow's statement of the rental and accommodation in 1543 is to be found in *Letter-Book Q*, fol. 71 b, and is printed above, p. 83.

The number of tenants on the upper floors varies, the building was completed in 1411, but the earliest reference to the upper floors is in 1460:

Year		Tenants			£	s	d	
In 1460 there were		7	tenants and the total rent was		£5.	4.	4.	p.a.
„ 1461	„	11	„	„	5.	6.	4.	„
„ 1464	„	11	„	„	4.	13.	0.	„
„ 1468	„	14	„	„	10.	4.	4.	„
„ 1472	„	19	„	„	10.	8.	4.	„
„ 1476	„	16	„	„	10.	4.	4.	„
„ 1477	„	14	„	„	10.	4.	4.	„
„ 1478	„	14	„	„	10.	4.	4.	„
„ 1479	„	16	„	„	10.	4.	4.	„
„ 1480	„	18	„	„	10.	4.	4.	„
„ 1482	„	16	„	„	10.	4.	4.	„
„ 1483	„	16	„	„	10.	4.	4.	„
„ 1484	„	18	„	„	11.	0.	4.	„
„ 1485	„		„	„	11.	0.	4.	„
„ 1504	„	19	„	„	11.	0.	4.	„
„ 1518	„		„	„	11.	11.	4.	„
„ 1519	„	{ 8 at East end / 11 at West end }	„		11.	11.	4.	„
„ 1536	„	do.	„		11.	11.	4.	„
„ 1537	„	{ 8 at East end / 11 at West end }	„		11.	11.	4.	„
„ 1545	„	do.	„		11.	11.	4.	„
„ 1555	„	do.	„		11.	11.	4.	„
„ 1562	„	17						

Afterwards let with remainder of building.

In *Londinopolis* by James Howel, published in 1657, it is stated that the rental of the Stocks building in 1507 was £56. 19s. 10d., and in 1543 that there were 25 boards or stalls for fishmongers at a rental of £34. 13s. 4d. and 18 boards or stalls for butchers rented at £41. 16s. 4d.; also that there were 16 chambers above rented at £5. 13s. 4d. "in all eighty two pounds three shillings."

Let us now consider the probable position of the market building.

The following are the principal maps. With the exception of Overton's plan they have all been considerably enlarged by photography; as a rule they have no scale and it is well not to place confidence on their accuracy.

Plan 3 is Braun and Hogenburg's map of 1572; this shows St Mary Woolchurch Haw and perhaps the Stocks market just above it, but it is impossible to tell. This part is similar to Faithorne's map of 1658. (Plan 6.)

Plan 4 is Agas's map, dated about 1570; this again is a perspective view, "Stokes" is written in the Poultry, and "Woolchur" below the church, the churchyard is shown south of the church.

Plan 5 is Norden's map of 1593, which is more indistinct than the two plans mentioned above.

Plan 67 is considerably enlarged from a map at the British Museum, the date assigned to it is 1640; it is headed "The Country-man's or Strangers ready helpe." It has no scale. The "Poultrie" and "The Stocks" are marked, the building is distinctly shown, and confirms Plans 3 and 6. This is the earliest map showing buildings immediately south of the church.

Plan 6 is Faithorne and Newcourt's map of 1658, the church and perhaps the market are shown; as also are the buildings immediately south of the church. It is of so great interest that a large portion of the city is given.

Plan 7 is Leake's plan of 1666; this is the most useful plan there is to show the market. It has a scale; it shows the way left between the church and the market; it is however obviously inaccurate, for there is no reason why the market building should have been erected with such irregular angles as shown; again the angles of the church were no doubt right angles. This plan has been used largely in preparing Plan 2.

Plan 8 is Pricke's map of 1667 and is very similar to Overton's map.

Plan 9 is John Overton's map of 1676, engraved by Hollar, this is not enlarged; it shows the extent of the great fire, the market and the church are roughly shown.

Plan 10 is Ogilby and Morgan's map of 1677.

In 1723 there was an action by Lord Micklethwaite against the Mayor, and in the papers it is stated that the ground where

"The Stocks formerly stood appears by the ancient surveys to have been laid into the Street near the King on Horseback, and this evidence is strengthened by the Act 19 Car. 2, cap. 3, sec: 23 which particularly decided that the Street and passage out of the poultry leading into the West end of Cornhill near the place called the Stocks should be enlarged, as also by the Act of Common Council of 12 Feby: 1667."

A reference to the site of the old Stocks building is made in a tender dated 3rd March, 1748. An estimate of £200. 10s. refers to the paving "before the North front of the Mansion House and void place where the old House was pulled down."

PLATE X

SOBIESKI: FROM REMBRANDT'S PORTRAIT, FORMERLY AT PETROGRAD
By permission of the Medici Society

PLATE XI

THE STATUE AS RE-ERECTED AT NEWBY HALL, RIPON

Chapter IV

St Mary Woolchurch Haw

THE following notes refer to the neighbourhood, up to the date of the great fire of 1666.

St Mary Woolchurch Haw and Parsonage.

The question of the level of the land in this neighbourhood before the fire is a little difficult to understand. We read in the Rules and Directions signed by the Clerk to the Comissioners and published in 1667, that it was decided to lower the site of the market building by two feet "and that abatement to be gradually extended in Cornhill, Lombard Street, Threadneedle Street and the Poultry, and a little way into Walbrook, which about the South End of the Churchyard of St Mary Woolchurchhaw is to be raised about 2 feet, that the current of water may be stopt and turned back into the Stocks whence it is to be conveyed by a grated Sewer into the main sewer not far distant." This south boundary of the churchyard of St Mary was about 110 feet, on the average, north of St Stephen's church. The level of the ground adjoining the north wall of St Stephen was lowered by Dance and there was trouble about it (see p. 121). There are other references to the open channel on the north side of the market, it was referred to in the case of Micklethwaite *v.* Mayor, etc., as the "Northermost Channel."

In the case of "Burford and others *v.* Burdett and others," it was stated with regard to St Mary Woolchurchaw that land was "taken away to levell same so that the corpses there formerly buryd lyd very near the surface of the Earth." At the time of the levelling the tomb-stones would be removed, but at least one was found when the Mansion House was built; there is an illustration of it at the Bodleian Library, Oxford; it was dated May, 1442.

Stow states that the beam was in the churchyard, and it is to be noted that the churchyard is sometimes referred to as the Church-Haw. Howel, in *Londinopolis* (1657), refers to St Mary Botham, or Boat Haw "adjoining to a Haw or Yard," and in the deed (p. 38) of 19th April, 1442, reference is made to the "Churchhawe grounde." This deed also states that the churchyard previous to 1410 extended right up to the south wall of the market building, which is referred to as the "Corne Market." The churchyard on the south of the church is shown on the maps of Braun and Hogenburg, and of Agas (see Plans 3 and 4). The deed of 1442 reads as if the parsonage had been erected before that date and was not being erected at the same time as the new church.

In the agreement dated 16th June, 1324, printed in the *Chronicles of London Bridge*, the site of the Stocks Market building is described as being on the north side of the "Cemetry of the Church of Woolchurch," the church was south of the cemetery and the haw or yard for weighing wool was south of the church.

Although the stocks were removed when the Stocks building was erected, they were re-erected in the parish. In the Churchwarden's Accounts of St Mary Woolchurch Haw we find the following interesting entries:

1560.	Item paid the XXIX daye of March for making the Arber in the Churchyard	xvi*d*.
1570.	Item paid for ringing the bells when the Queens Majestie throughe the citie to the Royall Exchange	vii*d*.
1586.	Paid to Thomas Addames dwellynge in the Duches place for cutinge and bindinge upe of all the trees in the churchyard	viij*s*.
1601–2.	Paid to Andrews for whipping the vagrants for one whole yeare	5*s* 4*d*
1603–4.	More paid for a pare of Stokes Iron worke and paintinge and a locke	£1. 17. 6.
1603–4.	More paid for removing the Ladders from the Stocks side into the Stocks against the Kings coming by and setting them up agayne	2*s* 4*d*
1607–8.	Paid Mr Godfrye for a double hanging lock for the prison Stocks	1 0*d*
1611–12.	Paid to Robert Andrews for yiorne worke for the whiping poste	2*s* 8*d*

1643.	Paid Robert Miles free stonemason for scaffold-ing and use of boards and poles with his and other masons and labourers wages in taking away the superstitious Images of the Virgin Mary and the Angels attending her and framing them into another decent shape in all as by agreement and his acquittance is	£9. 0. 0	
	Paid the carvers for work done by them in the like kinde in altering of images	£3. 8. 6.	
	Paid the carver for taking up and laying down with brass pins the Monuments and defacing the superstitious inscriptions and cutting others in their stead that are not offensive the some of	£4. 9. 6.	
	Paid Robert Miles for filling up the places where the superstitious images of brass were taken up and not fit to be put down againe	1. 4. 6.	
	Allowed for 77 lb of old brass taken out of superstitious monuments	4. 9.	
1644.	Paid an officer which brought an order to demolish the cross and other superstitious things about or in the church	1. 0.	
1663.	Paid Mr Robert Freeston for the Stocks and whipping post and for mending and painting them	£1. 16. 0.	
1666–9.	Paid to severall watchmen to secure what was left unburnt about the church	£9. 18. 0.	
	Paid for repairing Rigby's shed the things being broken by taking down the stocks	£2. 11. 0	

Memor. That after the fire 3 houses belonging to the parish of the aggregate rental of £70 were layd into the Markett by virtue of an act of Parliament full value was paid for them viz: £350.

We also learn that in 1616 a clock was given to the church "to strike on the great bell and with two dyales one towards the streate and the other within the church."

An account of the church is given in Newcourt's *Repertorium*.

I note that Michael Herring was churchwarden in 1643, John Seede in 1646, 1647, 1648, 1663. Captain Giles Travers in 1663, 1664; Thomas Langly in 1666, 1667; John Seede in 1671; Jonathan Botham and John Child in 1673; John Child in 1674. These names appear in the survey books of Oliver and Mills (chapter VIII, page 150).

There are two accounts in existence with reference to the ruins of the Church of St Mary Woolchurch Haw after the

fire of London[1]. The materials of the ruined church sold for
£191. 10s. and included "Bricks and Chalks," "Hard and
soft stones." £24. 13s. 2d. was paid for "takin down ye Church
and sorting stones," and the balance of £166. 16s. 10d. was
paid to the Vestry. One account is dated 22nd December, 1669.

With reference to the Parsonage House of St Mary Wool-
church Haw, an agreement was made between the Rector,
Samuel Angier, the Bishop of London, and the Mayor and
Commonalty of the City; it was dated 11th March, 1736, and
in 1737 a Private Act of Parliament was passed (Anno 10
George II, c. 19) entitled:

An act for confirming an agreement between the Rector of the
parish church of St Mary Woolnoth and of the united parishes of St Mary
Woolnoth and St Mary Woolchurch in the City of London, and the
Mayor, Commonalty, and Citizens of the said city, with the consent of
the patron and ordinary, for the grant of a parcel of ground therein
mentioned lying in Stocks Market, to the said Mayor, Commonalty and
Citizens, in consideration of a rent of 10 pounds a year, payable to the
rector and his successors for ever

In the act the market is referred to as "Stocks Market, otherwise Woolchurch Market," the security for the £10 p.a. was
the land of the Stocks Market and any buildings on the site.
The rent paid from the date of the fire until 1736 was £8 p.a.
This rent of £10 p.a. is still paid, it is sometimes humorously
referred to as the Ground Rent of the Mansion House, this is
of course incorrect.

Unfortunately it is impossible to make an accurate plan of
the church and churchyard from available data; the following
is a modernised copy of a deed at the Guildhall dealing with
the subject[2]:

The four viewers say that the void ground between the church called
Wolchirch and the said common ground of the Stokkes containeth in
length 4 score foot eleven inches of assize and in breadth 14 foot 7 inches
of assize and the post standing in the North east corner of the said new
building so there made by the said parson and parishioners is enforced
(forced into) and made there into the wall of the same Stokkes the thickness of the legement table that is to say in depth inward 5 inches and in
breadth 11 inches which is the breadth of the same post and in height
17 inches and a half. And over that they have broken the Water table
above of the same wall to let in the said post to stand straight upright

[1] Guildhall Library MSS. 306.1 & 306.2.
[2] Comptroller's Deeds A. No. 30.

with the withdraught of the same wall from the legement table upward. And also they have encroached in with their timber above the said legement table to the which draught of the said wall in breadth 6 inches and in length from the said post westward 9 foot of assize except the breadth of a buttress there and also the same new building jutteth outward above over the common ground and before the said Stokkes 4 foot large of assize because of which jutting outwards they have cut a part of the pentice serving there to the west end of the Store house of the Stokkes.

The date of the above deed was apparently during the fifteenth century, and shortly after the erection of the church. The length of the vacant land is stated to be 80 feet 11 inches. The deed of 19th April, 1442 (p. 38), gives the length as 72 feet, and in June, 1346, the Corporation conveyed to the church authorities a small piece of ground at the east end of the church having a length of 7 feet 6 inches; this added to 72 feet makes a total length of 79 feet 6 inches. The difference of 1 foot 5 inches is trivial and perhaps the space was occupied by a post.

In the above deed the width between the buildings is stated to be 14 feet 7 inches and lower down we read that the plinth had 5-inch projections, this makes exactly 15 feet as the width to the upper face of the wall and corresponds with the deed of 1442.

As plotted in Plan 64 the north boundary of the church and the small yard make a total length of about 96 feet and this corresponds with Leake's map; Oliver states that the passage on the east side was 14 feet wide (Plan 18). Consequently the total north boundary plus 14 feet was 111 feet, the following extract from *Journal* 46, fol. 210, dated February, 1667–8, gives it as 110 feet.

That the Stocks being removed and laid into the Street Woolchurch and Churchyard with the same ground of some small Tenements or sheds lately adjoining to the Churchyard and belonging to that Parish, will contayne about 150 foot on the East side, about 140 foot on the South side, about 105 foot on the West side, and about 110 foot on the North side, taking in the passages on the East and South sides which parcel of ground we conceive will be a convenient place to supply the former use of the Stocks and the lower part of Cheapside with fish, flesh, fruit and herbs, being encompased about with short posts and laid open to the High Street on the North, and Walbrook on the West and to Bearbinder Lane on the East and South.

The dimension of 150 feet on the east side, including

Bearbinder Lane, verifies Leake's map, but Leake's southern dimension is far in excess of 140 feet, and he gives the western boundary as about 90 feet. The dimensions given in the *Journal* have never before been published. Oliver gives the width of the passages on the east and south sides of the church as 14 feet, consequently it is reasonable to assume that the church and yard measured on the north side about 96 feet, on the east side about 136 feet, on the south side about 126 feet and on the west side about 91 feet.

Leake's plan shows the angles of the Stocks buildings and the church as anything but right angles, no doubt they were right angles, the plan is obviously distorted. The reader can compare the map enlargements and will see how unreliable they are, no two of them agree, the maps of Agas, Braun and Hogenburg, Norden and Faithorne are all views, some of them show the churchyard on the south of the church; the tower was at the west end of the building; the plan by Pricke shows the church as rectangular.

Plan 18 is a reproduction of Oliver's survey, from the Guildhall Library books, described elsewhere (see p. 150). There is no date to the survey, but two plans on the same page are dated in 1669 and the survey was obviously made some little while after the fire for we read of a "Corner House already built." Three of the sides of the open space are tied by diagonal dimensions, but unfortunately the line of Bearbinder Lane is not a defined straight line. It is however a most valuable plan, and Bearbinder Lane, Walbrook, and the lane on the east side of the space are all figured as 14 feet wide.

In the case of Micklethwaite *v.* Mayor, etc. (1723–1725), George Smith, Clerk of the City's Works, attempted to ascertain the area of the church and neighbouring property, he said he had no reliable data but "Suppose Stocks Market consisted of Several propertys, the Church 6832 square feet, the Churchyard 2970"; but these figures are clearly unreliable if we consider the dimensions given above.

An analysis of the evidence as to the length of the east boundary of the market may serve as an instance of the difficulty of attempting to make an accurate plan of the neighbourhood.

Let us take the distance from the line of the Churchyard of St Stephen and work north.

PLATE XII

Mr. Dance

S I R,

Y OU are defired to meet the C O M M I T T E E for

the Mansion Houfe

at *Guildhall*, one *Thurfday* next, being the *firft*
Day of *March* 1770 at *9* of the Clock in the
fore noon.

Hen: Groome

SUMMONS TO MR DANCE TO ATTEND A MEETING
OF THE MANSION HOUSE COMMITTEE, 1 MARCH, 1770

PLATE XIII

A View of the Lord Mayors Mansion House, shewing the .... Vüe de l'Hôtel du Lord Maire, qui comprend la
Front of the House and the West Side. Façade et le Coté Occidental

VIEW OF THE MANSION HOUSE, LOOKING EAST AND SOUTH

Oliver in his plan of 1669 gives the following dimensions:

	10' 0"	
"Parish"	54' 8"	To Corner of Bearbinder Lane
To N.E. Corner	169' 0"	
Total	233' 8"	

The following dimensions may be of interest:

	Oliver's survey of 1669	Dance's site Plan of 1735	Present day	Hooke and Oliver's dimensions of 1692
From Churchyard to south side of Bearbinder Lane	64 8	72 0	70 0	Not marked
From south side of Bearbinder Lane to corner of Lombard St by N.E. corner of the present building	169 0	168 0	154 0	170 6
Total	233 8	240 0	224 0	

Now let us turn to Ogilby and Morgan's map of 1677 (Plan 10):

From Churchyard to Bearbinder Lane	88' 0"
From Bearbinder Lane S. side to N.E. corner	160' 0"
Total	248' 0"

Ogilby and Morgan's plan is very inaccurate, the north opening of the Market scales only 109 feet, and on Oliver's map of 1669 it is figured 122 feet. Hooke and Oliver's plans of 1692 are figured 122 feet 2 inches for the boundary in question.

In the action of Lord Micklethwaite, in the abstract of the deeds to show the City's title to the Stocks Market, is one dated 6th December, 21 Car. 2d, made between the Parishioners of St Mary Woolchurch Haw and Sir John Lawrence and others. This refers to certain buildings "burnt down in the late Dreadfull fire," and mentions

one Messuage neare the North wall of the said church...three other Messuages or tenements next adjoining...three little Messuages or Cottages...one other Messuage lying neare the East wall of the said Church a piece of ground whereof they are jointly seized with the City whereon a Messuage burnt downe was situate...all which tofts and grounds together with the ground whereupon the Church of the said Parish and a Messuage called the Parsonage house...and the Churchyard.

The lease of the parsonage site in 1673 was for 99 years at a rental of £8 p.a.

Mr Andrew Crispe, the "Rector of Woolchurch," demanded £10. 14s. 4d. p.a. for tithes; this was in February, 1667–8, and counsel's opinion was taken. Tithe amounting to £13. 0s. 5d. p.a. is now paid.

On 14th February, 1687–8, a petition by the rector states that "for divers years last past he had received £18. 13s. 4d. p.a.," one eighth "for glebe and the remainder for the tithe of houses laid into Woolchurch Markett," and prays that the payment might be continued. On 14th June, 1688, a report was made to the Court of Common Council and it was decided not to pay £10. 13s. 4d., for tithes of houses laid into the Market, until the Common Sergeant had reported his opinion, but that £8 for the glebe ground was to be paid, as it was part of the Market. A copy of the case submitted to Mr Andrew Crispe is in existence but not the opinion.

The following is an extract from the *Repertories*, dated 25th February, 1668–9:

Whereas the standing of St. Mary Woolchurch being one of the Churches to bee removed is dangerous to passengers and an hindrance and a discouragement to the new buildings there abouts and an obstruction to the Markett which is to be setled in place of the said church, It is thought fitt and ordered by this Court that the churchwardens and parishioners of St. Mary Woolnoth to which the said parish of St. Mary Woolchurch is to be added shall take or cause the parts of Woolchurch yet standing to bee forthwith taken downe and employed in rebuilding their own parish church and as they proceed in taking downe the said Church shall cause the ground to be cleered of the rubbish and the same to be duly carried away.

Stocks Building.

The first building was erected by Henry le Waleis in 1282.

Fabyan, who died in 1512, wrote "And this yere (1410) the market hous called the Stokkys, standynge by the Church of Seynt Mary Wolchirche of Lōdon was begon to be edyfyed."

In *Chronicle of London* 1089–1483[1], under the years 1410–11, it is stated: "Also in this yere the stokkes between the Cornhull and the Poultrye was begonne to make, and in the yere next folwynge it was full complet and made."

In a Release dated 7th October, 1671, the building is

[1] Ed. by Nicolas.

described as "one great stone house called the Stocks...with the Flesh and Fish Market and Chambers."

In 1671 the Executor William Osbolston, assignee of Edward Ditchfield, accepted £140 in settlement of any interest he had in

the ground whereon before the Fire stood one great stone house called the Stocks, and also in the Lease thereof granted with the Flesh and Fish Market and Chambers belonging granted 22 January 1633 unto the said Edward Ditchfiled by the Mayor, etc.

There is a reference in 1345 to the "pent houses adjoining the enclosed space called the Stokkes[1]."

In the deed of confirmation of 16th June, 1342, it states that the building site of the building was "contiguous to the Wall of the Cemetry of the Church of Woolchurch, on the North side." This document is printed in the *Chronicles of London Bridge*, p. 168, and is referred to in *Letter-Book E*, p. 186, and there are several other references to it. In Leake's plan of 1666 the churchyard is shown on the south side of the church; but according to the Agreement of 1442 (see p. 38) the church was rebuilt further north, "as far as our Churchawe ground" and "savynge of more grounde of our Churchawe on the south side of oure said Churche."

We learn from this deed that there was a right of way on the south side of the churchyard, this was closed and there was a public right of way for foot passengers between the church and the market building during the day-time only; and that at the west end of it the parsonage was built over it and people passed into the Poultry "by the way and postern under the same parsonage."

There was an entrance on the west door to the Stocks building; this is mentioned in a deed dated 11th August, 1645[2].

In 1736 counsel's opinion being taken in connection with various matters, reference was made to the Act of Parliament, 19 Car. 2, cap. 3, giving power to the Common Council to enlarge the street and passage out of the Poultry leading into the west end of Cornhill, and a reference was also made to the fact that on 12th February, 1667, the Common Council decided that the Stocks building should be removed and laid into

---

[1] Riley's *Memorials*, p. 223.
[2] See chap. II, p. 63.

the street; and a statement was made that this was done; and further that "the present Stocks Market is not any part of the Ground called the Stokkes, that being entirely laid into the Street."

We know that Samuel Pepys constantly visited the city during the fire; the Stocks building was evidently a substantial stone erection and no doubt the roof collapsed but the walls were left standing, the spread of the fire was over by September 6th, 1666, and two years later, on September 16th, 1668, Pepys wrote:

So to the office, and thence to St. James's to the Duke of York, walking it to the Temple, and in my way observe that the Stocks are now pulled quite down: and it will make the coming into Cornhill and Lumber Street mighty noble

Plan 2 shows the north boundary of the church, and is plotted from a description in 1357, but it had been rebuilt in 1410; and the agreement as to lights was made in 1442. Apparently the building of 1410 covered the same area as the previous structure, for Leake's plan gives roughly similar dimensions.

Bearbinder Lane.

This extended up to the High Street, on the east side of the church and churchyard, according to the Common Council minutes of February, 1667, and also according to the claim in the action of "Burford and others v. Burdett and others," where the market is described as "an open Markett encompassed with Short posts, and laid open to the High Streete on the North, to Walbrooke on the West and to Bearbinder Lane on the East and South."

The papers in the case of Micklethwaite v. Mayor, etc. (1723–5), state that the Lord Mayor "caused a lane called Beerbinder Lane to be made of part of the...premises, before the fire of London the said Lane lay severall yards north of the place where it now lyes," and "before the said ffire old bear-binder Lane lay thirty one feet more northerly at the West end adjoining to Wall brook...and twenty feet more northerly att the East end where it enters into the said Markett than it does now." This statement seems to be inaccurate. Bearbinder Lane was apparently about 45 feet more to the north at the west end and the variation at the east end was very slight. In the answers of the Corporation it was stated that no plan was known showing the exact position of the Lane, and it was suggested that excavations should be made to search for foundations.

James Smith, part author of the *Rejected Addresses*, published the following verse in *London Misnomers*, 1840:

> I went to Cornhill for a bushel of wheat,
> And sought it in vain ev'ry shop in.
> The Hermitage offered a tranquil retreat
> For the jolly Jack hermits of Wapping.
> Spring gardens, all wintry, appeared on the wane,
> Sun Alley's an absolute blinder;
> Mount Street is a level, and Bearbinder Lane
> Has neither a bear nor a binder.

The portion of the lane now existing is unfortunately known as one of the many George Streets of London. It would be a good idea to return to the old name.

There is a plan at Guildhall Library, dated 1832, which shows the footway running north and south on the east side of the Mansion House as "George Street," this is now known as Mansion House Place.

On Horwood's map of 1799 both names are given, also in maps up to 1832. George Street is mentioned in Robson's *London Directory* of 1835, and both names are mentioned up to 1841. In Johnson's *Directory* of 1817 George Street is given, but not Bearbinder Lane. A reference is made in 1780 in committee documents to George Street.

According to Leake's map, which was engraved by Virtue, the lane was more than 31 feet more northerly at the west end and apparently about 12 feet more northerly at the east end. The plan was incorrect.

Premises South of the Church and Churchyard, between those premises and St Stephen's Church.

According to a deed dated 21st December, 1651, John Cropley was the owner and John Seed his lessee, Michael Herring the occupier, and the premises comprised "Gate rooms, yards and garden." Seed owned other properties in the neighbourhood, the corner of the Poultry near the Mansion

House was known as "Seed's Corner." The premises were burnt down during the fire and the Court of Judicature ordered that John Seed should rebuild; the rent before the fire was £46 p.a., and a premium of £200 was paid; the term was 31 years; after the fire the rent was to be £30 p.a. and the term increased by 40 years. Seed sold his interest to John Cooke. Other property owned by John Cooke and Timothy Wade and leased at £152 p.a. to Thomas and Joseph Lister, described as

A shop as it was then inclosed formerly part of the old Hall, a Warehouse as it was then enclosed formerly an old buttery, a cellar under the said Warehouse with an hole going under part of the said Shop, a kitchen as it was enclosed and a hole or buttery by the Chimney there, a little Yard adjoining to the said Kitchen, a Parlour adjoining to the said Entry with a Clossett in it, a paire of staires, a little Chamber at the Stairs-head over part of the Kitchen and little Yard, a Chamber over the Parlour and another Chamber adjoining behind it with the Garrett or Darke Room over them, a Great Chamber with two clossetts therein lying over the said Kitchen and Warehouse and another lesser Chamber adjoining over the said shop and all lights etc: together with ingress etc. thro the great Yard adjoining to the said Shop and the great Gates at the Entrance thereof.

The lease was dated Christmas, 1661, and the tenants had certain rights of loading in the Great Yard, etc.

John Cooke also owned other property which was leased in May, 1664, at £100 p.a. The tenant was Richard Hare, the property is described as

All those the severall roomes and Garden Plott...situate lying and being in Walbrooke...at the East end of the great yard...the particulars of which roomes and Garden Plott are (vizt.) On the ground or 1st. story One Entry or Passage, one little Closett on the North side the said Entry or Passage A staircase leading upon the Southside the said Passage into a Warehouse Chamber, the said Warehouse Chamber lying in part over the said Entry, in other part over Listers Shop, and in other pt over the little Parlour thereafter menconed, One Yard paved with ffreestone at the end of the Entry, The Garden, One Warehouse erected on part of the Westside of the said Garden, a little Yard to keep Poultry in on the Westside the said Garden, The Kitchen on the Southside the paved Yard, A little Parlour on oneside the said Kitchen, a Closett in the Kitchen, a faire large Dining Roome with a Closett in the same on the same ffloor with the Kitchen, the little entry on Passage between the said Kitchen and Dining Roome, the stairs leading out of the Kitchen into a Cellar lying part under the Kitchen & part under the Dining Roome, the staircase leading up between the said Kitchen & Dining

Roome into the 2^d. story, In the second Story one Chamber over the Kitchen One large Chamber over the Dining Roome...one little chamber on the...3rd story etc.

The above particulars are from papers in connection with the action by Lord Micklethwaite against the City. The original deeds were missing, and unfortunately there are no plans.

The City's title referred to three houses in Walbrook "called the White Beare, the Wheatsheafe, and a house between them," bought from George Townsend, Henry ffewterell, Grace Townsend, and states that the City authorities had enlarged the passage of Bearbinder Lane.

A reference is also made to the purchase of other properties burnt down during the great fire, one building near the north wall of St Stephen's Church occupied by Sharly, three other buildings adjoining, three little messuages or cottages, a building or shed near the east wall of the church. Also another building, occupied by E. Phillips, on the site of the Parsonage House, church and churchyard of St Mary Woolchurch Haw.

Allen's ground is described as being 1012 feet super; all this land was "sett out for enlarging the Comon Passage of Woolchurch Markett."

The Parsonage House of St Mary Woolchurch Haw was laid into the Market.

The Public Record Office has an account of the Chancery proceeding of Micklethwaite *v.* Mayor and Corporation of London, 1714 to 1756 (Bundle 59, No. 21), the above details are referred to. The premises occupied by Michael Herring were relet part to Lister and part to Richard Hare, and the description includes a yard 18 feet by 10 feet, a garden, a warehouse on the west side of it, and a yard "to keep poultry in." Another building was let to R. Hare, who paid 3s. 4d. a year to the parson of St Stephen's Walbrook

for the use of a pipe fixed to the North wall of the church for conveying rain water from the tiling of the premises and for the benefit of two lights lately made by John Cooke looking into Saint Stephen's churchyard.

So the premises must have backed on to the church and also on to the churchyard, if so they would have blocked up the entrance.

In the claim by the plaintiff the building before the fire is described as containing

at least on the ground floor nine rooms...and was four stories high, and on the ground floor had at least four warehouses, four yards, one a large yard with penthouses and a passage into Old Bearbinder Lane as the said Lane lay before the Fire of London and a garden: the premises were situated east west north and south of the cart yard and part of them abutted south on several parts of St. Stephen's churchyard, north upon old Bearbinder Lane, west upon the small freeholds belonging to Mr Rider, Mr Harvey and Walbrook and the ground contained from east to west about 150 foot and had two pairs of great gates...there were at least 6 several tenants and two of them Lister and Hare...paid at the rate of £109 for some part.

The reply of the defendants gives the usual denials of any knowledge concerning the premises, and states that "as to the plan in Vertue's hands, being improved that the same was engraved at the request and charge of private persons and was not to be relyed on," they had a plan made by the Clerk of the City's Works, but as that was made partly by "guess work" the old landmarks being entirely unmoved they refused to consider it.

THE Citie also paid besides the Sums aforesaid for other ground laid into that Markett as ffollows (vizt.)

		£	s.	d.
15° June 1669.	Paid George Lee of the Innere Temple Esqre. for ground laid into the New Markett place where Woolchurch formerly stood	25	0	0
5° Augt „	Paid to Grace Townsend and Henry Fewterell for ground laid into Woolchurch Markett	381	0	0
17° Decr „	Paid R. Thompson for ground in Woolchurch Markett place	80	0	0
16° May 1670.	Paid to the Parishoners of St. Mary Woolchurch for Parish ground laid into the New Markett place there	270	0	0
12° Apr. 1671.	Paid James Houblon for a part wall adjoining to the Piazza in Woolchurch Markett	36	13	4
6° March 1671.	Paid William Osbalston for his interest in the Stocks demolished &c	140	0	0

For these last Sumes of money I cannot find any Description of the Quantity of ground or any conveyances made to the City nor any other then the entries above in the Cities books.

It is clear that Lord Micklethwaite had considerable property, because on May 11th, 1756, the Court of Common Council considered the purchase of a ground rent of £150 p.a. of a lease for 999 years "for the greater part of the Ground on which the Mansion House is built."

In support of the City's title to the Stocks Market, an indenture was made on 16th June, 1669, that George Townsend owned three houses in Walbrooke called the White-Beare, the Wheatsheafe and a house between them, £455 was paid for the property and part was used for "enlarging the Passage of Bearbinder lane," and the remainder formed part of the market (see page 103).

Poultry.

It has been possible to make a plan of the frontage lines of the Poultry before the fire of London, and to claim for it that it may be considered fairly accurate.

The most convenient way to study the alterations is to work backwards. To-day the Poultry averages about 52 feet wide. I have before me a survey made in 1866 showing the improvements at that date, it is to a large scale and gives the frontage of each house, the width of the Poultry on the east side of Old Jewry was previous to that date 38 feet 3 inches, and it was about 39 feet wide opposite St Mildred's Church. On 29th April, 1667, an Act of Common Council decided

that the said street and passage at the East end of Cheapside leading into the Poultry shall be enlarged to be on a level line forty foot broad. That the said Street and passage out of the Poultry leading into the West end of Cornhill shall be enlarged to be of a breadth of forty foot.

Full particulars are printed in Maitland's *History of London*[1], and particulars are also given in Sir Walter Besant's *London in the times of the Stuarts*. Grocer's Alley in the Poultry was to be made 11 feet wide and Scalding Alley was to be made 9 feet wide. These improvements were carried out, the Poultry was made, practically, 40 feet wide shortly after the fire of London, and for about two hundred years it remained that width. The exact dimensions are given above. In 1866 the entire widening was made on the north side of the street. After the fire of London the widening was made on both sides of the street.

[1] Vol. 1, p. 443, Entick's edition, 1775.

John Oliver set out the foundations in the Poultry and has left some excellent plans such as Nos. 19, 20 A, 20 B; he shows exactly how much land had to be cut off to make the street the required width and by plotting that land we get the frontage line as it was before the great fire. He invariably gives the name of the owner on either side and at the back of the property he deals with. The dimensions agree as a rule, and a continuous line is possible.

It has however been impossible to link up the plots marked *A*, on Plan 64, so as to say exactly how far east or west they should be, but the line of frontage is definite. The breaks in the frontage were sometimes considerable, and instances are given in Cheapside and Fleet Street, etc., where the owner built on the public way so as to bring his frontage line up to the general line of the street.

With regard to Bucklersbury there were 20 surveys made by Oliver of properties on the south side of the street, and in no case was the width increased, one survey of a plot apparently at the corner of Walbrook gives a dimension of 14 feet 6 inches as the width of "Bucklersbury Street." This is the present width.

On the north side of Bucklersbury Oliver made 10 surveys and again there are no examples of a widening except at the junction with the Poultry.

With regard to the supply of water in the neighbourhood of the Stocks building the following extracts from the *Repertories* have never been published and may be of interest to the reader:

Tuesday 21 Sept 1527

Item this day Mr. Harry Dacres late alderman "of his own good mynde" on departing from his room of Alderman promised to spend upon my Lord Mayor and my masters his brethren at their recreation at the Condyttes 40s. And they shewed him that they would be at said condyttes on Monday next. *Repert.* VII, f. 288.

It is agreed that the Chamberlain go to Mr. Exmewe Alderman to demand of him 6 fother 16 cwt 3 quarters 21 lbs of lead pertaining to the store of the commonalty of the City according to the tenor of his bill obligatory dated 1 December 7 Henry VIII. *Ibid.*

24 Sept.

Mr. Rudstone and Mr. Chamberlain which were sent to Mr. Exmewe (as above) report that he answered that he will pay the money therefore and no lead. Wherefore the court will further be advised thereof. *Ibid.* f. 290.

1 March 1529

Forasmuch as the Conduit at the Stokkes occupieth a great room to the great "streyting" of the king's highway for horses and carts there to pass by therefore it is agreed that the conduit be taken down and that the Chamberlain shall cause there to be set up some other thing by his dis- cretion of less bulk with a cock running with water that people may there wash their hands.

As touching the conduit at Holborn Cross it shall be viewed by the Chamberlain who is to report on the costs for the perfection thereof. *Repert.* VIII, f. 27.

Thursday 24 April 4 Edward VI [1550]

Item this day Sir William Laxton Sir Marten Bowes knights, Mr. Judde Mr. Dobbs and Mr Hynde aldermen are appointed to "travayele" for the conveying of waste water of the conduit in Latheberye and of the great Conduite to St. John's in Walbroke and to London Wall or to one of those two places as they shall think most mete for the better serving of the citizens of this City of water. *Repert.* XII, f. 224.

Tuesday 7 May 36 Elizabeth [1594]

At this court it is ordered that Sir Richard Martyn knight, Mr. Skynner, Mr. Moseley aldermen Mr. Chamberlen John Blount Cloth- worker and Richard Proctor merchannt tailor or any fower or more of them shall finde out some convenyent place in Cheapside for placing of a cesterne there for the receipt of such water as shalbe brought thither by Bevis Bullmer Esquire. And Henry Woodwall to warne them to meet togeather and to attend on them. *Repert.* XXIII, f. 210 b.

Tuesday 12 November 36 Elizabeth [1594]

Item it is ordered that the twenty tonnes of Thames water which is to be brought into Cheapsyde by Beavis Bullmer Esq. shalbe brought to the Crosse there according to the reportes of Mr. Soame Mr. Moseley, Aldermen and other commytties formerly in that behalf appointed. And that the said Commytties shall have consideration for the altering of the stones and all other necessary thinges that are to be done at the said Crosse for the water worke there. *Ibid.* f. 313 b.

Tuesday 13 June 1592.

Item whereas Richard Hill fownder hath of long time kept the great conduyte in Cheape and had the keyes thereof in his custodye, wch con- duyt hath bin by him so negligently and carelessly looked unto, that very fowle disordered lewd and beastly parts have bin committed with in the said Conduyte head and cestern not fytt to bee spoken of for modestyes sake. And for that Sara Guy maid servant to the sayd Richard hath con- fessed that shee for her part hath at sondry tymes fowly and beastly abused the sayd Conduyte head and her sayd Mr. knew thereof and concealed the same; yt is therefore ordered decreed and adjudged by this court that the said Richard Hill and Sara Guy shall for their sayd misdemeanours on two market dayes next be sett on two several stages in Cheapsyde there to remain for the space of three howers a peice with papers on their heads declaring their offences and then to be committed to ward into one of the compters of this Citty there to remain during the pleasure of this court and the keyes of the sayd conduyte head to be taken from the sayd Hill. *Letter-Book A.B.* f. 92.

Tuesday 5 September 1609

Item it is ordered that Richard Wright Ironmonger William Bennett Fishmonger and John Davies haberdasher calling unto them the citty plomber and Founder to attend them shall forthwith view and see what decayed and defectes ther bee in the great cunditt in Cheapsyde either in pypes or other wise and they to make report thereof to this court in writing under their handes of thare opinions touching the same what is fitt to be done And Richard Midleton to warne them. *Repert.* xxix, f. 78 b.

Tuesday 19 Sept 1609

Item the plombers report concerning the repayring of the great Conduit in Cheapside being this day here read in Court and the same being conformed and veryfyed by Richard Wright etc. (see above) to whom the viewing of the decayes and defectes in the same conduit was by order of this court referred the fifth day of this instant moneth. And considering how needfull and how speedyly the same ought to be amended, it is ordered that Sir Stephen Soame knight Mr. Chamberleyn and the Comptroller of the Chamber shall take care that the same conduit be repaired and amended at the City charges in such sorte as they in their discretions shall thinke and fynd most fittinge. *Ibid.* f. 85 b.

There is a deed at Guildhall, dated 12th April, 1693, between the Mayor, etc., and Robert Aldersey, for providing a lead pipe from Tyburne to the city to supply the conduits in Cheapside and the Stocks Market. The contractor was to lay

one good and substantial pipe of lead from the...called the banquetting house...to the conduits in Cheapside...and from there to the high street called the Strand ffleet street Cheapside and the poultry...conduit in the Stocks Market,...

The cost was approximately £1000.

PLATE XIV

WEST FRONT OF THE MANSION HOUSE
Showing portico at the West Door—built 1775, afterwards removed. Published 1798 by T. Malton

PLATE XV

THE MANSION HOUSE FROM THE POULTRY

Chapter V

St Stephen, Walbrook

ST STEPHEN'S Church was originally built on the west side of Walbrook and Stow tells us that the site was used at a later date for a parsonage.

It has been possible to fix the site of this early church and it is shown on Plan 21. It is now known as No. 4, Walbrook. After the great fire Oliver settled the dimensions of this plot, on the plan he wrote as follows:

I sett out one foundation for Mr Jeramy Royston in Wall Brooke which was the ould Church of St. Steven as designed on the other side this 20th May 1674[1].

Oliver also settled the adjoining site and the alley is marked "Church way to ye Bull[2]." We know the church had a belfry[3], and the alley is still called Bell Court. The building is still parish property.

We know from *Letter-Book C*, p. 71, that in the year 1300 the parishioners were bound to repair the covering over the Walbrook as the chancel abutted on to the stream.

The following are translations of the original deeds relating to the first church on the present site. The deeds are deposited in the Guildhall Library, and have never been published.

Charter of Robert Chichele (xxi. 3).

Know all present and future that I Robert Chichele citizen and grocer of London; considering that the Church of St. Stephen of Walbroke in the City of London, which is of the advowson of the religious men the Abbot and Convent of St. John of Colchester, as it is said, is so narrow and straight that the parishioners of that church and others strangers flocking crowdedly to the same as well on solemn festivals as at other times to hear divine service, without waiting in great and greivous weariness cannot get in as they desire and are bound to do and that there is not space sufficient and near to the same church for the enlargement thereof or for making a cemetery or burial ground of the dead there; to

---

[1] Oliver's *Survey*, vol. II, p. 172.   [2] *Ibid.* p. 17.
[3] Riley's *Memorials*, pp. 13–14.

the honour of God and his glorious Virgin Mother Mary and in reverence of St. Stephen in whose honour the said church is dedicated, and especially that my own soul and the soul of Agnes my wife and the souls of William Stanndon formerly citizen and grocer of London and of Agnes his wife and of all others to whom I am deservedly bound, and of all and every Christ's Faithful departed may be specially had in recommendation by the prayers and suffrages of the foresaid parishioners, the royal licence in this behalf being first had and obtained; have given granted and by this my present charter confirmed to Thomas Suthwell clerk now parson of the foresaid church, a certain parcel or land or soil within the appurtenances lying in the said parish of St. Stephen in Walbroke in the City aforesaid, containing 208½ feet in length and 66 feet in breadth, as the said parcel of land or soil with the appurtenances lies between the tenement late of Thomas Hanhampstede's grocer on the northern side, and the tenement sometime Adam de Bwny's on the southern side and the tenement of the Mayor and Commonalty of the City of London which John Hende lately held on the Eastern side and the highway of Walbroke on the Western side: to have and to hold all the foresaid parcel of land or soil with the appurtenances to the foresaid Thomas Suthwell now parson of the foresaid church and his successors parsons of the same church forever in pure and perpetual alms of the chief lords of that fee by the services therefore due and by right accustomed to this intention viz:—that the foresaid parishioners may without delay cause to be newly constructed and built another church upon the said parcel of land or soil in honour of St. Stephen and a cemetery for the burial of the dead and also certain houses for the parson and his successors to dwell in and inhabit there by the licence of the ordinary of the place and of others concerned according to the tenor of our lord the king's letters patent of licence in this behalf had and obtained. In testimony whereof to this present charter I have put my seal, Henry Barton being then Mayor of London, John Abbot and Thomas Dufhouse then sheriffs of the same city, and Robert Whityngham alderman of that ward. Witnesses, Thomas Knolles junior, Thomas Cateworth, William Bothe, grocers, John Lemman, John Trethewy skinners, citizens of London and others. Dated London 8 May in the 7th year of King Henry the Sixth after the conquest of England.

(Enrolled in the Hustings Monday before 5th Barnabas 7 Hen. VI.) (1429)

Sir Henry Barton was Mayor 1428–9, when Abbot and Dufhouse were Sheriffs; he was previously Mayor 1416–17.

Abstract of the King's Licence for R. Chichele's gift (xxi. 4).

The King having due regard to the honour of God, considering that the Church of St. Stephen's Walbroke, in the gift of the Abbey of St. John Colchester, is so narrow that parishioners and others frequenting it on festivals and other times cannot get in to hear without long waiting, and that there is no place sufficient and near enough for its enlargement and for a cemetery and having regard to the pious and devout intention of Robert Chichele, citizen and grocer of London who, kindled with zeal and wholesome charity intends to help the parishioners in their behalf, to the honour of God and in reverence of St. Stephen, that he (the king) may participate in the prayers and suffrages of the parishioners; grants licence, with the assent of his council that R. Chichele in his own life or his heirs or assigns after his death may give a certain parcel of land or soil with the appurtenances in the parish of St. Stephen Walbroke containing 208½ ft. in length and 66 ft. in breadth, held of the king in burgage like all the City of London and worth yearly 13s. 4d. according to the inquisition thereon returned by Henry Barton the Mayor and Eschaetor of London to Thomas Suthwell clerk now parson and to his successors forever to the end that the parishioners may build on that parcel of land another church and make a graveyard and erect houses for the parson and his successors to dwell in, with the licence of the ordinary of the place and others interested, and that the Abbot of Colchester and his successors may be patrons of the new church of St. Stephen to be built, and as often as the church is vacant by death or resignation of the parson may present a fit parson to the ordinary, and licence to the said Thomas Suthwell that he may receive the land from Robert Chichele the Statute of not placing lands and tenements in mortmain, notwithstanding.

Dated at Westminster. 1 July 6 Henry VI.

By writ of privy seal and for 5 marks paid into the hanaper (With the royal seal still attached.)

Faculty of the Bishop of London for the New Church of St. Stephen (XXI. 5).

William by divine permission Bishop of London to all the sons of holy Mother Church to whom the present letters shall come and especially to Robert Chichele citizen and grocer of London and to the parishioners of the Church of St. Stephen of Wallbroke of the foresaid city, greeting. Know that whereas our Lord King lately of his special grace and with the advice and assent of his council and at the devout supplication of the forementioned Robert Chichele citizen of London, has granted and given licence that he Robert in his own lifetime or his heirs or assigns after his death may give a certain parcel of land or soil with the appurtences in the parish of St. Stephen of Walbroke in the city of London containing in itself certain feet in length and certain feet in breadth to Thomas Suthwell clerk now parson of the foresaid church forever to the end that the parishioners of the same may cause to be newly built and constructed another church on the said parcel of land in honour of St. Stephen and a cemetery for the burial of the dead and houses for the same parson and his successors to dwell in and inhabit with the licence of the ordinary and other persons interested on this behalf, as concerning these and other things is fully contained in the letters patent of our said lord the King thereof made: we indeed, the gracious and meritorious grant of our said lord the King, so far as in us lies, desiring to follow in this behalf, and the pious and devout intention of the foresaid Robert Chichele in this behalf deservedly commending, to you the foresaid Robert Chichele citizen and grocer of London and the parishioners aforesaid of the said church of St. Stephen of Walbroke aforesaid that you may cause to be built and constructed another church on the said parcel of land or soil in honour of St. Stephen. We grant our special licence by these presents, saving in everything the episcopal rights and customs, and the dignity of our church of London. In testimony whereof we have caused to be made these our testimonial letters patent given in our Palace of London 4th day of July A.D. 1428 and the third year of our consecration.

(With the seal (broken) attached.)

Stow quotes from the above charter and states that the site given by Robert Chichley was "one plot of grounde, containing 208 foote and a halfe in length and sixtie sixe foot in breadth." He adds that when the church was completed in 1439 it was 125 feet long by 67 feet wide, and the churchyard 90 feet long by 37 feet wide. That would make the total length 215 feet instead of 208 feet; but the churchyard was only 37 feet wide instead of 66 feet. Stow evidently referred to the frontage to Walbrook.

The following is a modernised copy from the deeds of the church, the original deeds were printed in the *Transactions of the London and Middlesex Archaeological Society*, vol. v, p. 332.

This is the bounding of the ground of St. Stephen's Church upon Walbrooke:

Imprimis. Saint Stephen's Church is of breadth at the East and from Paul's Rent to William Whetenhaly's Rent, grocer, 67 foot and more.

Also it is of breadth at the west end by the street upon Walbrook, between the rent of Paul's and Whetenhaly's rent 66 foot and more.

Also it is of length on the south side by Paul's rent, from the street upon Walbrook, unto the garden-wall of Paul's rent 115 feet and more.

Also it is of length, on the north side by William Whetenhaly's rent, grocer, from the street of Walbrook, unto the outer (further) side of the door in the churchyard, 125 feet and more.

Also Saint Stephen's Churchyard is of length on the north side from William Whetenhal's rent, grocer, to the rent that was sometime John Hendes, draper, 90 feet and more.

Also it is of length on the south side from the same church wall unto the rent that was sometime the said John Hendes, draper, 84 feet six inches and more.

Also it is of breadth at the East end by the said John Hendes rent, 35 foot and more.

PLATE XVI

A VIEW OF THE MANSION HOUSE, 1751

Drawn and engraved by T. Bowles

PLATE XVII

THE MANSION HOUSE FROM THE BANK, 1830

Drawn by T. H. Shepherd, engraved by W. Wallis

Also it is of breadth at the west end, by the said Church from Paul's rent *to our new Churchyard wall* 37 foot and 4 inches and more.

Also our stone wall that is our defence between us and Whetenhale, grocer, is of length from our churchwall on the north side of the said church, unto Whetenhale's rent at Berebynder (Bearbinder) Lane's end, 70 foot and more.

Also the east side of the same ground by William of Graschirch's house, is of length from Berebynder Lane to our churchwall 60 foot and 8 inches and more.

The breadth thereof at the north end by the street side is 16 foot and more.

The breadth thereof at the south end by our *churchyard* is 20 foot and 2 inches and more.

The length of all our ground from Berebynder Lane to the wall of Paul's rent is 98 feet and more.

The length from Walbrook unto the said rent of John Hende is 215 feet and more.

The church was commenced 1429. The dimensions in the above deed give a total length on the north side of the property, of 215 feet, which is about the present dimensions.

In addition to the above there was the land between the north side of the churchyard and Bearbinder Lane, this had 16 feet frontage to Bearbinder Lane, it was 60 feet 8 inches on the east side, 70 feet long on the west side, and 20 feet 2 inches on the south side where it joined the churchyard. Stow makes no mention of this strip of land but he states that Chichley paid "the charges of all the timber worke on the procession way, and layde the lead upon it at his owne cost, he also gave all the timber for the rooffing of the two side Iles." It is possible the entrance from Bearbinder Lane was the procession way referred to, this strip of land is now occupied by the south-east corner of the Mansion House and the public way. See Plan 17.

We learn from the Inventory at Guildhall that there was a cloister and that there were hedges to the churchyard.

There is a reference to the approach to the church from Berebynder Lane in 1508, Thomas Reede was to be buried in the alley, etc.

In a letter dated 3rd March, 1748, the Rector of St Stephen's, Walbrook, stated that the passage to the churchyard was

a Road which the Rectors of the Parish have enjoyed for three hundred Years, and was granted to them by the Gentleman that gave the Ground, and Confirmed in Mortmain under the Great Seal.

Dance realised that the church property joined the Mansion House site, for in February, 1749, he made an estimate

of work necessary to open up way behind Mansion House to Bearbinder Lane to remove the ground and level part of the churchyard with the passage, to erect and make good the old door case.

In an action of "Burford and others *v*. Burdett and other Farmers of the Markets and the Mayor etc." it was stated in the claim, dated 10th October, 1692, that the farmers (*i.e.* tenants) of the market had erected several "Shedds upon that part of the Markett which was formerly the Church and Churchyard."

In 1694 there was a conveyance from the Grocers' Company of two small pieces of ground. This deed is with others belonging to the parish deposited at the Guildhall. Both pieces fronted Walbrook; one was about 20 feet square, on the south side of the tower, the other had about 7 foot frontage and was about 14 feet deep. The deed states that it was a piece of ground "whereon parts of the said Church stood before the late dreadful fire."

In the deeds at the Guildhall is the following:

XXIII. 1. Faculty from the Bishop of London for William Stonestreet, Rector and William East and James Saunders churchwardens of the parish Church of St. Stephen's Walbrook to build a parsonage house, on a void piece of ground about 20 feet square adjoining the church "whereon part of the said Church stood before the dreadfull fire, which ground is of no use to the parish," the Grocer's Company as petrons of the Church having already consented. Dated 20 Feb. 1691–2.

The following is a modernised copy from the Inventory of the fifteenth century.

(Robert Chechile laid the first and second stone etc.)
...with whose good (money) the ground that the new church stands now on and the houses with all that then stood thereon, and the churchyard with the tenement annexed thereto, which has its boundary at Bere bynder (Bearbinder) Lane was bought by the said Robert Chechile for 200 marks of the Wardens of the Grocers of London and at that time was let yearly for 26 marks.

When the rebuilding of the city after the great fire was considered, certain rules were made with regard to the widening and levelling of streets. The site of the Stocks Market building was lowered two feet, and it seems probable that the level of the churchyard of St Stephen is now the level of the yard before the fire, it is now about 3 feet above the public way at the back of the Mansion House, on a level with the floor of the church, and about 6 feet above the level of Walbrook. There are no less than 14 steps up to the floor of the building from the Walbrook level, and as a rule Wren built his churches with the floor line only slightly above the level of the street. We know the pre-fire church was of the same width, the old foundations were doubtless used and I think we may assume that the floor line of the medieval church was at about the same level as that of Wren's church, which is about the same level as the churchyard.

When the Mansion House was built there was a serious complaint that the Corporation had trespassed on the property of the church; this is related later in this chapter (pp. 120–122).

It is much to be regretted that there is no history of the present and previous buildings; much information is to be obtained from Mr Milbourn's papers in the *Transactions of the London and Middlesex Archaeological Society*, vol. v, already referred to and in those of the *St Paul's Ecclesiological Society*, vol. i. Plates II and III show that there was an entrance on the north side of the church opening on to the Stocks Market. An examination of the panelling shows where the mouldings, etc., were cut for the return of the woodwork for the door enclosure, and there is a "straight joint" in the masonry which can be seen from the exterior.

There are many references in old documents to the Piazza which was built along the north wall of the church for the shelter of the market people and it is shown on maps by Ogilby and Morgan and others (see Plans 10 and 11), and in Plates VI and VII. The foundation stone of the present church was laid on 16th October, 1672, but in the following March there was a request that the steeple might be placed on the market land and it was agreed on 26th March, 1673, that "so much ground as is by them desired shall be conveyed over to the said parish upon such terms and for such rates as the City purchased the same," but it is obvious that nothing was done.

The following is an abstract from the minutes of a vestry meeting held on 15th October, 1673:

Mr. Robt. Waigh, Mr. Christ: Flow^r. Mr. Jno Pollexsen and Mr. Jno Lilburne, put in theire severall bills to bid for ye parsonage ground and twas consented he y^t bid most should have it to build one Merch^{ts} house ye perticulars discorsed of were Mr. Andrewes many lights and encroachm^{ts} ye Grocers Company their claime in a small part of ye Ground to ye East Joyning to ye Church Alley Mr. Batemans wall at ye west and to be free to ye build^r to put in his timbers twas agreed ye builder should have ye assistance of ye vestrey to cleare ye differences and incumberances but ye build^r to bare ye whole charge and in case Mr. Batemans wall be not free to ye Build^r and Companyes consent obtained y^n ye builder to bee free from his bargaine if he thinke fitt Mr. Waigh Mr. Pollexsen and Mr. Flow^r bid 15^{li} p Ann Mr. Jno Lilburne 15^{li} 5s p Annum twas agreed Mr. Lilburne should have it at ye Price and ye said Mr. Lilburne excepted of ye same.

From the description it is clear the parsonage ground was the site of the old church on the west side of Walbrook, Oliver's survey was made on 20th May, 1674 (see Plan 21), and the Mr Andrews who had ancient lights is shown on the plan as being the owner of the property on the south side of the parsonage ground. Church Alley is called "Aley" on the plan, and the dotted dimension of 4 feet by 15 feet apparently shows the land claimed by the Grocers' Company as "a small part of ye Ground to ye East Joyning to ye Church Alley." Stow states the parsonage house was on the site of the first church of St Stephen.

Among the deeds relating to St Stephen's is one dated 3rd January, 1773, this refers to a building at the west end of the church on the south side of the tower, "called the Rector's or Parsonage house," and also the "small house erected and built —on the north side of the said tower," this we know was the clerk's house. The rector was to have power to let the parsonage house.

In the *Repertories*, dated 28th April, 1668, we find a complaint by the churchwardens of St Stephen's church that Daniel Andrews was erecting a wall on the foundation of the ground belonging to the parsonage house, and the alderman and others were instructed to inquire into the matter. This was evidently the "Mr Andrews" named on the plan by Oliver (Plan 21).

The following is copied from the parish documents:

Whereas the Church of St. Stephen Walbrook was begun be rebuilt in an^o 1672 And whereas the Parishion^{ers} have advanced the sume of 3000^{li} towards rebuilding of their sd Church & Tower And whereas the Tower remains att the hight of 85 steps, and the Vestry stands soe adjoyning to it that it cannot be made usefull without rebuilding the same,

and the Scoffolds if struck will be chargeable to bee hereafter erected It is therefore Ordered that the said Tower be carried on, and the Porch of the Church standing conspicuous to the high street while the same shall be finished out of the Ordinary as it shall come in course. July 10th. 1679. JAM: EDWARDS, Mayor.
H. LONDON.

The following petition is of interest, Sir John Moore being Lord Mayor in 1681.

To the Right Honourable Sir John Moore Knight, Lord Mayor of the City of London.

And to the Right Worshipfull Court of Aldermen.

The humble Petition of the Parishioners of St Stephen's Walbrooke, London

SHEWETH

That the Steeple of the said Parrish Church was by the ffirst design thereof to be made ffronting the high street or Stocks Market, for a public Ornament to this City, but afterwards for some Considerations, known to this Honble Court, it was order'd that a handsome and Ornamentall Porch, fronting the Market aforesaid should be built in steede thereof And in pursuance an Order was then Signed, for the building by the then Lord Mayor and Lord Bishop of London, bearing date the 10th. July 1679. Whereupon Sir Christopher Wren made a draught for the said Porch for a Generall ornament as aforesaid, and hath often expressed his readiness to proceed therein, if Ground were assign'd for the Same: For obtaining whereof a Petition was then presented, but was opposed by the ffarmers of the Marketts Now the said Porch not being designed for any advantage to the Inhabitants of the said Parish but for a public Ornam^t to the said Church and this Honourable City. And your Petition^rs haveing been at great trouble and charge in beautifying the said Church answerable to the said intended Porch, and doe humbly conceive the said Ground to be of small benefitt to the City, being at present imploy'd for Slaughterhouses, Stables, Comon Jakes, and such like uses, to the very great anoyance of all the Neighbourhood, and others resorting to the said Church.

May it therefore pleas your Lordship and this Honble Court, to take the premises into your serious consideration whilst ye loan of ye publick money may be had, soe that y^o Peticon^rs receiving your finall resolves, may be concluded thereby, and be noe further troublesome to this Honble Court.

And yor Peticon^rs (as in duty bound) shall ever pray &c.

13th. December, 1681

The Peticon of the Prishioners of St. Stephen Walbrooke now prsited to this Court for leave to erect a Porch to their Parish Church upon parte of the Market Ground there Is by this Court referred to the consideracon of Sr Patience Ward Sr Robt. Geffery & Sr John Shorter Kn^{ts} & Aldern or any two of them And they to call before them the ffarmers of the Marketts & heare what objections may be made against the same And to certify unto this Court in writing under their hands how they find the same & their Opinions And John Doley to warne & attend them.

WAGSTAFFE.

18th. July, 1682.

This day a Report formerly made unto this Court touching the Portico desired by the Parishioners of St. Stephens Walbrooke to their Pish church was here againe openly read and taken into consideration by this Court the tenor whereof is as followeth—

To the R^t Honble the Lord Major and court of Aldren.

In obedience to the order of this Honble court wee whose names are subscribed have severall times viewed ye Pish church of St. Stephen Walbrooke and considered the desires of ye Pishioners for some of the Markett ground whereon to erect a Portico And we are of opinion that a Portico there will be very ornamentall and are informed that the charges thereof will not exceed CCC^{li} And therefore we humbly recomend it to y^r Lo^p to move the Lord Archbishop of Canterbury and Lord Bishop of London that an order may be issued out to Sr Christopher Wren for building the same if the pishion^{ers} will be oblidged (as they have promised) to sett up a clock and handsome dyall thereupon as the said Sr Christopher Wren shall direct And it is our further opinion that the ground whereon such a Portico shall be built be purchased out of the money appropriated for building of churches and annexed to the said pish church And that the ffarmers of the Marketts be required to take downe so much of the Piazzoes there as shall be requisite for the said Porch the said pishioners paying them for the same the sume of xx^{li} (as they agreed to doe) with which the said ffarmers have declared they will be satisfied for their Claime both to the ground and roome for so much of the Piazzoes as shall necessarily be taken downe All which nevertheless wee humbly submitt to the grave Judgment of this Honble court this 2nd. of May 1682.

P. WARD.   ROB^t. GEFFERY.
JN^o SHORTER.

And this court having also received informacon from the R^t Honble the Lord Major and seen a Note attesting the same under the hand of Peter Kidd one of the said ffarmers That the said ffarmers have received full satisfaction from the church Wardens of the said prish for the markett ground whereon the said Portico is to be erected And have given their consent that soe much of the said ground as shall be thought necessary may be used for that purpose This court doth therefore agree with the said Comittees in the said Report and doth recomend it to the R^t Honble the Lord Major to move for the building of the said portico accordingly And that soe much of the said ground as may be necessary for building thereof be purchased as in the said Report is mencoed.

WAGSTAFFE

Unfortunately Wren's design is not among the parish documents, but there are five designs for a clock. There is no trace at St Paul's of the documents, etc.

In the description of the church in the *Gentleman's Magazine*, 1813, p. 542, the oval windows are described as "having Doric architraves, and key stones of cherubim heads," "the lower half a blank wall," these no longer exist.

It is interesting to note that according to Ogilby and Morgan (1677) the main body of the church is shown, but there is no indication of a tower or porch or vestry; a small forecourt is indicated at the west end of the church (Plan 10).

Sir Christopher Wren designed a porch to open on to the Stocks Market, owing to opposition the porch was not built, but we know the doorway was used, for at a vestry meeting on 11th September, 1685, complaint was made that the "Intended doreway for a porch into the Stocks Market was at present a great añoyance to the church by reason of the offensive Stinks and Sents yᵗ come from Several Shedds yᵗ Joyned to it as a Slaughter house, herbe shop," etc.; it was ordered to be bricked up. The internal views, Plates II and III show the enclosure inside the church and the panelling still shows the mitres and indicates the alteration made when the lobby was removed.

At a vestry meeting on 17th June, 1681, it was decided to petition the Court of Aldermen for "demolishing yᵉ house of office wᶜʰ is in yᵉ Stocks Market by yᵉ north dore of yᵉ Church."

The Ordinances of the Court of Assistants of the Grocers' Company have the following entries:

Court held Tuesday 20 December 1692.

Also at this court Mr. William Stonestreete minister of St Stephen's Walbrook appeared and intimated to the court that the parishioners of the said parish were willing to build him a house for his residence in the same upon a wast peece of ground neare the Church. But that the parish desired the concurrence of this Court before they made any progress therein. This Court upon consideration thereof do empower and appoint the Wardens together with Mr. Stacee etc. (3 others named) a committee to view the said peece of ground and also to treat with the Church Wardens and inhabitants of the said parish about the said house and to report their proceedings thereon to the court of Assistants.

Court held Monday 16 *January* 1693.

Three others are added to the committee appointed to view the ground (as above).

Court held Friday 10 *February* 1693.

Alsoe this court doe order and agree that lycence be given to the Church Wardens and inhabitants of St. Stephen's Walbrooke, London to erect a house on the waste peece of ground adjoining to the Church there for the sole use and benefitt of Mr. William Stonestreet the present incumbent and his successors soe long as he or they shall live or reside in the same parish And upon condition that the said Church Wardens and inhabitants doe seale and execute or cause to be sealed and executed such instrument or writing for performance of the same as councell Learned in the law shall advise Between the parish and company necessary in that case to be done.

Court held 6 *July* 1694.

Alsoe this court doe empower and appoint Mr. Crosner and Mr. Sedgwick a committee to advise with counsell on the Deede lately drowne relating to the parsons and Clerke's houses of St. Stephen's Walbrooke (but at the charge of the said parish) and in case they shall be advised it may not be prejudiciall to the company to consent, the parish may goe on and finish the small house now erecting for the clerke of the parish.

Court held 17 *July* 1694.

Alsoe this day Mr. Sedgwick informed the Court that pursuant to an order of this court the sixth instant relating to the deede lately drawne Between the company and trustees of St. Stephen's Walbrooke touching the erecting of two houses for the Minister and Clerke of the said parish, he had attended Mr. Grainger and had advised with him on the said deed and produced his opinion in writing which being read and considered of this court doe order and agree that the said deed doe passe the common seale of this company and the Wardens with such members as is usual in like cases are thereby empowered to open the seale and seale the same accordingly.

The parsonage was built adjoining the church on the south side of the porch, and the clerk's house was on the site of the little bookseller's shop on the north side of the tower.

When Dance commenced to build the Mansion House he apparently had little respect for the church property; this is shown by the petition by the rector of St Stephen's.

COMMON COUNCIL. 14th. September, 1738.

Journal 58 fo. 103.

Petition of Rector and Inhabitants of United Parishes
of St. Stephen Walbrook and Bennet Sherehog

SHEWING

That workmen employed by Committee for building a Mansion
House have not only pulled down the Stone Porch that led to their
Church Yard but have conveyed away the same and Pavement;

That they have carried away the soil adjoining the Church although
the Ground belonged to the Church;

That the Walls of the Church had thereby been laid bare almost to
the Foundation which causes the rain-water to settle against the Church
and make its way through part thereof into the cellars of some of the
Inhabitants on the other side of the Church;

Read, and referred to the Committee to examine and report.

Mr Wilson, the rector, had written a letter previously,
which was considered on 16th May, 1738, and the committee
replied that they

will not invade Mr Wilson's property, that the digging mentioned in his
letter was by order of the Commissioners of Sewers, to make a drain into
the great sewer in Walbrook.

The above petition is more fully referred to in the minutes
of 14th September, 1738, it is stated that the

soil next adjoining the Church of about twelve feet and a half in Breadth
and about seventy four feet in length and about ten feet and a half in
Depth, altho' the said Ground did undoubtedly belong to the said Church,
as will appear by the Grant and plan annexed and confirmed under the
Great Seal of England.

The above dimensions are confusing, for the strip of land
between the church and Bearbinder Lane was 70 feet long for
its greatest length and an average of about 18 feet in width.

On the 3rd March, 1748, a letter was submitted from the
Revd Dr Wilson to the Court of Common Council.

To Sir John Barnard,
    Deans Yard, Westminster.
        Febry. 27th. 1748.

Sr.

I beg the favour of you to mention to the Comittee for building
the Mansion House, That about a year ago, I waited upon the Gentlemen at Guildhall to Represent to them, That by their pulling down the
Houses that joyned to a little House of mine next to the Church Steeple,

it w^d endanger mine, I was called in by the late Lord Mayor and assured by His Lordship, that if any Damage was done to me by the taking down those Houses, They w^d make it good.—As I then apprehended, That part of my House is fall'n down and has so damaged the rest, That I shall be oblig'd to Rebuild the whole from the Ground;—I have often spoke to Mr. Dance both before and since it fell, but he was very positive, contrary to the Opinion of Two Eminent Surveyors, that my House would Stand, tho' the others were remov'd and has since treated me in a Manner very unbecoming a Person in the Employment he is in.

To induce you, Sir, and the Comittee to favour Me upon this Occasion, I beg leave to Mention that ever since the Foundation of Mansion House has been laid, The Passage into the Church Yard, and so into the Church has been Shut up; By which Passage my Predecessors, had, in one Article avail'd themselves, of a Considerable Perquisite And this was a Road which the Rectors of the Parish have Enjoyed above three hundred Years, and was Granted to them by the Gentleman that gave the Ground, and Confirmed in Mortmain under the Great Seal, Mr. Dance has also pull'd down a Porch that belonged to the Church Yard Door contrary to my protest, and has actually built a part of the Mansion House upon the Wall of the Church Yard.

I mention these things at present not so much by way of Complaint but rather to induce the Gentlemen of the Comittee to be kind to me upon this Occasion, as I have been so great a looser, as being only Tenant for Life, and as I have Laid out above nine hundred Pounds upon My Rectory House and Glebe Houses, two of which have been unlet for many Years, and this and many other Inconveniences have arose from the Shutting up the Street and wayes leading to my Parish.

I submit the whole to your Candour and Judgement, not doubting but you will do me Justice and Represent this affair to the Comittee in a much better manner than I am able to do, which will add very much to the many favours You have already laid upon

     Sr.

       Your most Obedient & Most obliged Humble Servt.

           Thos. Wilson.

          Rector of St. Stephens, Walbrook.

The above grant in Mortmain is dated 6 Henry VI, and the above letter clearly shows that the rector claimed the strip of land between the present churchyard and Bearbinder Lane, which land was also at that time used as the churchyard, and that a porch existed on what at present is the public way on the south-east corner of the Mansion House. Dance refers to the old "door case" and confirms the statement as to the churchyard now part of the public way.

Apparently there was no satisfactory solution to the complaint of 1739, and the question of the porch was again referred to nearly 10 years later.

Dance reported in February, 1749, on the work necessary to open up way behind Mansion House to Bearbinder Lane which he estimated at £50. "To remove the ground and level part of the churchyard with the passage, to erect and make good the old door case, to bring up a brest wall three feet high above the passage," etc.

There is an account in the *Gentleman's Magazine* of August, 1738 (p. 434), stating that the rector and others waited on the Lord Mayor and complained in the terms of their petition.

Unfortunately no record of the solution of the difficulty can be found.

There is a view of the clerk's house, see Plate XIV, date 1798.

The priced building accounts for the erection of St Stephen are printed in *Archaeologia*, vol. LXVI, from these accounts we learn that the previous church was not completely destroyed during the fire of 1666. We find that "Ye East walls, and the pillars and arches on the North side,...the Outside wall North and South" remained, but in addition we find that the tower had to be pulled down, and also the steeple, and the west end; they were so slightly damaged by the fire that "ye Roofe floor bells and frames" had to be taken down. Needless to say a church so damaged to-day would be restored and the ancient parts preserved. The Guildhall was quite as much damaged but was restored and the marks of the flames can be seen on the fifteenth century stonework. The previous church must have been a most interesting structure, this we know from the ancient accounts which still exist, but Wren and his employers seemed determined to make a clean sweep of the old Gothic churches and as a rule did not trouble to preserve the tombs.

We also learn from the accounts that apparently the old foundations were used. There is one charge digging and clearing foundations of the east wall, this is accounted for by the fact that the west end of Wren's church is about 119 feet from Walbrook, and the previous structure was 125 feet long on the north side and 115 feet long on the south side. There is also a charge for making a vault at the west end.

The first date was Midsummer, 1673, the hoarding was charged for two years ending Midsummer, 1675. The plastering to the dome was completed in September, 1677. The doorway to the rectory was made after the wall was built, for there is a charge for pulling "downe the wall for ye new dorcase to be in next ye Parsons ground."

There is a charge for making a gutter about 24 feet long to bring water from Mr Polixphen's house.

The joiner's bill is only for doors, the panelling is not included.

There is a charge for 14 feet 9 inches "of rough purbeck Step out of ye North dore in ye Street." Then there is a charge for 16 feet of brickwork under the "Steps."

We read of a wall at the east end with "2 dorecases in ye same."

There is no account for any porch or doorway from the churchyard into the market. The piazza of the market was damaged and the market tenants were paid £10. 10s. including expenses, the sum was settled by three arbitrators.

It is interesting to note that Henry Chichele was presented to the Rectory of St Stephen in 1396; at a later date he became Archbishop of Canterbury, his tomb is in the choir of Canterbury Cathedral and is maintained at the expense of All Souls College, Oxford.

PLATE XVIII

THE MANSION HOUSE FROM THE POULTRY

PLATE XIX

VIEW LOOKING EAST

Showing Cornhill and Lombard Street and the enclosure to and steps of the Mansion House

Chapter VI

The Statue

AFTER the fire of London the open market was laid out and a statue of Charles II was erected on the north side; this is shown on Plans 9, 11, 12, 13, 23, 24, 25, 26, and on Plates IV, V, VI, VII, VIII and IX.

The following is an extract from the *London Gazette* of 30th May, 1672:

> London May 29. This day being the great Anniversary of His Majesty's birth, as well as the Glorious Restoration, has been celebrated in this City with all imaginable demonstrations of Public Joy, and to adde to the Solemnity of the day a new Conduit of a Noble and Beautiful Structure was opened (in the Stocks Marketplace, near Lombard-street) plentifully running Claret for divers hours, adorned with an Excellent Figure of His present Majesty on Horseback having a Turk or Enemy under foot. The Figure all of the best White Genova Marble, and bigger than the Life. The whole erected at the sole charge of Sir Robert Viner, from whom his Majesty was pleased to accept it some years since, although but now finished, as a Mark of the particular Devotion that worthy person is used to express on all occasions, for the honor of His Majesties Royal Person and Government.

The conduit again ran claret when an heir was born to James II.

In 1674, two years after the statue was erected, Sir Robert Vyner was Lord Mayor, he had offered a statue to the Gresham Committee, who declined it on 29th March, 1669; and it is thought that the statue was the one under consideration.

It is stated that the pedestal was 18 feet high, and that on the pedestal were the arms of Sir Robert Vyner "within a compartment of fishes." See Plate VI. In *A New View of London*, published in 1708, vol. II, p. 800, there is a similar description of the statue and pedestal.

In the *Gentleman's Magazine* of 1790, Part 2, p. 888, there is a description of the statue, stating "it was cut at Leghorn, in Italy, and reported to be designed for Cromwell."

It was stated that Sir Robert Vyner was knighted in consequence of his having erected the statue, but that is incorrect for Sir Robert was knighted in 1665, and the work was not completed until 1672.

The figure on the horse was originally Sobieski, and was converted into a likeness of Charles II; Plate X is a reproduction of the portrait of Sobieski by Rembrandt, the prostrate figure is supposed to represent Cromwell, originally a Turk, and if any alteration was made to the Turk's head, the turban still remained. It is quite possible that in the seventeenth century an Italian working at Leghorn may have imagined the usual head dress of Oliver Cromwell to have been a turban. Sir Robert Walpole states that the statue came over unfinished and a new head was added by Latham, but apparently the head was only altered, and not renewed.

Sir Robert Vyner was soon in financial difficulties and advertisements appeared in the *London Gazette* of March 17th, 20th and 24th, 1683, calling together his creditors. The advertisement of March 20th was as follows: "The creditors of Sir Robert Viner are desired by him to meet at the Cock, lately called the Cardinals-Cap Tavern in Lombard St. on the 25th day of this Instant March at Nine of the Clock in the Morning, to consider the best way for the satisfaction of their Debts."

Sir Robert was a sheriff during the great fire and died in 1688, he was buried in St Mary Woolnoth, next to his house of business in Lombard Street. Plan 22 is a plan of the property set out by Oliver in 1670.

The statue is shown on the maps of Morden and Lea of 1682, Lea and Glynne (about) 1690, Overton 1676, also in the general views referred to above.

Plate VI is dated 1753, Plates IV and V are undated; Plate VI is more carefully drawn than the others, this is clear from a comparison with the recent photograph Plate XI. In Plates VIII and IX there are no "breaks" to the pedestal. The figures in Plates IV and V are also ridiculously small and entirely out of drawing, apparently with the intention of making the statue look very large; this silly trick can be seen in many hotel advertisements in a modern railway guide.

The statue with plan to scale is shown on Plans 24 and 25,

consequently we know the exact size; the pedestal was about 17 feet by 13 feet, and stood on a base about 29 feet by 23 feet, this was raised about 6 inches above the ground level. The photograph Plate XI shows a modern base about 3 feet high. Plate VII is a photograph of a view which is hung in the Parlour of the Bank of England; it was purchased in 1896 by Mr C. Arbuthnot, a Governor, and presented to the Bank. I believe it has never been published[1], but was recently exhibited at the Burlington Fine Arts Club. The picture is 50 inches by 37½ inches; the figures were painted by Joseph Van Aken (1709–49) and are very charming, but the architecture is very bad, the central window of St Stephen's church is semicircular, but it looks like half an egg. The lean-to shed for market purposes built against the north wall of the church is clearly shown. Van Aken painted so many figures in the picture of other artists that he was nicknamed Schneider Van Aken.

Plate XI is a view of the statue re-erected at Newby Hall, Ripon, the sub-base is modern and it will be noted that the statue is at a much lower level than it was originally.

In the *Grub Street Journal* of 8th August, 1734, in "A Continuation of the Critical Review of the Public buildings, etc., examined by Mr. Hiram" we read as follows:

that lump of stone made for John Sobieski King of Poland, and set up by the citizens in honour of their king, but to their own disgrace, converted into pavement, and the statute of the ever glorious William III erected in the centre of that area: had, I say, all this been effected this place would have been the *real center of beauty to the city*, as our critic terms it, etc.

This critical review commenced on 11th July, 1734, and runs through several numbers.

The position of the statue with regard to the present building may be of interest; it was at about the centre of the present façade, and mainly under the portico.

When Sir Robert Vyner was Lord Mayor the King dined at the inaugural banquet, the following account, which appeared in *The Spectator*, No. 462, 20th August, 1712, was probably written by Steele. It is often referred to.

He (Charles II) more than once dined with his good citizens of London on their lord-mayor's day, and did so in the year that Sir Robert

---

[1] Since the above was written the view has been used as an illustration in the *Catalogue* issued by the Club.

Viner was Mayor. Sir Robert was a very loyal man, and if you will allow the expression, very fond of his sovereign: but, what with the joy he felt at heart for the honor done him by his prince, and through the warmth he was in with continual toasting health to the royal family, his lordship grew a little fond of his majesty, and entered into a familiarity not altogether so graceful in so public a place. The king understood very well how to extricate himself in all kinds of difficulties, and, with an hint to the company to avoid ceremony, stole off and made towards his coach, which stood ready for him in Guildhall yard. But the mayor liked his company so well, and was grown so intimate, that he pursued him hastily, and, catching him fast by the hand cried out with a vehement oath and accent "Sir, you shall stay and take t'other bottle." The airy monarch looked kindly at him over his shoulder, and with a smile and graceful air (for I saw him at the time, and do now) repeated this line of the old song: "He that's drunk is as great as a king," and immediately returned back and complied with his landlord:

Chaffers in his *Gilda Aurifabrorum* of 1883, p. 67, states, I do not know with what authority, that the statue lay for many years neglected in a builder's shed, till an enterprising inn-keeper set it up in his backyard. It is also stated that it was kept in Aldersgate Street until 1779, when Mr Robert Vyner took possession of it, but I can find no authority for that statement.

In Cunningham and Wheatley's *London Past and Present*, vol. III, p. 317, it is stated that there were two statues in the Market, one of Charles I and one of Charles II; what authority there is for that statement I do not know. Only one statue is shown in all the plans and views I have seen, and I find no reference to two statues in any eighteenth century documents.

In the *Gentleman's Magazine* of July, 1737 (p. 449), we read

At a Court of Common Council at Guildhall, Resolved: That Stock Market be enclosed with boards on the 30th. September next, in order for beginning a Mansion House for the Lord Mayor, that the Fleet Market shall be open'd the same Day, and that a Carcase Market, Pumps, and all other Conveniences be immediately made to it; and for the Encouragement of those who intend to take Shops, Stalls etc. they are to pay no Rents or Taxes whatever for 6 Months, to commence from 30th. of September.

In the *Monthly Chronologer* of October, 1737, we read

On the 28th. of last Month the Stalls belonging to the Herb Square in Stocks Market were pulled down as on the next Day were likewise the Butchers Shambles in the Meat Market, in order to clear it for building a Mansion-House for the future Lord Mayors. And on the 30th. the Fleet Market was proclaimed a free Market, and opened accordingly.

PLATE XX

A VIEW OF THE MANSION HOUSE AND CHEAPSIDE, LOOKING WEST

PLATE XXI

A VIEW SHOWING THE OLD BALUSTRADE TO THE MANSION HOUSE
And looking East, along Cornhill (showing St Michael's Church and the old Royal Exchange) and Lombard Street
Drawn by T. H. Shepherd, engraved by S. Lacey

When it was decided to build the Mansion House the statue had to be removed and the following advertisement appeared in the *Daily Post* of Monday, 28th November, 1737:

The Committee appointed by common council to erect a Mansion House for the Lord Mayors of this City for the time being do give notice, that they intend to dispose of the Timber, Boards and Tyles belonging to the several Sheds and Houses that lately stood on the Ground where Stocks-Market was used to be held, in different Lots, (that is to say) the Timber and Boards in one lot, the Tyles in another, and the materials belonging to the Conduit, Pedestal and Horse in another lot. All persons therefore who are willing to treat with the said committee for purchasing the same are desir'd to deliver their proposals in writing, seal'd up, to the said Committee, who will sit in the Council Chamber of the Guildhall, on Tuesday the 6th. of December next, at Four o'clock in the afternoon, for the disposal thereof: and in the meantime any Person, by applying to Mr. Dennison at the Globe in Walbrook, may have an opportunity of viewing the same.

This was followed by another advertisement which appeared in the *Daily Post* on December 9th, 10th and 12th, 1737, as follows:

London Dec: 8. 1737.

The Committee of Common Council appointed to erect a Mansion-House for the Lord Mayors of this City for the Time being give Notice, that they intend to dispose of the Materials belonging to the Conduit, Pedestal and Horse at Stocks Market, in one Lot: that if any Persons are willing to contract for the same they are desir'd to deliver their Proposals, seal'd up, to the said Committee who will sit in the Council Chamber of the Guildhall, on Tuesday next, being the 13th. Instant, at Four o'Clock in the Afternoon, for the Disposal thereof: any Person in the mean time applying to Mr. Dennison at the Globe in Walbrook may have an Opportunity of viewing the same.

On 13th December, 1737, John Hoare and Mr Long both wanted the horse; Long's best offer was £12. The matter was adjourned.

On 17th February, 1737–8, the minutes of the Committee dealing with the Mansion House state that the Lord Mayor informed the Committee he had talked with Mr Vyner at the House of Commons with reference to his claim for the horse, "A stone Pedestal Horse and Statue of King Charles II said to have been set up by Sir Robert Viner, an ancestor of the said Mr Vyner," and the Committee said he could have it. But apparently Mr Vyner had made no claim for the statue, for on 3rd March, 1737, it was recorded that the Town Clerk and Comptroller had waited on Mr Vyner, who said that the statue was erected by "Sir Robert Vyner, by the consent of the City, as an ornament, and that it should remain their till waisted, or Devoured by time, and that he would have nothing to do in removing it, or taking it down, nor would he Receive the same," and the consideration of the matter was adjourned.

On 17th March the Committee decided that the horse and pedestal were to be placed in the engine house. This was a little building about 7 feet by 14 feet on the west side of Walbrook and about 50 feet north of Bucklersbury. See Plan 29.

In the *Monthly Chronologer* of Saturday, 4th March, 1738, we read

> The Workmen began to clear and take away the Pavement of Stocks-Market, in order to lay the Foundation for the Mansion-House for the Lord Mayors. And soon after the Statue on Horseback of K. Charles 2nd. was taken down.

The same statement appeared in the *London Magazine* of a similar date.

The Committee reported on 20th April, 1738, that at Michaelmas, 1737, the Stocks Market was "shut up and enclosed," the statue, horse and pedestal taken down and the ground cleared.

In the *Gentleman's Magazine* of 1779, 28th May, we read:

> A letter from Robert Vyner Esq: to the Common Council of London, was read in Court, requesting the equestrian statue of Charles II, put up in Stocks Market by his ancestor Sir Robert Vyner Bart: lord mayor of London in 1673, and taken down in 1738 for the purpose of erecting a Mansion-house, might be given to him for his use. The Court complied with his request.

The statue was re-erected in Gaultby Park, Lincolnshire, and removed in 1883 to Newby Hall, Ripon.

Broadsides 13. 127. at the Guildhall Library, consists of one headed "For the Creditors of Sir Robert Viner." It is dated 22nd March, 1683–4, and refers to the proposals made on the 12th December of that year.

The erecting of a statue, or indeed almost any other public event in the eighteenth century, was seized upon by the poets, and the following are some examples.

An Elogium preserved at the British Museum, dated 1674, contains the following lines:

> King Charles his Monument amaz'd to see
> And Lumbards Temple, lately built by thee.

In 1674 was published "A dialogue between two horses" by Marvell, which is very long and very coarse in parts. The following lines indicate the two horses referred to:

> The horses I mean of Wool-Church & Charing
> Who told many truths worth any man's hearing,
> Since Viner & Osborn did buy and provide 'em,
> For the two mighty monarchs who now do bestride 'em.

Chapter VII

The Stocks Market after the Fire

THE following is an extract from the *Repertories*:

Thursday 3 October 1667.

It is thought fitt and ordered by this Court that the building called the Stockes in the Poultrey bee forthwith taken downe and the materialls therof sold or otherwise disposed of to the best advantage of this Citty by the Committee for letting the Citty lands.

The following is taken from the *Journal* 46, f. 210:

Common Council 12th. February, 1667–8.

This day the Committee formerly appointed to consider of places most convenient for the publique Marketts of this City did deliver theire Report in writing under theire hands touching the same the Tenor whereof followeth.

To the right hono^ble the Lord Maior Aldermen & Commons of the City of London in Comon Councell assembled.

Wee whose names are subscribed Comittees appointed (amongst others) by a late Order of this Court to consider off and find out fitt and convenient Markett places for this City Doe humbly Certifye That in obedience to the said Order Wee have veiwed such places as wee did conceive might bee fitt for such uses and have treated with all or the greatest part of the owners thereof and haveing fully considered of that affaire doe find—

That there are two Gardens adjoining to the South west Angle of Leadenhall one belonging to the late dwelling house of Mr. ffarringdon and the other of Mr. Stock being one hundred ffoot square vizt. each one hundred ffoot in length and ffifety ffoot in breadth into which may be made three convenient passages one out of Leadenhall Eight foot wide one out of Limestreet Eight foot wide and one out of Gracioustreet fourteen foot wide, which wee conceive wilbe a very convenient place for an Hearbe and fruite Markett instead of that lately kept in Gracioustreet.

And we find that Leadenhall and the Green Yard wilbe sufficient for a fflesh Markett for the East part of the City and alsoe to receive the Markett out of Leadenhall street reserving the ground of the Houses now unbuilt on the West side of the Green Yard which belongeth to the City.

That the Stocks being removed and laid into the street Woolchurch and Church Yard with the ground of some small Tenements or Shedds lately adjoyning to the Churchyard and belonging to that parish will conteine about one hundred and ffifety foot on the East side about one hundred and fforty foot on the South side about one hundred and five foot on the West side and about one hundred and ten foot on the Northside takeing in the passage on the East and Southsides which parcell of ground wee conceive wilbe a convenient place to supply the former use of the Stocks and the lower part of Cheapside with ffish fflesh ffruite and Herbs being encompassed about with short posts and laid open to the high street on the North and Walbrooke on the West and to bearbinder Lane on the East & South.

That milke street Church and Church Yard and Hony Lane Church with the passages about them togeather with soe much of the Grounds adjoyning and now staked as will conteine two hundred ffoot in length from East to West and one hundred ffoot in breadth from North to South haveing one passage enlarged through Hony Lane out of Cheapside ten ffoot wide and the passage made ffifeteen or sixteene ffoot wide and of St. Lawrence Lane and the whole West end left open to Milkestreet (save onely an inclosure of some short posts to distinguish it from the street) wilbe a very convenient and spatious place for a Markett place instead of that formerly placed in Cheapside which ground soe staked out to be annexed to the Ground of the said Churches Church Yard and passages belongeth to the proprietors hereafter mencoñed and in manner following (that is to say) to Sir John Robinson one thousand sixty and six foot To the house between Sir John Robinson's house and Milkestreet Church four hundred tweenty three foot To[1]   owner of the Ground on the South of Milkestreet Church six hundred seaventy five foot To Deputy Griffith four hundred and ffifety foot To[1] next his Ground two hundred Eighty five foot To Deputy Knott 2412 foot to Mr. Maxy six hundred and sixty foot To Mrs. Hatton 1085 foot To Mr. Edward Waldoe 1624 foot.

That the Ground of severall Gardens on the back part of the late Tonn Taverne in Newgate Markett togeather with the ground of some back houses adjoining conteining a square of ground of two hundred ffoot long on every of the four sides into which may be made four convenient passages That is to say one ffoot passage out of Pater Noster Row ten foot wide one foot passeage out of Ivy Lane ten foot wide one Cart passeage out of Newgate Markett sixteene foot wide and one Cart passeage out of Warwick Lane sixteen foot wide is the most convenient place for a white Markett in the stead of that lately kept in Newgate Street And that the same Square of ground wilbe sufficient for an Hearb and ffruite Markett in stead of that now held in Aldersgate Street and alsoe for a Meale Markett which Ground belongeth to the Church of Saint Pauls and the Church is willing the same should be made use for this purpose if this Court can obteine an Act of Parliam[t] for the same.

<hr>

[1] *Sic.*

All which nevertheless wee humbly submit to the grave Judgem^ts of this Hono^ble Court Dated this 10th. day of ffebruary Anno Dñi 1667 And in the Twentueth yeare of his Maties Reigne.

Nicholas Delves (and 14 others).

The which Report being openly read was allowed off and ordered to be entered and in all points accordingly performed.

And it is referred to the same Committee to consider for improving and setling the Markett of Leadenhall and all other the old and the aforesaid new intended Marketts to the best advantage of the Chamber and of reforming all abuses and irregularities in the said Marketts And to report their proceedings to this Court And the Clerkes of the Marketts to warne and attend them.

The above report is of interest as it deals with all the city markets after the fire, and gives the dimensions of the church and churchyard of St Mary Woolchurch Haw with the passages on the east and south sides, which we learn were both known as Bearbinder Lane.

The next report of importance is dated 20th December, 1668; it refers to the consent of the Archbishop of Canterbury and the Bishop of London to allow the site of St Mary Woolchurch Haw to be used for a market, and is as follows:

To the Right Honble the Lord Maior Aldermen and Commons of the City of London in Common Councell assembled.

THE COMMITTEE appointed by a late Order of this hono^ble Court to improve and settle the old and new intended Marketts of this City; DOE HUMBLY CERTIFY That in obedience to the said Order they have mett severall times about that Affaire and fully considered of the same and treated and agreed with allmost all the persons concerned in the Ground to be made use of for that purpose And have caused Draughts or Maps to be made of the manner of setling the same Marketts and forasmuch as the late Act of Parliament for rebuilding the City[1] It is provided That the Scites and Materialls of such Churches as are not intended to be rebuilt together with the Church yards belonging to such Churches shalbe and are vested in the Maior and Aldermen of the City of London for the time being, to the End soe much of the said Ground as shall not upon the Rebuilding of the said City be laid into the street be sold and disposed of by the said Maior and Aldermen or the Major part of them for the time being with Consent of ye Arch Bishop of Canterbury and Bishop of London for the time being and the money raised by such sale shalbe by the said Major and Aldermen or the major part of them with the consent of the said Arch Bishop and Bishop disposed of and imployed for and towards the

[1] *I.e.* 18 & 19 Ch. II, c. 8 (*Statutes of the Realm*, v, 609).

Rebuilding of such parish Churches as by the said Act was intended to be rebuilt and for noe other use or purpose whatsoever Thereupon the said Committee did thinke fitt to waite on his Lordship the Bishop of London for obtaining his Grace the Arch Bishop of Canterburies and his Lordships consent for the disposall of the Ground of Woolchurch and its Churchyard Milkstreet Church and its Churchyard and Hony Lane Church and Churchyard for the making of markett places according to a former order of this Court And accordingly some of the same Committees did attend his Lordship the Bishop of London about ye same who was pleased to declare it to be his opinion That the City may lay those Churches and Churchyards into ye Streets And that his Grace the Arch Bishop and himself had noe power to dispose of the same otherwise then by the Act is appointed AND DECLARED that Woolchurch is one of thirty nine Churches by them agreed on to be rebuilt But if the City thinke fitt to lay it to the Street (being soe much for the Cities Advantage) his Lordshipp declared he believed his Grace the Arch Bishop would not contend with the City about it And that his Lordshipp for his part should not provided it be not made use for a Shambles.

Since which time the said Committee have ordered the taking downe the walls of the said Churches and levelling and laying open the Ground That thereby the severall proprietors of the Ground adjoyning may be the better enabled and encouraged to build their houses And as to the further setling and improving these marketts the said Committee humbly submitt and leave the same to the grave judgement of this hono^{ble} Court Dated this one and twentieth Day of December 1668 And in the 20th. yeare of his Mat^{ies} Reigne.   Nicholas Delves (and ten others).

It has been impossible to trace any documents giving the consent of the Archbishop and Bishop to allow the site of the church and churchyard to be used as a market; there is no document at Fulham, Lambeth, or Canterbury referring to the matter, probably verbal consent was given.

The formation of the market proceeded slowly, for the following extract from the *Repertories* is dated 31st August, 1669:

Diverse of the Common Councell men and other inhabitants of the Ward of Walbrooke now present making suite unto this Court foe speedy levelling fitting and preparing the ground intended for the new market place at Woolchurch which now lyes heaped and disordered with earth rubbish and other filth to the damage and common annoyance of the inhabitants and passangers thereabout this Court doth referre it to the committee for letting of the City lands to take speedy and effectuall course and order for fitting and setting the said Markett place and removal of all hindrances and obstructions thereunto as a matter of especiall concernment not only to the neighbourhood of the place but to the interest of the whole Citty.

This petition had some effect for the following extract is dated 21st October, 1669. Here again we get evidence that the market building was removed and the site paved. Pepys had noted the walls were taken down a year before this date (see p. 100).

Thursday 21 Oct 1669.

It is ordered by this Court that Mr. Chamberlain shall pay unto George Dixon his bill of charges amounting to £34. 12s. 11d. for levelling and clearing and paving the ground of the late Marketthouse called the Stocks in the Poultry near Woolchurch which was ordered and allowed by the Committee for Sewers as by their subscription under the said bill may appear. *Repert.* LXXIV, f. 315.

The following extract deals with the site of the parsonage house referred to on pp. 38, 40, and 153.

Teusday 14 December 1669

This day the counterpart of one writing pourporting a demise or grant made by Mason Dr, in Divinity parson of the late parish church of St Mary Woolchurch London to the Mayor Commonalty and Citizens of the said City of the scite of the late parsonage house of the said parish now laid into the new ground intended for a market place there for the yearly rent of £8 to be paid to the said Dr. Mason so long as he shall continue his right and title to the said parsonage was here sealed with the common seal of the City.

On 18th January, 1669–70, the *Repertories* note that "This court being informed of the backwardness of the Markett places at Woolchurch and Honey Lane for want of paving," desired help from the Paviors Company. On 5th April, 1670, the Ward of Walbrook petitioned for "a Markett house and other conveniences," and on 4th October, 1671, the City Landes Committee reported as follows:

This day a report touching placing of Markett people in the new Marketts and other matters therein contayned made by several Members of this Committee was read and confirmed, And it is thereupon agreed and ordered by this Comitee in pursuance of the said report, That such Market people as shall hereafter think fit to repair to Woolchurch Market to sell white meal shall be accommodated with stations for that purpose under the Piazzas there And that between the said Piazzas Butchers & fishmongers be placed in two severall Ranges in lieu of those formerly at the Stocks now taken away And that the remaining part of the said Market formerly the Church and Churchyard be duely employed to sell herbs and fruit.

The following document clears up the question of claim in connection with the old Stocks building:

RELEASE and QUIT CLAIM
of William Osbolston of all right to The Stocks Market—1671.

KNOW ALL MEN by these Presents That I William Osbolston Executor of the last Will and Testament of Robert Osbolston late Citizen and Haberdasher of London deceased Assignee of Edward Ditchfield Citizen and Salter of London for and in consideration of the sum of £140 of lawful money of England to me in hand paid by the Mayor Commonalty and Citizens of the City of London the receipt whereof I do hereby acknowledge Have remised released and for ever quit-claimed and by these presents do for me my heirs and executors and administrators absolutely and clearly remise release and for ever quit claim unto the Mayor Commonalty and Citizens of the City of London their successors and assigns all manner of right title claim interest and demand whatsoever which I now have or my executors administrators or assigns or any of them may have hereafter in the ground whereon before the Fire stood one great stone house called the Stocks with all and singular the appurtenances situate and being in the Parish of St. Mary Woolchurchhaw of the City of London and also in the Lease thereof granted with the Flesh and Fish Market and Chambers thereunto belonging granted 22 January 1633 unto the said Edward Ditchfield by the Mayor Commonalty and Citizens of the City of London.

Dated 7th. October, 1671 (*Comptroller's Deeds E*, 63).

The following report refers to the trees shown in Plan 23.

18th December 1673.

Report to the City Lands Committee.

We have also viewed Woolchurch Market and offer concerning it that it will be both pleasant and convenient that it be planted round with Lime Trees. That the pease carts be hereafter placed in the square where the pump now is and that posts be set up neare the Street to prevent Carts entering where now they do and that the Rates and Regulations for the standing of the Gardeners be the same that are reported concerning Newgate Market. Dated December, 1673.

Upon reading whereof it is ordered that Mr. Chamberlain and the Comptroller do take care that there be an addition of Lyme trees round about Woolchurch Market according to the Report that such persons who have already laid out money in that object be reimbursed their expenses.

The city granted a lease of all the markets for 5 years, dated 17th September, 1674, rent £3850 p.a., increasing £100 p.a. every year.

A fresh lease was granted in 1677; this refers to the eight stalls with the letters P, Q, R etc. near the statue (Plan 24). The rent was £2500 p.a. and a scale in connection with the duties on hides. In 1686 the farmers, or tenants, applied for a new lease, no rent to be paid in the event of a "Generall plague," and asked for a reduction of rents; the petition was refused.

In 1676 there was a petition against the proposal to make a market at Shadwell, and in 1682 another petition against a proposed market "at Conduit Meade near Albemarle House," as it would damage Smithfield market.

The following were the charges made in the year 1677:

For every stall or standing of Eight ffoot long and four ffoot broad for sale of fflesh-meat or ffish under Publick Shelter in the beefhall at Leadenhall not exceeding three shillings pr week and for every stall or Standing of the Same dimentions for the like Comodityes in all and every of the other Publick Marketts afore mentioned under Publick Shelter not exceeding two shillings and six pence pr week for every Stall of Standing of Six ffoot long and four ffoot broad for the like Comodityes in the said Beefhall not exceeding two shillings and Six pence per week and in all other Publick Markett not exceeding two shilling pr week for every Stall of Standing of Six or Eight ffoot long and four ffoot broad for other Comodityes under Publick Shelter threepence pr day or twelve pence pr week at the Election of the Markett people that use the same ffor every horseload of Provisions upon Stalls or under Publick Shelter three pence pr Day or twelve pence pr week and not upon stalls nor under Publick Shelter two pence pr day or Eight pence per week at the Election of the Market people as afsd.

For each of the eight fixed Stalls marked P Q R S T V Y Z , and four in Honey Lane marked 5 6 7 and 8, two (?) shillings a week.

In November, 1682, we learn that the "pavement in the high street before Woolchurch Markett" was "very ruinous."

On 1st November, 1684, John Oliver and three others reported on "needful and necessary works" to "The Severall Marketts in Leaden hall Woolchurch on ye Stockes market, Newgate market and Honey Lane market." The following refer to the Stocks Market:

Woolchurch Market to make good ye Oaken Floore of the Piatizo at ye East corner of the market a great part of it being falen in and ye styles to the cellar there   £30. 00. 00

The Slatting about the severall places of that to be made good.   £06. 00. 00

To empty ye house of Easement there   £10. 15. 00

To mend ye Pavement there stones, gravell and workmanship.   £10. 08. 00

In the *Repertories* dated 14th April, 1687, there is an account of a petition by the inhabitants near the market that the farmers of the market had commenced to build a house with 40 feet frontage and 20 feet in depth, proposed to be four storeys high "on part of the ground where the piazza did stand." The previous building was two storeys high. The committee reported in April, 1687, that they thought the higher building would not be a detriment to the neighbourhood.

Oliver's plan (Plan 18) has already been referred to, it was probably made in 1669. Plans 23 and 24 are two plans of the market and were checked by Hooke and Oliver. The scale dimensions do not agree with the figured dimensions; the plans are incorrect, unfortunately Hooke and Oliver only checked the boundaries and made no record of "cross" or "tie" dimensions so dear to a surveyor, consequently even with Hooke and Oliver's corrections it is impossible to make a correct plan. Plans 23 and 24 are however interesting. Plan 24 appears to be the plan as it existed, the stalls marked A, B, C etc. are referred to in a document at Guildhall. Plan 23 seems to indicate a scheme, showing an enclosure with posts, the trees along the east side of the enclosure, and various open shops facing the market. The south-east corner with the dimensions 54 feet 8 inches, 16 feet, 18 feet, is marked "Parish" on Oliver's plan and the adjoining land, figured 10 feet, is not included in the market; but on the 1692 plans this property formerly belonged to St Stephen's Church and is shown as market premises. The fifteenth century description of the church property gives the frontage to Bearbinder Lane as 16 feet; this is the dimension on Oliver's plan. The length on Oliver's plan is about 64 feet 8 inches, and the ancient description is 60 feet 8 inches on one side and 70 feet on the other.

About the year 1690 two men went round the market telling the stall holders they ought to be there rent free; they were taken before the Lord Mayor who told them they were "impudent fellows and Saucy rascals, with many other ill words." I wonder what those "ill words" were!

The following are notes from some papers in connection with the actions of Burford and others *v.* Burdett and others. One document endorsed "on hearing 10th Oct: 1692," states that the plaintiffs were various owners at or near the Stocks Market, that St Stephen's Walbrook was built with a piazza for the shelter of the market people, that the tenants of the market pulled down the piazza and built warehouses and slaughterhouses and sheds upon that part of the market which was formerly the church and churchyard.

A petition addressed "to the Right Honble: George Lord Jeffryes Baron of Wemm Lord high Chancellor of England" states that the Corporation had power to buy land for the purpose of a market and pay for it by a duty to be levied on coals, that Woolchurch was one of the 39 churches appointed to be rebuilt by the first Act of Parliament for rebuilding the city, but that the consent of the Archbishop of Canterbury and the Bishop of London was obtained to use the site as a market; that Margaret Allen owned land "Joined to" Walbrook Church which was worth £1000, but the jury awarded her £300; that portions of the ground formerly the church and churchyard were used for market purposes; the latter portion being used for selling vegetables.

There were various complaints and petitions to the Corporation with respect to certain grievances of the market people. On 29th May, 1696, the "Oppress'd Petitioners" stated that

Before the Great Fire of London the markets were kept in the Common Streets and High-ways and the Butchers and Poulterers paid only One Penny every time they came to Market, which was then called a "Pitching Penny" and One Penny for a board whereon to place their goods (if they had a board provided for them) and this they paid to three city Officers, called the Serjeant of the Channel, Yeomen of the Channel, and Foreign Taker who bought their places of the Lord Mayor at about £600 each, and they divided the money....The markets were farmed at £3,850 p.a.: and are now Farm'd to Mr. Burdett, Mr. Kilner and others at £3,600 p.a.

A note is made in the margin of the petition

That Mr. Burdett is a profest Papist concern'd in procuring a Vessel to carry the Lord Preston and Mr. Ashton into France, in the execution of their treasonable practice, as appears in their Printed Tryals, for High Treason.

The petitioners stated the charges had greatly increased, and that the farmers of the markets had erected enclosed shops and let them to haberdashers, milliners, turners, toy-sellers, etc., and that the market space had been curtailed. The petition was properly dealt with, and an inquiry held.

In 1716 there was another petition from the parish authorities stating that rates were not paid "Nor payment to the Convex Lights." Passages were obstructed and markets not properly cleansed; an inquiry was held and there is a report of the evidence.

At a vestry meeting held on the 25th August, 1715, it was decided by the parish of St Mary Woolchurch Haw to petition the Corporation. "Several of our parish visited at Garraways Coffee house" and complaint was made that carts stood in the streets all night and inhabitants could not "pass to and from their own houses with safety on foot for many hours together"; that the middle man sold in the markets, not the farmers, "all the ground in the Market is lett out by the foot to fforestallers"; that vegetable refuse was left in such heaps in the streets "That Coaches and Carts are in danger of being overturned." A later vestry meeting was "held at the Eagle and Child in Stocks Markett," and further complaints were made and it was decided to take action. It was noted

That severall standing are allowed betwixt the boundary of the Market and the Channel in the street just in front of the market before the King's statue...and...it is with difficulty to pass the high street towards Stocks Markett....That formerly there was a Piazza all open alongside of Walbrook Church and so to Bearbrinder Lane...which is now built upon and converted into wharehouses....We pray that all the fixed stalls round the Market may be pull'd downe.

This petition was signed at a vestry meeting of St Mary Woolchurch Haw, held 14th August, 1716.

Meat, fish, fruit, vegetables and herbs were all sold in the market.

For the year ending Michaelmas, 1732, the profits of the market were as follows:

Leadenhall Market	£2,273
Newgate „	2008
Honey Lane „	1063
	£5,344. 0
Stocks Market for the year 1728	£1,103. 15s
TOTAL	£6,447. 15s

In 1739 "a certain large piece of ground lying behind Leadenhall Street and adjoining to part of Leadenhall Market" was "called Tokenhouse Yard." It was decided that this was suitable land to add to the market.

In the eighteenth century certain men were known as Fruit Meters, and a complaint was made that there was a loss of £200 p.a. to the Stocks Market in consequence of the Fruit Meters "taking their Dutys at the Waterside."

The market was evidently very badly kept according to modern ideas; the Commissioners of Sewers had some references as a result of complaints. On 16th March, 1710, there was "a great breach or hole" in the paving and precautions were taken to prevent accidents. In July, 1713, certain inhabitants of Lombard Street and Cornhill complained that carts waited in the streets. In May, 1730, it was found necessary to have a night watchman and a sentry box was erected for him.

PLATE XXII

A VIEW OF THE CHURCH OF ST MARY-LE-BOW AND CHEAPSIDE

Showing the Mayor's Nest and the Noah's Ark in the distance

PLATE XXIII

A PERSPECTIVE VIEW OF THE MANSION HOUSE

Probably prepared for the competition

Chapter VIII

The Surveys after the Fire

IN 1667 there was an Act of Parliament "for erecting a Judicature for Determining of Differences touching Houses buried or demolished by reason of the late Fire which happened in London[1]." It decided that judges could settle disputes between landlord and tenant, apportioning the rent, deciding the time for rebuilding, or determining the leases. Powers were very similar to those under an Act passed during the late war; but the Act of 1667 gave greater power to the judges.

Under sect. 23 of cap. 3 there was authority to widen certain streets, among them the "Street and Passage" at the east end of Cheapside leading into the Poultry, and also the "Street and Passage out of the Poultry leading into the West end of Cornhill"; this was the widening of the High Street in front of the Stocks building and included the passage which was a public right of way, between the market premises and the church wall of St Mary Woolchurch Haw. The Court of Common Council made an Act in 1667 carrying out their various powers and dealing with the improvements in greater detail. It was decided that the "street and passage" at the east end of Cheapside should be widened to 40 feet (see Plan 64), and that the "street and passage" leading out of the Poultry at the west end of Cornhill, should be the same width. Ogilby and Morgan's map of 1667 shows the width of the Poultry to be 40 feet although as shown on Plan 64 it was not widened quite so much.

Under the Act 22, Car. 2, cap. 2, sect. 5, surveyors were to be appointed to apportion the cost of rebuilding between the various parties concerned; and under sect. 16 the sum of 6s. 8d. had to be paid to the Chamberlain of London for setting out each site, and on the production of the receipt the surveyor had to do so within three days.

[1] 18 & 19 Car. 2, cap. 2.

Grocers' Alley, now Grocers' Hall Court, was to be made 11 feet wide, and Scalding Alley, now St Mildred's Court, was to be made 9 feet wide. Chapel Place was the entry to the Compter.

As so much doubt exists about the appointment and duties of the City Surveyors I give below extracts from the records showing how and why certain men were appointed; Hooke is first mentioned because of his plan for rebuilding the city.

Bolton, Mayor, 31 September 1666, Jor 46. fo. 121.

Mr Hooke having upon Mcõn and encouragement of this Court prepared and presented an exquisite Modell or Draught for rebuilding of this City, This Court doth declare their good acceptance of the same.

4th Oct, 1666. Jor 46. fo. 123.

Sir Thos: Adams and others of the Committee appointed by order of this Court to attend the Committee of Lords touching the great business of rebuilding the City declaring that they have there upon attended the Right Hon the Lord Chancellor and other Lords of his Majŝtys most honorable Privy Counsell and received from their Lordshipps his Majesty's pleasure.

That for the better and more expedition of this work he hath pleased to appoint, Dr Wren, Mr May and Mr Pratt to joyne with such Surveyors and Artificers as should be appointed by the City to take an exact and speedy Survey of all Streets, Lanes, Alleys, Houses, and places destroyed by the late dismal fire, that every particular...interest may be ascertained and provided for the better judgment made of the whole affair.

This Court doth therefore Order that Mr Hooke Reader of Mathematics in Gresham College Mr Mills and Mr Edw. Jerman do joyne with the said Dr Wren, Mr May and Mr Pratt in taking the said Survey, and that the Deputy's and Common Councellors have notice of the Surveys where the same shall be taken in every Ward to the end they may be in readiness to take care for the interest of themselves and the Inhabitants of their respective Wards.

31st Oct. 1666. Jor 46. fo. 129.

This Court doth nominate and appoint Mr Hooke, of the Mathematics in Gresham House, Mr Peter Mills and Mr Jerman from time to time to meet and consult with Mr May, Dr Wren and Mr Pratt Commissioners appointed by his Majesty concerning the manner, forme and height of Buildings in this City, the Scantlings of Timber, removing of Conduits, and Churches, and alterations of the Streets.

And it is Ordered that from time to time they report such their Consultation to this Court and give no consent or make any agreement therein without the special Order of this Court.

Common Council. Journal 64. fo. 152. 29th April 1667.

Surveyors to be paid £50 a year for the time past till Lady Day last, and One Hundred and Fifty Pounds a year, same to be paid out of the Chamber of London out of such Monies so to be raised by Quarterly Payments, and the said Committee or any three of them, whereof one of the Alderman to be one, are hereby impowered to order the Chamberlain to pay out of the said money such other charges as they shall find to be reasonable and incident to the carrying on of the work.

Jor 46. fo. 188 b. 25th Oct 1667.

Upon reading the Petition of Mr Mills and Mr Hooke Surveyors for an augmentation of their Salaries this Court doth referr the same to the Committee for building who are desired to consider thereof and report their opinions therein to this Court and John White to warne and attend them.

Tuesday 28 January 1667 19 Charles II

This day John Oliver citizen and[1] of London formerly elected by common council to be one of the surveyors of the new buildings within this City and liberties according to the act of Parliament for rebuilding the City of London was here sworne for the due execution of the said place. *Repert.* LXXIII, f. 62.

Peake, Mayor, 12th Feby 1668–9. Jor 46. fo. 263 b.

This Court doth nominate and appoint the Right Hon the Lord Mayor, Sir John Lawrence, Sir Wm. Hooker, Sir Dennis Gauden Kt, Ald. Lampson Esq, Deputy Cade and Mr Kaives Commoners or any one of the Aldr̃n, and two of the said Comoners to be a Committee to manage the affairs of rebuilding the City according to the late Act of Parliament in that behalfe, and to hear and examine all causes of complaints touching the same or any irregularity in any building and to proceed to finish which is to be done by virtue of that Act and make report of their proceedings therein to this Court.

And it is ordered that the Surveyors thereunto appointed by the Court shall from time to time attend the same Committee and that the same Committee shall have liberty to call such Counsell and other persons to their assistance as they shall think fitt and reward them from time to time out of the money to be raised on Foundations, and the Chamberleyne is ordered to pay such monyes as shall be ordered to any person for any paine or service about the workes by the Quorum of the said Committee out of such monyes to be raised by the Foundations, and John White to warne and attend them.

Jor 46. fo. 148. 13 March 1667–8.

At this Court Mr Peter Mills, Edw. Jerman or Jarman, Mr Hooke, and Mr Oliver are chosen to be Surveyors and Supervisors of the houses to be new built in this City and destroyed by the late dismal fire according to the late Act of Parliament in that behalfe.

[1] Blank in MSS.

And it is ordered that the said Surveyors do further proceed to the stakeing out the Streets as is ordered and directed by the Court in pursuance of the said Act.

Order of the Court of Common Council for Payment of the Salary of Mr Oliver one of the City Surveyors. 23 July 1668.

It is ordered by this Court that Mr Chamberlain shall pay unto Mr Oliver one of the Surveyors appointed by the Common Council of New Buildings within this City and Lybtȳs, his Sallary from time to time according to the allowance made to the rest of the said Surveyors for their Services in that Employment.

Peake. Mayor. *Rep.* 73. fo. 237.

Jor 47. fo. 20. 4th Feby 1669.

It is ordered that a Common Councell be held this day sevennight and that the Surveyors of new buildings for the Citty doe then deliver in several tofts or particulars of such tofts of ground as are unbuilt in their severall devisions and who are interested therein and preserving particularly such as they conceive will not be built unless proclamation be made thereon according to the late Act of Parliament for rebuilding this City.

Jor 48. fo. 57. 19 May 1674.

And it is ordered by this Court that the Surveyors doe take a speedy and exact account of all other Tofts of ground unbuilt within this Citty with the names of the present and past Proprietors of such Tofts and how many Tenements formally stood thereupon and have the same in readiness without fail at the next Court that Proclamation be likewise ordered to be then made thereupon according to the directions of the said Acts of Parliament.

There are four very interesting books in the MS. department of the Guildhall Library[1]. Each is bound in vellum and is about $8\frac{1}{2}$ inches by $12\frac{1}{2}$ inches by $\frac{7}{8}$ of an inch.

On the front of volume 1 is written "A Day Booke for ye receipts of money for ye stakeing out of Foundations in the Ruins of the Citty of London." The first page is headed "Received of severall Persons for Stakeing out the Foundations of their Houses within the Ruines of ye Citty of London as followeth." In the margin is written "Mr. Peter Mills and Mr. Robert Hooke Surveighers" and under that statement the words "Mr. John Olliver" are written. The first receipt is dated 13th May, 1667, and is as follows: "Received of Mr. John Midgely for one foundation in ould ffish street set out by Mr. Mills VI–VIII."

There are very few instances where the name of the sur-

1 MSS. 275–8.

veyor is not mentioned; the payments are at the rate of 6*s.* 8*d.* for each foundation and in several instances more than one building is referred to. At the foot of each page the total number of foundations is recorded and carried over. At the end of volume I the total is carried on in volume II as also the cash received and the totals are continued in volume III. The account is balanced in volume III; it was evidently considered that the work was concluded, and the last survey is dated 21st May, 1683. The number of surveys was 8354, and the total receipts were £2784. 13*s.* 4*d.*, out of this amount the expenses of the surveyors were £2677. 19*s.*[1] and the balance of £106. 14*s.* 4*d.* was "Charged in the Chambers Cash Sept. 4. 1683." But although the account was considered closed a few further surveys were made and the last entry is dated 16th July, 1691, the total being 8391. As a rule about six or seven surveys were made each day, but on at least one day 16 foundations were set out.

At the end of volume I are some receipts by the surveyors; the first is as follows:

Received the 30th Day of December 1667 by me Robert Hooke Gentleman, one of the Surveighers appointed by the Comon Councell according to the Act of Parliament of S^r. Thomas Player Knt. Chamĕlen of London the sum of Seventy five pounds for my sallary, for half a Year ended at Mchas. 1667 payable unto me by virtue of an Act of Comon Councell dated the 29th day of April 1667.

It is signed Robert Hooke.

The next entry is dated 7th January, 1667–8, for a similar amount for the same period and was received on behalf of "Mr. Peter Mills," who is not described as a gentleman, but his salary is the same as the "other Surveigher." The first seven surveys were made by Mills; three on 13th May, and four on 14th May, 1667. On 15th May, Robert Hooke made his first survey.

Robert Hooke is the last surveyor mentioned, and the receipt is dated 19th January, 1683–4. The last receipt for his regular salary is for three months ending Christmas, 1672; on 17th June, 1673, he was paid £15 on account of salary and although the receipt is not recorded the balance sheet concludes with this entry: "1673 December 24. Paid by an order dated

---

[1] This must have included certain expenses as the actual payment to the surveyors was £52. 19*s.* less: see page 149.

the 18th December, 1673, advanced to them being the Arreare of Sallary due to them at Xmas 1673 £270. 0. 0." John Oliver has also received £15 on account so the £270 was £135 each and the £15 each would make up the £150 p.a. The further receipts for surveys only amounted to £12. 6s. 8d., so the balance was on the wrong side, the loss being £150. 19s.

Peter Mills died and the last payment was for salary due at Michaelmas, 1670, and the receipt is signed by William Bright, one of his executors on 8th October, 1670; Peter Mills only signed one receipt and that was in the previous June; all the other money was signed for on his behalf.

There are various interesting entries of payments made during the time the work was in hand. On 4th January, 1666–7, a payment of £3. 15s. 4d. was made for "clearing of the Streets being over and above £100 sent by his Majesty for that use."

There are several entries for "disbursements in attending Judges at Cliffords Inn," and for stationery and for the judges. A Mr Jennings, "Surveigher who was employed to draw the line of the Thames," died and his widow was paid £2.

Peter Mills was paid £50 for a half year's salary due at Lady Day, 1667. Robert Hooke was paid the same amount for the same period, so at first the salary was at the rate of £100 p.a., but after the first six months it was raised to £150 p.a.

The lives of Hooke, Oliver, Mills, and Jerman are given shortly in the *Dictionary of Architecture*. Jerman's name is sometimes given as Jarman and the general idea is that Jerman was a surveyor with an appointment similar to the other three men, but there is just a little doubt expressed by one writer in the *Dictionary*. The books under consideration prove without a doubt that Jerman, who died in November, 1668, did not act as one of the surveyors although he was appointed under the Act, his name is not given at the head of p. 1 of volume 1, and the surveyor's name is mentioned for each survey (with a few extremely rare exceptions) and Jerman's name is not to be found. Neither did he sign any of the records of the viewers in the books mentioned later, except in one instance mentioned below. Again on the two receipts for £20 and £30 respectively Jerman is not called a surveyor.

With regard to Robert Hooke the *Biographia Britannica*

states that with regard to his appointment "The profits of it were from the money which was given him by the several proprietors of the ground for dispatch. The whole amounted to several thousand pounds in gold and silver." In these days that money would be regarded with suspicion, as it was received by an officer who was paid a salary. He was employed throughout the entire period and received a total sum of £1062. 10s. from his employers. We learn that the money was found after his death in an iron chest that had not been opened for 30 years. The total outlay of £2947. 19s. is made up as follows:

	£	s.	d.
Mr. Robert Hooke	1062	10	0
Mr. Peter Mills	575	0	0
Mr. John Oliver	937	10	0
Mr. Edward Jerman	50	0	0
Mr. Jno: White, Officer to the Committee	82	10	0
Sundries	240	9	0
Total	2947	19	0

These volumes contain thousands of names of owners of property, in every case it is stated who paid the money for the survey, and volume IV is a careful analysis of the previous volumes, it is arranged according to the various streets, and the following are the numbers of foundations set out in the neighbourhood of the Mansion House:

Bucklersbury	40 foundations.
Bearbinder Lane	21 ,,
Poultry	75 ,,
Walbrooke	54 ,,

The list includes the names of many localities now unknown, such as Anchor Lane, St Ann's Lane, Poulsons Gardens, Staininge Lane, Butcher's Hall Lane, Black and White Court, Bear-Key, Five Foot Lane, Way House in Cornhill, Barken Alley, Bosse Alley, Black Boy Alley, High Timber Street, Bishop's Court in Coleman Street, Bishops Court in ye little ould Bayly, Blowbladder Street, Poppingay Alley, Cozen Lane, Greens Rents, Cheqz Yard Thames Street, Dice Key, Ebgate Lane Thames Street, Emperours Head Alley, Gunpowder Alley, Jerusalem Alley, Lilly-Pott Lane, Lyon Key, Pittcocke Lane, Paved Alley, Ram Alley, Smither's Lane, Smarts Key, Tennis Court Alley, and Curriers Alley.

With reference to the total number of surveys mentioned above as 8391 the books of survey described below have particulars of about 2272 by Mills, and about 1172 by Oliver, total about 4044; this would leave about 4347 as Hooke's work, for Jarman's name does not appear in the receipt book. I find one reference to his work; in Mill's *Survey Book*, vol. 1, there is an entry "Memorand^m That upon the 6th day of October 1667 I Peter Mills with Mr Edward Jarman did view," etc.

There are also four large books and an index in the Guildhall Library[1]; these are the records of the work done by Oliver and Mills principally with reference to setting out foundations. The following are the headings:

Olivers Survey of Ground Staked out after the ffire of London. Vol 1st containing No 1–2–3–4–5 & 6.

Olivers Survey of Ground Staked out after the Fire of London. Vol 2nd containing No 7–8–9 & 10.

Mills Survey of Ground Staked out after the ffire of London. Vol 1st containing No 1–2–3–4 & 5.

Mills Survey of Ground Staked out after the Fire of London containing No 6–7–8–9 & 10.

There is an index for locality, and another index for the names of the owners. The entries are copies, for there is a second index to the original ledgers, which cannot be traced. To the student of London before the fire these four volumes have information not to be found elsewhere, and as far as the writer knows they cannot be equalled and are of absorbing interest.

The first date in vol. 1 of Oliver's *Survey* is February 3rd, 1667–8, the last date in vol. 1 is 26th May, 1669. The first date in vol. 11 is 21st August, 1669, and the last date is in 1672.

The first date in Mill's *Survey*, vol. 1, is 23rd March, 1666–7, the last date in vol. 1 is 29th August, 1668. The first date in vol. 11 is 25th February, 1668–9, and the last date is 19th July, 1670.

Oliver's work is far more valuable than that of Mills. Oliver gives a careful plan of which Plans 18 to 22 are examples, he also gives the name of the owners of the site and the adjoining premises, he is careful to note the points of the compass, he marks the old frontage line and shows in certain cases how

[1] MS. 84.

much land is to be added to the street. Both surveyors note the actual amount of land given up when certifying as to compensation. As an instance in vol. 1, p. 51, of Oliver's *Survey* we read "Mr Oliver this is to certify that you Mr Baptist Pigott hath lost Nineteen ffoot of Ground in Length in front and Two ffoot of ground in Depth in the Poultry." In addition to the particulars of foundations all the volumes contain a certain amount of miscellaneous information, such as the disputes; in vol. 1, on 26th May, 1669, a reference to some property "Mr Mills, Mr Hooke and myself did vue." There are references to the sites of many city halls, but none to churches, there is also a reference to defects at the Almshouses at Greenwich.

Mills' work is not so exact, he gives very few plans, he simply describes the site and it is often impossible to tell on which side of the street it was, but he gives a plan when recording the land dealt with for public improvements. Mills' district was principally Fleet Street, St Paul's, St Martins-le-grand, and Thames St, and he, as well as Oliver, records cases where the owner of the property advanced his building line over the public way so as to make it continuous with the adjoining property. Mills is very irritating, he gives the frontage and the width at the back of the plot but he does not mention the depth, in some cases he simply states he set out the foundation and gives no description; luckily Oliver dealt with the neighbourhood of the Mansion House. An interesting note in Mills' *Survey* is that "Wee began to stake out the streets in ffleet street the 27th March 1667." Again there are a series of recommendations as to closing certain public ways. In August, 1667, the surveyors recommended closing St Bride's Alley, Black Horse Alley, Turnagain Lane, Queenshead Alley, Paved Alley, Grocer's Alley, Scalding Alley, Tennis Court Lane. With regard to Scalding Alley we know it was not closed; the surveyors stated it was decided it was "to be opened on the Court side to 9 feet," but submitted that in their opinion it was "not fit to be opened," having "no throw passage." Unfortunately both Oliver and Mills ignored the importance of a dimension to tie in the boundaries, the result is that as a rule it is impossible to make an accurate plan of each site. The plan of the Stocks Market (Plan 18) has some tie lines, but no accurate dimension along Bearbinder Lane.

In the *Viewers Book* the order of signature is always Mills, Hooke, Oliver.

As examples of land taken from the public way and built upon, Mills gives the following instances:

Page 94. Frontage 15 feet: depth 4 feet, "Taken from the street in Cheapside by Mr Peter Gray which he is to pay nothing for because his cellar walls and floor was the longer before the Order for that ground.

A plot in Cheapside near Bread Street with 34 feet frontage and 4 feet in depth, another at the Bow Lane end of Cheapside with 34 feet frontage and 7 feet 6 inches in depth were taken in from the street and built over.

There are also three bound volumes each about 10 inches by 1 foot 3 inches by 1¾ inches, written on vellum. In these books are written the decisions of the viewers and each has the names of the viewers, not the signatures, at the end of the decision[1].

The first award refers to the "four sworn viewers" or any three of them, and it was signed by Mills, Hooke, and Oliver. It refers to a dispute as to damage to light; it is in the form of a report addressed to the Lord Mayor and the Court of Aldermen. The second report states they examined witnesses. A report of 16th September, 1668, was signed by Mills, Hooke, Oliver and John Wildgos. Another report was signed by Mills, Hooke, and Oliver, "the three Surveyors for this City," and it was also signed by John Burridge, John Wildgos, John Tanner and John King, "the former viewers of this Citty." One report is signed only by Oliver, several are signed by Mills and Oliver. Another report dated 4th March, 1669–70, was signed by Mills and Oliver "2 of the 3 Surveyors."

The last report was by Robert Hooke, dated 6th November, 1691, it is loose in the book and only part of it is copied.

Reference has been made to the fact that Bearbinder Lane is now known as George St. and Mansion House Place and several other old names of streets and alleys are mentioned above. I suggest that where the old streets etc. exist that it might be an advantage to return to the old names, and so add to the interest of various landmarks in our ancient city.

[1] City's Records, Town Clerk's Office.

Chapter IX

Purchase of Property

WITH regard to the purchase of property to clear the site, there are many entries in the transactions of the Corporation. The following is a list of the properties acquired:

Site of Parsonage of St Mary Woolchurch Haw.

The building was destroyed during the Great Fire and in 1673 the site was let for 99 years to the City authorities by the "Minister of St Mary Woolchurch-haw—if he should so long continue Minister." Rent, £8 p.a.

An agreement was made on 11th March, 1736, by the rector, the Bishop of London and the Corporation, for the site to be let on a perpetual rent charge of £10 p.a. This arrangement was confirmed by a Private Act of Parliament, 10 Geo. II, c. 19 (1737).

In 1736 it was stated in a case submitted to counsel that it was impossible to ascertain the size or position of the plot, but the building was evidently at the west end of the church and partly over the gateway between the Poultry and the right-of-way immediately south of the Stocks building (see pp. 38 and 40 and Plan 64).

A deputation waited on the Bishop of London during the year (1736) and he stated that "he was ready and willing to consent to do anything for the better assuring of the Parson's Glebe to the City."

Mr Calvert's Property.

This is shown on Plan 25. It was a public house known as the Sign of the Plough. The freehold belonged to the Corporation, it was leased until Michaelmas 1752 at £10. 15s. p.a. and in 1736 the Committee reported that Calvert was willing to surrender his lease if he were paid £450; the Committee considered the amount reasonable as Calvert had paid a premium of £210 and had spent much money on the property. The money was paid. The house was "situate on the North

East Corner of Walbrook fronting North on the market," this is evidently the building shown in the views of the Stocks Market (Plates VI and VII).

The back part of the house over the piazza belonged to the Clothworkers' Company.

The Swan Tavern.

This was immediately south of Calvert's property. It was formerly two houses, the first portion, facing Walbrook, belonged to the Clothworkers' Company and a Mr Harvey; the back part was built out over the butchers' shambles, 15 feet wide,—this being Corporation property. It was also built over the gateway leading into the market, and had been let at a rental of £1 p.a. This lease had expired. The building was adjoining the passage from Walbrook into the Market.

In June, 1745, the Committee agreed to give £500 for the southern house forming part of the Swan Tavern.

In October, 1747, the Corporation agreed to take a lease from the Clothworkers' Company for 21 years from Michaelmas, 1747, at £14 p.a. with power to renew for another term of 21 years.

Calvert's leasehold interest was worth £60 p.a.

In 1747 the Clothworkers' Company suggested for the purchase of this house "late part of the Swan Tavern," an annuity of £16 p.a.; the Corporation suggested £14 p.a., lease 21 years, renewable for ever, and this was agreed.

Mr Ryder's Property.

This consisted of two houses bounded on the north by the passage into the market and on the south by St Stephen's Church. The back portion of the property was built over the shambles in a similar way to the Swan Tavern. With regard to Mr Ryder's property the following letter, written by a lady in the middle of the eighteenth century, may be of interest.

Lydcott near Looe, Cornwall.
June the 12th. 1744.

Sr.

This Comes to return you thanks for the favour of yours of the 5th. instant which I should have answered last Post, but that my Son Mr. Ryder was abroad twenty Miles distant from this Place, with the Lady he is to have, so till now I had no Opportunity of letting you and the Gentlemen of the Comittee know his thoughts as well as mine, I have showed him the Letter and he joins with me in opinion that the Offer is very low, Considering how small the Yearly income of four hundred Pound must be in Comparison with fifty four pound a Year under which Rent yearly the Globe Alehouse was never let exclusive of that part of which Samuel Ryder Esq. deceased had a Lease of the City and the Money now offered by the Committee is very little more than was Usual to give according to the Old Practice all over London, at the Entrance of every new Tenant (especially in Publick business) for good will Money, without any Deduction of the Yearly Rent aforementioned, and one very material Article is, that as the City would not be so kind as to make an Offer before they gave me Notice of taking down their part at the Expiring of their Lease, it put me to a great Expence to Support and Repair the Building, to prevent the Damage that might be done in Seperating the City's part from mine, so that when this Expence is joined with that, that I should have of a New Tenant for the Goodwill Money, I think the Offer is nothing for the Land, and it is my Son's and my own Opinion that if the Comittee are not willing to give five hundred Guineas for the Freehold, it is better to let it remain as it is, than to give it away for nothing, especially as my business will in no long time call me to London, which is my Native place where I lived above twenty Years, I dont doubt but to Let it much more to my Advantage than the Offer of the four hundred Pound; I bless God my Circumstances are far from Streight to Induce me to Accept of any Sum of Money to be afterwards an Illconveniency, and can as well afford the Loss of the Rent of Years to come as I have for years past (which the City has been the Cause of) if it were a great deal more; As affairs are now in speedy Action relating to my Sons Marriage, I must add some further particulars to save time; that is, if the City comes in to my Proposals they must transact the whole affair from beginning to End, except the cutting of the Entail, to pay all expences for so doing, and the Money to be paid into my Hands without any deduction for which my Son is desirous, I hope Sᵣ. you will be so good as to let me have an Answer to this as soon as possible for my Son and I are likely to Remain but a short time together occasioned by his being likely to Settle soon in a new State of Life, which will then put it out of his or my Power to Dispose of Land upon any terms whatever, what I have set forth is with a great deal of Truth as well as reason, & if not according to the expected form, to be laid before so many worthy Gentlemen, yet I hope the Chief Substance will be understood, and they will Impute it to my Ignorance, it being a great undertaking for a Woman to transact such an affair, having no person to Assist me, so that whatever particulars are here omitted if the Gentlemen will be so good as to direct me in any thing I shall take Care to Observe their Orders, and I shall be very careful to answer all particulars they please to Enquire into.

I am,

Sᵣ. Your humble Sevᵗ.

(Signed)   ANN HILL.

The house had a value of £54 a year; the Committee eventually paid £450 in settlement.

There was a plan on Martyn Ryder's lease dated 15th February, 1721, the building referred to had a cellar under the piazza, which was 13 feet wide, and there were three floors over the piazza, the length of the premises was 23 feet. The building between this structure and Walbrook was Ryder's freehold. The rent he paid for the Corporation property was £12 p.a. and he had paid a premium of £30.

Duke of Bedford's Property.

It was soon seen that it would be an advantage to purchase the property at the corner of the Poultry and Walbrook, and in 1738 an Act of Parliament was passed giving the Duke of Bedford power to sell (see Plan 27).

In April, 1739, the Committee reported in favour of buying three houses at the corner of the Poultry. The house facing the Poultry was let to a linen draper at £80 p.a. and had the sign of the Unicorn. The corner house was also let to a linen draper at £140 p.a. The third house faced Walbrook and was divided into two, one part was let to a basket-maker at £50 p.a. and the other part to a cheesemonger at £30 p.a.

On 28th May, 1739, it was reported that the only house required was the corner house let at £140 p.a., and that the Duke would sell for 18 years' purchase, the Court of Common Council agreed. The Duke had first asked 20 years' purchase for the three properties, a sum of £6000; when the Corporation said they only wanted one house, the Duke's agent replied that he was glad, and the Duke would keep the rest.

In February, 1741, there was an account delivered for one house as follows:

To two years rent from Michaelmas 1739 to Michaelmas 1741 at £65 p.a.	£130	By half a years land tax to Lady day 1740	£4
		By a years do: to Lady day 1741	£16
		By two years allowance as paid extraordinary viz:—	
		Water £1. 0. 0	
		Lamps £1. 0. 0	
		Rector £1. 10. 0	
		Window lights £1. 10. 0	
		Repairs £5. 0. 0	
		£10. 0. 0	£20

To Balance due at Michaelmas 1741 £90.

In May, 1747, the Committee found that even when the house of Mr Martin in the Poultry was pulled down the passage way or junction of Walbrook with the Poultry would only be 16 feet wide and they suggested purchasing the property to make it 40 feet wide.

In February, 1755, the matter was revived and the Duke's agent wrote that the two remaining houses, one being divided into two, were then let for £120, and that the price was £2200. The Committee offered £1800, the reply was that the Duke was "very glad the City had no occasion for the houses he offered them, being much more inclined to keep them than to dispose of them at the price he offered them for." The Committee reported to the Court that £2200 should be paid and this was agreed to. In July, 1739, there was a warrant drawn for £2520. This evidently included costs, and the Town Clerk was paid 30 guineas "for his trouble."

In 1759 a portion of the property was taken down and a reference is made to a proposal to build a coach house and stables for the Lord Mayor, on the adjoining land facing the Mansion House, and Dance prepared the plans (see Plan 32).

It is interesting to note that in 1683 the crypt of the Guildhall was used as a stable and coach house, and three members were appointed to inquire into "the mischiefs arising therefrom" and the "annoyance and inconvenience thereof." At that time the Lord Mayor kept his mayoralty at his private house, and it is unlikely that the stable and coach house were used by him.

Property of the Clothworkers' Company on west side of Walbrook.

In 1750 the Company was anxious to deal with five houses facing the Mansion House; they calculated they were worth a total rental of £105, but were all empty on account of the works at the Mansion House. The Committee considered a rental of £50 ample, and in 1754 the Clothworkers' Company agreed.

In June, 1754, the Corporation treated for the purchase of three houses facing the site of the Mansion House. Plan 28 is a plan of the property taken from the Company's Plan Book and dated 1612; it is also shown on Plan 64. The Company had no power to sell the freehold but were willing to let for a term of 21 years renewable for ever at £30 p.a. They were willing to let three other houses on similar terms at £20 p.a.

In 1755 the Ward presented a petition with reference to the site of the above five houses which they state the Corporation had acquired, the site being vacant and a nuisance.

In 1760 the churchwardens of St Stephen's Walbrook stated they had "two water engines" and that there was no room for them in the church or in the churchyard, and asked permission to build an engine house on the land facing the Mansion House and which was vacant. Permission was given, the position being "Where the doorway into the Court of Bucklers bury is placed." The building is shown on Plan 30.

This plan is traced from a lease dated 31st July, 1775; it shows the various properties and the land added to the public way on the west side of the Mansion House.

Generally as to Purchase.

The *Gentleman's Magazine*, vol. XVIII, p. 234, May, 1748, states the total cost of Mansion House was £42,638. 18s. 8d., including £3900 paid for purchasing property.

In Gwynn's *London and Westminster* there is a similar statement as to cost.

Mr Thursby's interest.

In March, 1737, Mr Thursby was offered £450 for his interest in the house he had. In April, 1739, it was increased to £500. In May he refused £500 and wanted £750. In June, 1745, he agreed to accept £500 for his interest "late part of the Swan Tavern."

With reference to the action brought by Lord Micklethwaite, it appears that in the year 1727 he leased certain property for 999 years, rent £150. There was a house occupied by Herring, apparently afterwards occupied by Seed; it was burnt down in 1666, neither party to the action knew the dimensions of the property; the old lease was burnt or lost. In May, 1756, a report was presented to the Court of Common Council advising the purchase of a ground rent of £150, term 999 years for the large sum of £4650 on 31 years' purchase. The description is vague and refers to "the greatest part of the ground on which the Mansion House is built." This was obviously an exaggeration, even supposing the property were the whole of the land south of Bearbinder Lane.

PLATE XXIV

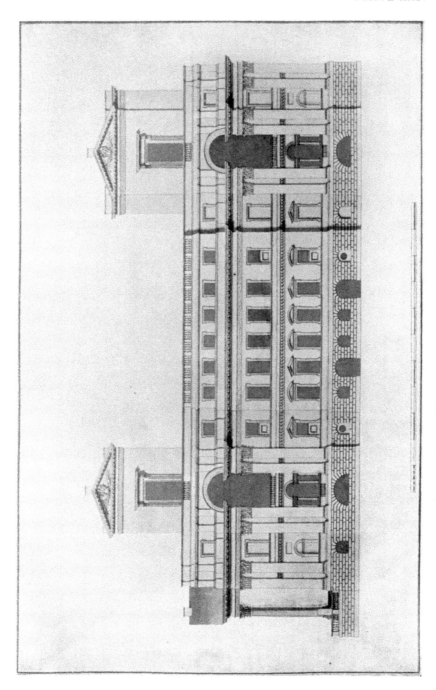

WEST ELEVATION OF THE MANSION HOUSE
Showing the Mayor's Nest and the Noah's Ark

PLATE XXV

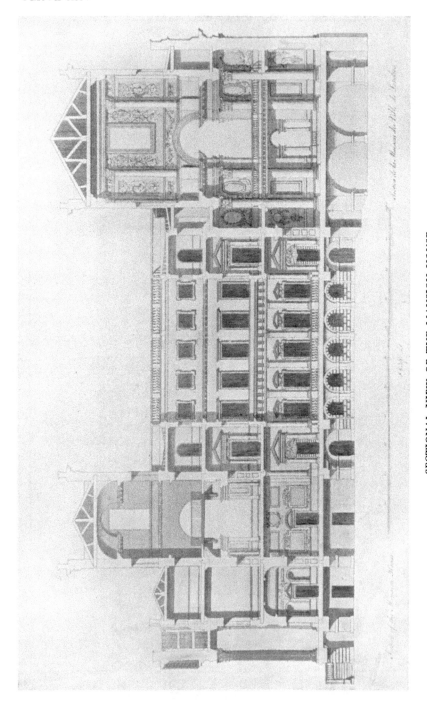

SECTIONAL VIEW OF THE MANSION HOUSE

Showing the extraordinary height of the Ball Room and Egyptian Hall, before the upper portions were removed

Drawn by T. Woolfe

Chapter X

The Plans for the Mansion House

IN the documents of the Corporation there are several references to the "Lord Mayor's House" many years before the
erection of the Mansion House was contemplated. In those
days it was the custom of the aldermen and the citizens to live
at their business premises. Stow states that "Leadenhall was
first a Mansion House belonging to Sir Hugh Neville anno
1309 and in 1408 it was purchased by Richard Whittington
(who was afterwards Lord Mayor in 1409)."

The following is a list of some of the residences:

John Gyssors, Founder of Bethlehem Hospital, was Mayor in 1245
and 1246; he lived at Gissors or Gerard's Hall which stood on the south
side of Baring Lane. The site is shewn in Carmar Street on an ordnance
map.

Richard Whittington lived in Hart Street, Mark Lane, in Sweedon's
Passage, Grub Street, now Milton Street and in College Hill, Upper
Thames Street. He was Mayor in 1396, 1397, 1406 and 1419.

Sir Thomas Bowes was elected Lord Mayor in 1545; he lived in
Lombard Street in a house on the site of Glyn's bank; he was a goldsmith
and pawnbroker.

Sir John Spencer was Lord Mayor in 1594; he lived at Crosby Place,
Bishopsgate. This building was pulled down in 1907 and re-erected at
Chelsea on the site of the garden of Sir Thomas More's house.

Sir Thomas Viner was Lord Mayor in 1653; he lived in Lombard
Street close to St Mary Woolnoth Church. Plan 22 is a plan of the
property taken after the fire of London.

Sir Robert Clayton was Lord Mayor in 1679; he lived in Fredericks
Place, Old Jewry. The building was afterwards the first home of the
London Institution, later it was used as a Lord Mayor's Court. It was
pulled down in 1863.

There is a MS. book in the Guildhall Library[1], written in
1609, giving a list of all the Mayors of London, and in many
cases their places of residence are mentioned; the following are
extracts:

[1] MS. 2077.

Mercers Company.

Simon Francis, Mayor 1343. "He dwelled in yᵉ Old Jewry in the same house, where Sir Thomas Benet now dwelleth."

Sir William Estfeld, Mayor 1430 and 1438. "He dwelled in Aldermanbury, where Sr. John Swineston now dwelleth."

Sir Robert Large, Mayor 1440. "He dwelled in Lothbury in the same house which is now the Windmill and standeth in two parishes."

Sir Geffrey Felding, Mayor 1453. "He dwelled in Milkstrete."

Sir John Tate, Mayor 1474, 1497 and 1514. Buried at St. Antholin, "dwelled at yᵉ est end of the same church."

Sir Hugh Clopton, Mayor 1492. "Dwelled in Lothbury where now the windmill a Taverne is."

Sir William Purchas, Mayor 1498. "He dwelled in St. Lawrence Lane, where Mr. Morley now dwelleth."

Sir John Gresham, Mayor 1548. "He dwelled where Sr. Leonard Holiday now dwelleth."

Sir Rouland Hill, Mayor 1550. "He dwelled on yᵉ west syde of Walbrooke, over against St. Stephens Church."

Sir Thomas Leigh, Mayor 1559. "He dwelled in yᵉ Old Jewry, his house joyning on the north of yᵉ Mercers Chapell."

Sir Humphrey Weld "now L. maior dwelleth in yᵉ same house, which he hath new builded of Brick."

Sir Richard Mallory, Mayor 1565. "He dwelled in Cheapsyde at Soper Lane end, where now the Golden Key is."

Sir Roger Martin, Mayor 1568. "He dwelled in yᵉ west syde of Soper Lane."

Sir William Allen, Mayor 1572, "dwelled when he was Sheriff in Bow Lane, when he was Maior in Tower strete."

Sir Lionel Ducket Mayor, 1573. "He dwelled in Woodstrete in St. Peters Parish."

Grocers Company.

Simon Dolsey, Mayor 1360. "He dwelled in yᵉ same house which is now Cutlers hall."

Sir Richard Lee, Mayor 1461 and 1470. "He dwelled in Walbroke near unto St. Stephens Church."

Sir William Tayler, Mayor 1469. "Buried in Aldermary Church 1483. He builded and dwelled at yᵉ est end of yᵉ same Church. In w̄ house Sr. Wm. Caxton dwelled since."

John Winger, Mayor 1505. "Buried at St. Mary Wolchurch nere the Stocks."

Sir William Laxton, Mayor 1545. "He dwelled in Budge Row, at ye est end of Aldermary Church."

Sir John Lyon, Mayor 1555. "He dwelled in Bucklersbery and was buried in St. Sythes Church w toucheth on the south syde of his house."

Sir John Whyte, Mayor 1564. "He dwelled in Lothbury at Bartelmew Lane end where Sr. Henry Anderson Late dwelled."

Sr. John Rivers Mayor 1574. "He dwelled in Bartelmew Lane, where Mr. Baldwin Derham now dwelleth"

Sr. Thomas Ramsey Mayor 1578 "He dwelled in Lombardstrete where Sr. Martin Bowes dwelled"

Drapers Company.

Simon Eire Mayor 1446 "Buried at St. Mary Wolnoth in Lombardstrete which standeth over against ŷ house where he dwelled"

Sr. William Chester Mayor 1561 "He dwelled at ŷ upper end of Lombardstrete, over against the George, near St. Edmunds Church where he was buried"

Sr. Richard Pype Mayor 1579 "dwelled in Aldermary churchyard:"

Sr. John Branch Mayor 1581 "He dwelled in St. Nicholas Lane nere Canwickestrete, in ŷ parish of St. Mary Abchurch"

Sr. Thomas Pallison Mayor 1585 "He dwelled in Budge Row"

Fishmongers.

Sir William Hampton Mayor 1473 "He dwelled next to St. Christopher's Church Dore"

Sir Thomas Carters Mayor 1558 "dwelled at ŷ upper end of Lombardstrete"

Goldsmiths.

Sir Drew Baxentine Mayor 1339 and 1409 "He dwelled in foster Lane, over against the Goldsmiths hall, from w he made a Gallery over ŷ Lane, to his owne house"

Sir John Shaw Mayor 1502 "He dwelled in the upper end of Woodstrete"

Skinners.

Sir Richard Dobbs Mayor 1552 "Buried at St. Margret moses in fryday strete, where he dwelled"

Sir Wolston Dixy Mayor 1586 "He dwelled where Sr. Leonard Holiday now dwelleth"

Merchant Taylors.

Sir Henry Hoblethorne Mayor 1547 "He dwelled in ŷ very next house to LeadenHall where Sr. Wm. Bowyer sometimes dwelled"

Sir Thomas White Mayor 1554 "He maried the widow of Sr. Ralph Warren in whose house he dwelled in St. Sythes' Lane"

Sir Thomas Ofley Mayor 1557 "He dwelled in Lymestrete, towards the north end of it not far from St. Andrews undershaft"

Sir William Harper Mayor 1562 "He dwelled in Lombardstrete (where Mr. Butler now dwelleth)"

Sir Thomas Row Mayor 1569. "He dwelled in Bishopsgatestrete, where his sonne Sr. Henry Row, now dwelleth"

Haberdashers.

Sir George Bayne Mayor 1553 "He dwelled in Bartelmews Lane, where Sr. Wm. Capell once dwelled"

Sir William Gerrard Mayor 1556. "He dwelled at the Conduit by ỹ stocks, in St. Christopher's parish"

Sir Nicholas Woodroff Mayor 1580 "He dwelled nere Leadenhall, in the parish of St. Andrew undershaft"

Sir Thomas Blanck Mayor 1583 "He dwelled a little above Billingsgate, hard by St. Mary hill"

Sir George Barne Mayor 1587 "He dwelled in Lombardstrete over against the George, in the house which was Sr. Wm. Chesters"

Sir George Bond Mayor 1588 "He dwelled in Walbroke, where Sr. Rouland Hill dwelled"

Clothworkers.

Sir Rouland Heyward Mayor 1571 and 1591. "He dwelled in Phillipp Lane by Creplegate, his house adioyning on Sr. Alphages Church"

Sir James Hawes Mayor 1575 "He dwelled nere to the Conduit in Cornhill"

Sir Edward Osborne Mayor 1584 "He dwelled in Philpott Lane, in Sr. Wm. Hewetts house, whose only daughter he had married"

As early as 15th of November, 1670, a Mansion House was contemplated. The following is an extract from the *Repertories* of that date:

This Court being further moved touching an house to be erected and continued for the constant habitation of the Lord Maiors of this Citty doe think fitt and order that Sir Richard Chiverton, Sir Jn° Lawrence Sir Wm. Peake Sir Richd Ryves Sr Robert Hanson, Sr William Hooker, Sr Joseph Sheldon, Sr Francis Chaplyn and Sr John Smith knts. and Aldermen or any three of them doe consider of what hath been or may be said or offered for or against the providing or erecting of such an house and if they think fitt to proceed therein to consider of the advantage and conveniencyes of the place in Cheapsyde now proposed for that purpose and certofye unto this Court in writing under their hands how they find the same and their opinions.

Apparently nothing was done at the time, but the following is an extract from a letter dated 1 Mars, 1679, addressed to "Monsieur" by "votre tres-humble et tres-obeissant Serviteur":

They tell me that Oates is to have a statue at the Mansion House. Do write the inscription I will give you sufficient materials. The more ample narrative which will appear shortly, will supply the varnish. In England two witnesses are necessary to establish a charge of high treason.

Hence the appearance of a second informer, named Bedloe, the son of a village fiddler, and a thief, rogue and debauchee[1].

On 19th November, 1689, it was proposed that a Committee of Aldermen might be appointed to consider the question of the Hall of the Grocers' Company being "a dwelling house constantly for the Lord Mayor." This no doubt arose from the fact that it was customary for the Lord Mayor to entertain at the hall of his principal company, and the Grocers' Hall was frequently used for that purpose.

In 1697 the markets were assessed as follows:

Leadenhall Market	£2900.	0.	0
Honey Lane ,,	1034.	6.	4
Newgate ,,	3500.	0.	0
Stocks ,,	900.	0.	0
Total	£8334.	6.	4

On May 24th, 1728, the Court of Common Council unanimously decided

that a Committee be appointed to find out a proper place for erecting the said Mansion House, to procure planns of such intended building and to consider of Ways and Means to defray the Charge therof.

On 5th June, 1728, the Committee reported that they had viewed several places and were of opinion

that that square part of Leadenhall Market now used for the Leather Market together with the Ground whereon now stands the Boching and Colchester Halls and several other Buildings adjoining or the Stocks Market will be a convenient place.

On 30th April, 1730, it was decided that "all moneys which shall hereafter be paid—as a fine for not holding the office of Sheriff shall be appropriated for the building of a Mansion House," and in the *London Magazine* of July, 1736, we read:

By an exact List of Persons who have fin'd for the office of Sheriff of London, there appears to be now in Hand, deducting £500 paid to five sheriffs in the year 1730 and 1732, the Sum of £20,700 towards building a Mansion House for the Lord Mayor, which being laid out in 3 per cent Annuities, the interest thereof is every Half Year to be made Capital.

On March 5th, 1734–5, a Committee was appointed

to consider of a proper place or places, whereon to Erect a Mansion

---

[1] *Historical Manuscripts Commission, House of Lords MSS.* vol. XVII, p. 99.

House for the Lord Mayor of this city for the time being, and to procure a Plan or Plans, for such intended Building, together with the Estimates of the Charge thereof &c.

The Committee consisted of the Lord Mayor, five aldermen, and 12 commoners, and promptly met on the 13th of March. It was known as the Mansion House Committee.

The selection of the present site for the building gave rise to considerable discussion, for in the Bodleian Library there is a pamphlet 24 pages long entitled

An answer to the Letter from a Common-Council-Man containing His observations on the Report of the Committee appointed to consider of a proper Place for a Mansion-House of the Lord Mayor: By a Member of that Committee.

The letter I have not been able to find but the writer evidently objected to the Stocks Market site, he admitted the Gresham College site was not suitable, but he was in favour of the Leadenhall Market scheme and made calculations to show it would be cheaper. The reply is very clear and no doubt the Stocks Market was the best site. The pamphlet has an interesting reference to the competition of the architects. It states: "there were nine or ten different Plans, two of each Place, and some of them in different Forms by each Architect." Although the reply was a long one, 24 pages, the complaint was evidently longer for there is a reference to the 28th page.

The Sword Bearer and Common Crier were ordered to report and deliver a list of the accommodation considered necessary for the new building. The rooms required were as follows: hall, great parlour, two small parlours, cause room, sword bearer's room, officers' room, cocket office, porter's lodge, kitchen, larder for housekeeper, housekeeper's room, store room for pewter, scowering room, a room for yeomen of the wine cellar, butler's room, servants' hall, three or four large rooms for the ladies, a tea room, lodging room, etc.

They quoted the fact that at the Fishmongers' Hall the great parlour was 45 feet by 21 feet, the hall 63 feet by 34 feet, the two middle rooms above stairs 31 feet by 17 feet, three outward ditto 45 feet by 17 feet, and one inward ditto 25 feet by 17 feet. Plan 31 shows the scheme.

It was decided to have a limited competition and Mr Gibbs, Mr James, Mr Leoni were summoned to attend the Committee; they were three well-known architects. It is strange that Dance was not invited for at this time he was acting for the Corporation in the office of Clerk of the City's Works (see Chapter XIII). On March 18th a letter from Mr Batty Langley was read, "but the Committee make no order thereon." The letter was as follows and addressed to Sir Edward Bellamy, the Lord Mayor.

Sir,
      That the intended Mansion House may be a just representation of ye Magnificency, Granduer, Riches, Trade &c. of London, the most famous Metropolitan in ye World; I am therefore making a Plan, Elevation, and Section for ye same, according to my promise made in my new Critical Review of the Publick Buildings &c. published in the Grub Street Journal of the 6th. of Augt. last, which in about 20 days time I shall begg leave to recommend to your judicious consideration.

I am,

Your Humble Sevt,

(Signed)   HIRAM.

Westminster.
   17. March, 1734.

Batty Langley also sent the following letter:

My Lord,
      Being not very well, I cannot attend your Lordship and the Gentlemen of the Committee this afternoon, as I would gladly have done; wherefore I beg leave to inform your Lordship and ye Gentlemen of ye Committee, that as the Just Rules of Architecture have always been my study; and as thereby I have demonstrated the many beauties and defects in our Publick Buildings; of which I lately published an acct. in the Grub Street Journal under the name of Hiram—I therefore begg leave to inform yr Lordship and ye other Gentlemen of the Committee, that as I know my self able to compose a Design for a Mansion House with greater Magnificency, Granduer, and Beauty, than has been yet express'd in any; nay, even in all, the Publick Buildings of this City, taken together—I am therefore making a Plan, Elevation and Section for ye same (supposeing it to be erected in Stocks Market) which in abt. three weeks time I shall have completed; and now beg leave, that then, I may be permitted to exhibit ye same unto this Committee for consideration.
     Mr. Justice Blackerbee of Parliam^t. Stairs is my near Neighbour, and who will further inform yr Lordship of my abilities &c. if required.

I am,

Yr Lordship's obed^t. Sevt.

(Signed)   BATTY LANGLEY.

Parliament Stairs,
   18. March, 1734.
      read in Comt^{ee}. 18. 3. 1734–5.

Batty Langley wrote a series of articles in the *Grub Street Journal* commencing on July 11th, 1734, the last appearing on March 6th, 1735. He stated when considering the "Critical Review of the Public Buildings, etc." by Ralph:

I observe in general, that the author has had the boldness to condemn almost every building, without assigning one single reason. It is therefore surprising to me, that no person has hitherto thought it incumbent on him to correct the insolence of this pretended critic.

The following is the modest statement of the critic, dated August 8th, 1734:

But however grand such a design might have been it is now too late, since the Bank is rebuilt in another place; and therefore to make the best of a bad market, I shall consider the whole for the lord mayor's palace only. As London is the capital city of the world, certainly the palace should be (of the kind) the most magnificent, elegant, and rich. To describe the manner in which I would express the magnificence, elegancy, and riches of this city, by external and internal parts of this intended edifice, would be a means of furnishing some persons with ideas, which they would probably afterwards claim for their own. And indeed, as the designs of buildings and their effects, cannot be so well understood by verbal description, as by real plans, elevations and sections, lineally described, I shall therefore forbear giving any such description; especially since, very shortly, I shall present the right hon: the lord mayor and court of aldermen, with a plan, elevation and section for that building; which I make no doubt, but these gentlemen, like the noble and virtuous old Romans, will impartially consider.

On April 1st, 1735, Leoni wrote from "Vine Street by Piccadilly" that his plans were ready. On May 8th, 1735, Mr Gibbs and Mr Leoni both attended and handed in a "Draught of a Plan"; and it was decided that a sub-committee should view the sites of Gresham College, Leadenhall Market, and the Stocks Market.

On May 13th the Committee met at the South Sea Coffee-house, and considered the question of purchase of properties adjoining the Stocks Market, and a deputation was formed to wait on the Duke of Bedford who, as we have seen, owned three houses at the corner of Walbrook and the Poultry; these were eventually purchased. On June 13th it was reported that with regard to the Stocks Market that the Clothworkers' Company would sell if they had power, and the properties to be purchased would be

One house belonging to the Clothworkers Company, one other belonging to Mr. Harvey, Two Houses belonging to Mr Rider, who is a

Minor Sir Francis Drake his Trustee and Guardian, The Interest of
the Farmers of the Market, Mr. Calverts interest in a house which he
holds of the City by Lease being the Sign of the Globe, and the Glebe
belonging to the Parson of St. Mary Woolchurch which is of the yearly
value of £8.

The architects were consulted on July 3rd and gave the
following dimensions for their schemes on the Stocks Market
site.

Mr Gibbs said he would leave "15 feet between the intended building and Walbrook Church," his design was 94
feet in front and 224 in depth. Mr James stated he proposed
a passage 11 feet wide, his dimensions being 95 feet in front
and 222 in depth. Mr Leoni's plan was 100 feet in front and
232 feet in depth.

The Committee abandoned the idea of the Gresham College
site as it "is too difficult to be procured."

Batty Langley was very persistent and wrote to the Town
Clerk as follows:

July ye 6th. 1735.
Parliament Stairs.

Sir,

My Lord Mayor has informed me, that His Lordship has given
you orders, for to give, or send me notice, of the time, when the Committee appointed for building the Mansion House, have their next
meeting. If you'l please to send to me at Parliament Stairs, near Old
Palace Yard, Westminster, such notice will be rec'd,

By Sir,
Your Humble Servant,
(Signed)   BATTY LANGLEY.

The result was that Batty Langley was called before the
Committee on July 17th "at the Lord Mayor's request," and
presented a plan; it was decided at this meeting that Dance
should also compete and the following letter was sent to the
five architects.

Sr.,

The Committee for the Mansion House desire you to Draw a
Plan of a House for the Ground in that part of *Leadenhall Markett*
between the four Towers where the Leather & Hide Marketts are now
held, the Demension of which Ground as Rep[ted] to ye Com[tee] is in ffront
next Leadenhall Street from Tower to Tower about 130 feet in Depth

about 228 feet & ye back from west to ye arch next Gracechurch Street about 120 feet.

18 July, 1735.   Sent to James.
                                          Gibbs.
                                          Leoni.
                                          Langley &
                                          Dance.

   The Committee's report to the Court was as follows:

> To the Committee of Common Council appointed to consider of a proper place or places whereon to erect a Mansion House for the Lord Mayor of this City for the time being &c.

   In p'suance of ye order of the 8th. of May last Wee have mett and viewed severall places whereon the said Mantion house should be erected and are of opinion that the most propper places are the ground now used as the Markett called Stocks Markett or the ground within the four Towers now used as part of Leadenhall Markett But if this Committee should be of opinion that the said Mantion House should be built on the ground called Stocks Markett there will be a necessity of p'chasing A Lease from this City granted to one Martin Rydor Esqre. of a piece of ground lying behind a Freehold Messuage belonging to him & Lett therewith which Lease will not expire untill Michas. 1742. A Lease also granted by this City of a Messuage or Tenem^t to Felix Calvert Esqre. which will not Expire untill Michmas 1742. The Freehold Messuage or Tenement belonging to the said Mr. Rydor and other Freehold Messuage or Tenement belonging to John Harvey Esqre. another Freehold Messuage or Tenem^t belonging to the Worp'full Company of Clothworkers. A piece of ground on which the Parsonage house stood & was in 1674 granted this City by the Minister of St. Mary Woolchurch Haw for 99 years if he should so long continue Minister and the interest of the Farmer of the Markett whose Lease will Expire at Michmas 1737 the improved rents of all which according to the best account wee could gett are as follows (vizt.)

Mr. Rydor Leasehold and Freehold	54 p. annum
Mr. Calverts Leasehold	60
Mr. Harvey's Freehold	30
The Clothworkers' Co. Freehold	30
The Glebe Land	8
The Markett	1500
in all	1682

   It is interesting to note from the above that in 1737 a fair sized house on the site of the Mansion House let at about £30 to £60 p.a.

On November 19th, 1735, the Committee saw the architects. James and Gibbs and Batty Langley submitted plans for the Leadenhall site. Leoni's plans were not ready. Dance delivered plans for the Leadenhall Market scheme and also for the Stocks Market site. At this meeting a Captain De Berlain attended and offered a plan, the Committee "did not think fit to Receive it, and the same was delivered back to him and he was dismist." The following is the "Memorial" he submitted and which was read to the Committee:

To ye R^t Honble ye Lord Mayor, & ye Gentlemen of ye Honble Comity, appointed for ye building of ye City mansion House, on Stocks-Markett.

Capt De Berlains Memorial.

My Lord, & Gentlemen,

Having had ye honour to serve ye Nation above 40 years, & being a Mathematician, Engineer, & Architect, I made bold to draw a Frontespiece, with its Ichnographic which will fitt ye ground proposed for such a Noble Building, on Stocks Market; that is composed of ye Corinthien, ye Britanical, or Protestant, & ye Dorick Orders, which if so builded, will excell, in beauty, rigularty, & Simetric, any Building in ye World, for its bigness, where there is 20 Rooms on ye ground floor, for such use as your Honble Comity shall judge most proper for conveniency, beside ye great Hall, of 82 feet & 58, ye Salon of 39 Square, ye great and Small Stairs, ye Lodge, & 2 yards of 18 & 9, besides an advant Court, where ye Statue Stands, & on ye first floor 16 Rooms besides ye Dancing Gallery of 82 & 39, with 2 places for Musiciens, & as many on ye Second for Servants, which I brought to shew your hon^ble Comity whom I gladly approch, it being composed of so wise and learned Gentlemen which will judge of this Small work favourably, it being only to be a perpetual Monument to posterity for ye happy Revolution, & for ye delivrance, of Popery.

(Signed)   D. De Berlain.

What a pity that plan cannot be found!

On December 18th, 1735, the Committee submitted a long report to the Court of Common Council, giving particulars of the Stocks Market, and Leadenhall Market sites. They said the five architects had submitted plans for each site and they were ready for instruction. Finally they recommend the Stocks Market site as the most suitable. The matter was adjourned and on March 28th, 1736, the Court decided on the present site.

The Committee at once took up the matter, the Common Serjeant and two other counsel were asked their opinion "at a fee of five guineas each." The rector of St Mary Woolchurch

Haw was approached, the Committee met at the Swan Tavern, and viewed the various properties.

In June, 1736, the Committee reported they had taken counsel's opinion as to any possible objections there might be against building the Mansion House on the site of the Stocks Market, and it was pointed out that "the present Stocks Market is not any part of the Ground called the Stockes, that being entirely laid into the Street." The question of the site of the parsonage house was also satisfactorily dealt with, and there was no objection to the proposal.

On July 6th, 1737, the Committee considered the designs, and the following were the estimates:

Mr Leoni about £26,000

 „ Gibbs „   £30,000

 „ James „   £30,000

 „ Dance „   £26,000

It is stated that "One Mr. Ware attended at the door, was called in" and presented a design to cost £23,000.

On the 27th of the same month the Committee submitted all the designs "together with one prepared by Mr. Ware without any directions" to be laid before the Court of Common Council. They recommended Dance's design, and also that the Stocks Market should be closed at Michaelmas.

Batty Langley is not mentioned in that report to the Court, for some unknown reason he retired from the contest, for according to the report of 18th December he had prepared plans for the Stocks Market site.

There was evidently some wire-pulling in those days, and the following memoranda are amusing:

After Dances Plans were approv'd and resolv'd on Dowbiggen by the instigation of Cordwell went with Drawings of another kind to several Members of the Court of Common Council particularly to Alderman Barber and to Mr. Ridge in order to prejudice Dance.

Branson hath a particular grudge against Dance and hath villified him and endeavoured to prejudice him ever since the trouble he had with the City about his bill for Plaisters Work.

Please to ask Dowbiggen
if after Dance's Plans were resolv'd on by the Committee he did not privately apply to several Gentlemen of the Court of Common Council, particularly to Alderman Barber and Mr. Ridge in order to set aside Dances design and to introduce other plans, and if he did not do this at the instigation of Cordwell.

In *A Critical Review of the Public Buildings of London and Westminster*, in the 1738 edition, we read as follows:

When it was resolved in the Common Council to build a mansion-house for the lord mayor, lord Burlington, zealous in the cause of the arts, sent down an original design of Palladio, worthy of its author, for their approbation and adoption. The first question in Court was not, whether this plan was proper, but whether this same Palladio was a freeman of the city or no. On this great debates ensued, and it is hard to say how it might have gone, had not a worthy deputy risen up and observed gravely, that it was of little consequence to discuss this point when it was notorious that Palladio was a papist and *incapable* of course. Lord Burlington's proposal was then rejected nem. con. and the plan of a freeman and a protestant adopted in its room.

The above is an early version of a ridiculous story that appears at intervals; there is no record of any such plan being submitted or of any such debate. The site was peculiar, certain conditions were laid down for the architects with regard to the plan, these are referred to above, and how could Palladio, who died in 1580, have prepared a plan with prophetic instinct to comply with these conditions? Lord Burlington's wonderful collection of Palladio's drawings is now owned by the Duke of Devonshire and for many years they have been on loan to the Royal Institute of British Architects. The author has examined these drawings and not one of them would have applied. He has also examined the designs of Lord Burlington in the same collection and none was made for the Mansion House site. There is another point, Leoni was an Italian, and probably a Roman Catholic; he was invited by the Corporation to compete and there is no record of any question as to his religion. Again, James Gibbs was a Roman Catholic.

In the same paragraph Ralph states that Dance was originally a shipwright—this is not supported by any life of Dance.

Giacomo Leoni was probably a protégé of Lord Burlington, he was a great authority on Palladio, but unfortunately his design cannot be found; I doubt if it was ever published. He died in 1746. In the Committee documents there is no trace of any communication with him.

Isaac Ware published his designs, which are reproduced in Plans 33, 34, 35 and 36. They are particularly interesting as he shows the optional scheme for Leadenhall Market.

Four schemes by John James are in existence for the Stocks

Market site; there is a plan of the Guildhall, for one floor of each scheme and one elevation—these have never been published. Plans 37, 38, 39 and 40 are samples of his work. There is a mistake on the drawing of Plan 39, the plinths to the two centre columns are omitted.

The plans of three floors for the Stocks Market site by James Gibbs were found by the writer at the Radcliffe Library, Oxford. Plan 41 is the ground floor plan and Plan 42 is an elevation although it does not exactly correspond with the plan. Plans 43 and 44 are also elevations by Gibbs. Plans 45 and 46 are the plans at the Guildhall for his Leadenhall Market site. Plan 47 is the elevation for this scheme. All the elevations are in the Radcliffe Library, Oxford.

Batty Langley's plan (Plan 48) is at the Guildhall; there is also a first floor plan. Plan 49 is the elevation taken from an engraving. Langley made a plan he considered suitable for either site. It is interesting to note that there was a Tokenhouse Yard near Leadenhall Market. The reader can compare the architect's opinion of his design on p. 166 with the result.

Had there been a big debate with reference to the design for the Mansion House and Lord Burlington's supposed suggestion, the journals of the time would doubtless have referred to it, for they gave considerable space to the discussions about the various contracts. The *Daily Gazetteer* of July 29th, 1737, gives an account of the meeting, sets out the names in full of the Committee for letting the stalls at the various markets and other matters, but simply states:

The Mansion House for the Lord Mayor for the time being is to be built according to a plan of Mr. Dance at Stocks-Market: for which purpose the said Market will be shut up from Michaelmas-Day next, at which time the Market in Fleet-ditch will be opened, the Shops in which the tenants are to have for six months without paying any rent.

The *Daily Post* had a similar account, but omits the reference to the Mansion House.

On March 3rd, 1737, the Committee agreed to pay

Mr. Gibbs one hundred guineas for his trouble in attendance, and drawing plans by order of this Committee, Mr. James...seventy five guineas...Mr. Leoni...fifty guineas, and Mr. Batty Langley twenty guineas.

On April 18th Mr Ware applied "for payments as Leoni and others; it was decided that as he had done the work without instructions he was not entitled to anything." Batty Langley's small honorarium is in keeping with the fact that he made no special design for the Stocks Market site.

The notice for clearing the market was as follows:

London August 5th. 1737.

This is to Give Notice that the Stocks Market will be discontinued shut up and Inclosed on the 30th. day of September next In pursuance of an Order of Common Council made the 28th. day of July last and that the New market near the Fleet called Fleet Markett will on the said 30th. September be opened. And all such persons who shall think fit to take any Shops Stalls Shambles or Standing in the said Market, for exposing any Goods to sale therein, may apply to the Committee of Common Council who will meet at the Guildhall London on Tuesday and Thursday in every week, at four of the Clock in the afternoon, until the 30th. of September to treat and agree for the same. And for the Encouragement of such persons as shall be minded to use the said Market, It is hereby declared that all and every such person and persons as shall take any Shop Stall Shambles or Standing in the said market and use the same for selling any goods therein, shall hold the same rent free and without paying anything for the same until Ladyday next; provided they do on or before the first of March next, Give Notice to the said Committee whether they will continue to hold the same after Ladyday, at such rent as shall be agreed on to commence from Ladyday aforesaid.

N.B. All Country Carts and Highers are to be at liberty to *sell* their Goods rent free as above.

With reference to the removal of the tenants from the Stocks Market to the Fleet Market, Hogarth's picture, "A Fleet Wedding," shows a portion of a stall with the words "from Stocksmarket" painted on it.

The inhabitants of Bearbinder Lane were evidently afraid there would be no passage at the back of the Mansion House, for in October, 1737, they petitioned for a footway from Bucklersbury to Bearbinder Lane "either thro' the Market or round by the Old Sheds."

In the *Gentleman's Magazine* of May, 1738 (p. 218), we read "Court of Common Council confirmed selection of Dance's plans, 'proposals' to be asked for carrying out the work by Artificiers...who must be Freemen of London."

A bundle of receipts for small disbursements during 1737–8 is interesting; the following are samples:

A Committee for the Mansion House the 20th. day of September 1737

Coffee Tea	12.	0
Chocolate	2.	9
Bread and Butter	1.	6
Tobacco		4
	16.	7

28th. July 1736

At Scotland yard Coffee house waiting on the Bishop of London 4. 6

With Mr. Sandford at Bishop of London. Coach and hire 4. 6

A Committee to view the Modall of the Mansion House of 21st. of June 1738

Coffee and Tea		10.	0
Bread and Butter		1.	6
Tobacco			4
		11.	10
Smelts		5.	0
Asparrowguse		5.	0
Bread Ale Butter cheese			
& Radishes		2.	0
Orranges			6
Bristoll Water		1.	0
Tobacco			6
Sherry		1.	6
Clarritt	1.	0.	0
Oporto		11.	0
Veale Cutlets		1.	6
	2.	8.	0
Servants		1.	0
	2.	9.	0

Nearly all the bills were for tea, very few for lunches or dinners.

Plate XII is the reproduction of a summons for attendance at committee. Not many public bodies meet now as early as 9 o'clock in the morning.

PLATE XXVI

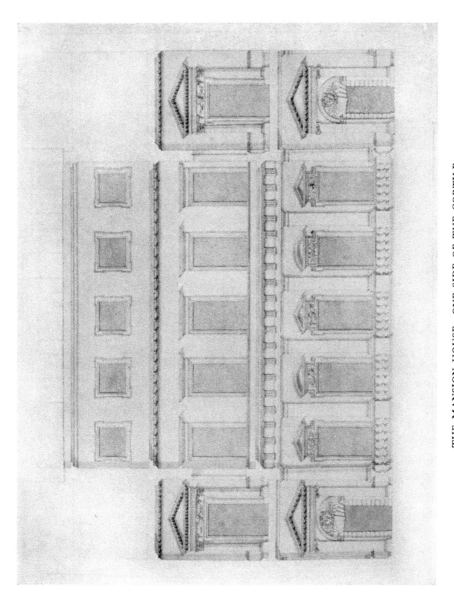

THE MANSION HOUSE. ONE SIDE OF THE CORTILE
Showing delightful architectural treatment now hidden

PLATE XXVII

THE EGYPTIAN HALL

Chapter XI

The building of the Mansion House

NO conditions for remuneration were stated by the Committee when the architects were invited to compete. When Dance was appointed he was asked what he expected "for his trouble and care in Surveying, and ordering the intended building and he said the usual allowance was five pounds per cent. on the money laid out"; this of course has been the usual remuneration for large buildings until quite recently when the Royal Institute of British Architects raised their scale.

Subsequently Dance's duties were set out in detail. He agreed to "keep a proper Person at my own charge, continually upon the Spot, to take care that no bad Materials of any kind be used in the Building." This man is now known as a Clerk of Works and his salary is paid by the employer and not by the architect.

There was no contract for the whole building similar to the London custom of to-day, the work was tendered for by various firms during the progress of the works. The obvious disadvantage of such a system is that the building owner does not know the cost of his building before it is commenced.

Advertisements appeared in the *Daily Post* of February 23rd, 24th, 28th and March 1st and 3rd, 1738, asking for "Proposals" for removing the stones of the Stocks Market and for excavating.

Five tenders were received for the excavation and the contract was 1s. 6d. per cubic yard for "digging the foundations and carrying away the earth and soyle," and the time was limited to two months. Dance's depth was 10 feet and he estimated it would cost 1s. 10d. a yard, total £739. 6s. 8d. Only those persons who were free of the City by servitude or patrimony were allowed to tender. Dance referred to piling and planking as "wharfing."

Advertisements were inserted in the *Daily Post* of April 28th and May 1st, 1738, for mason's, bricklayer's and carpenter's work, and on June 2nd, 1738, the Committee reported they had received the following tenders:

Mason's Work, Thomas Dunn & Co., £18,000.
  „   John Townsend, Christopher Horsenaile and Robert Taylor, £18,000.
Bricklayer's Work, Five Tenders, the lowest being £5. 3s. 6d. per rod.
Carpenter's Work, Four Tenders, the lowest being £1240 by John Cordwell.

The Court of Common Council accepted those of £5. 3s. 6d. and £1240.

Robert Taylor, who tendered with others for the mason's work, was the sculptor who afterwards became an architect.

Cordwell, Taylor, Townsend and Horsenail were all members of the Court of Common Council.

At a meeting of the Common Council on June 2nd, 1738, the Committee submitted the two tenders for the mason's work. Messrs Dunn and Devail £18,000, and Messrs Townsend, Horsenail and Robert Taylor for the same amount. The last three men were members of the Court of Common Council, and two tenders only, each of the same amount, suggests collusion. At a meeting of the Court "fresh proposals were submitted," Messrs Dunn & Co. £16,975, and the three members of the Court £17,200. The latter firm was accepted after a division.

The following appeared in the *Gentleman's Magazine* of 7th June, 1738, p. 321:

On the 2nd and 7th of this Month happened great Disputes in the Court of Common Council of the City of London concerning Proposals for performing the Masons Work of the intended Mansion-House for the Lord Mayor; and on the Divisions, one Party appeared in behalf of the Proposal of Mess. Townshend, Horsenail, and Taylor, three of their own Body, to do the said Work for 1720l. and the other Party for 250l. cheaper. Some Persons thinking it extraordinary that Gentlemen should be for the highest Price, and also that it might carry a Reflection, as if those proposed to take the lowest, were not able to do the Work so well as the others; inserted in the News Papers the Oath of a Common-Councilman, distinguishing the Clause following in a different Character.

"Good and true Counsel ye shall give in all things touching the Commonwealth of this City, after your Wit and Cunning: And that for

Favour of any Person, ye shall maintain no singular Profit against the common Profit of this City." A List also was handed about of 7 Alder-men, and 110 Commoners who divided for the highest Price, all, but about 20, of which List are distinguished to be of some of the Committees for administering the City Affairs; and, what is pretty remarkable, they are distinguished, who voted on the first Division for the lowest Proposal, viz. Sir John Barnard, (Lord Mayor) Sir Robert Godschall, Daniel Lambert, and Robert Westley, Esq., Aldermen. Dep. Joseph Ayliff, Dep. Tho. Sandford, Dep. Sam. Tatem, Mr. Robert Henshaw, and Mr. Hen. Sisson Common Council-men.

The first Division, (June 2.) was,

For the highest Price   80.

For the lowest   63.

The second Division, (June 7.) was,

For the highest   110.

For the lowest   87.

But on the 7th some of the Aldermen insisting on their right, as prescribed as Act of Parliament, to put a Negative on the Commons, they divided, and 7 were for the highest Price, and 15 for the lowest; which Right of a Negative in this Affair being disputed, it was agreed to apply to Council for an Explanation of the Act relating thereto.

The following appeared in the same Magazine on 18th July, 1738:

The Printer and Publisher of the *General Evening Post* attended the Court of Aldermen, by Order, to answer for printing the List of Alder-men, &c. who voted for the Mason's Work of the Mansion House to be done at the highest Price (See p. 321). He acknowledged printing the Paper, but would make no Submission. And tho' a certain Alderman moved to resolve that the said Paper was false, scandalous, and malicious, the Majority insisted on the previous Question, upon which he withdrew his Motion, and the Printer and Publisher were dismissed without the least Reprimand. But the matter did not end here; for several Letters were pub-lished in the *Daily Advertiser*, calling upon that Alderman to justify his Conduct in this Respect, and his Principles in declaiming for the Liberty of the Press in National Affairs, yet notoriously attempting to destroy it in those of a Corporation only.

In 1738 a pamphlet of 34 pages was published entitled A Modest Enquiry into the Conduct of the Court of Aldermen in which the true Reasons that induced them to put a Stop to the Building of The Mansion House, by their Negative Vote on the 7 of June last in Common Council, are respectfully sought for, but not found. With some Short Reflections on the Use and Abuse of the Negative Power of that Court. To which is added, A seasonable Caution to the Commoners of London, to beware of too great a Growth of Power in the Court of Aldermen.

It refers to the vote of the Common Councillors to pay £225 to one firm more than the estimate of another firm who tendered at the same time; this was in connection with the mason's work. Dunn and Deval's tender was the lower; Horsenail, Townsend and Taylor's tender was the other "proposal." Letters appeared in the *Daily Advertiser* of July 25th and August 10th. There was evidently water in the excavation at the time for the writer refers to the "Duck Pond now made at Stocks Market." Horsenail & Co. had estimated the cost as £17,200, and Dunn and Deval £16,975.

In 1738 another pamphlet was published entitled "A Guide to S^t. Thomas's Day," being "An address...on the Subject of the Mansion-House"

to which is added a List of those Gentlemen, who appeared in Common-Council on Behalf of the Proposal of Messr. Townsend Horsenaile and Taylor, to do the Masons Work—for £17,200, in opposition to the Proposal of Mess: Dunn and Deval to do the same work, with equal Security, and subject to the same Inspection for £16,975.

It quotes the advertisement dated April 28th, 1738, and states that the higher tender was accepted, although strongly condemned by several members of aldermen. The aldermen objected and by the right "interposed the Negative," this power is given in 11 Anni. Reg. Geo. I. The list comprised 7 aldermen and 110 commoners who voted for the higher tender, and included John Cordwell, who was the City Carpenter and a contractor at the Mansion House; Child (Deputy), who was also a contractor, William Cooper, the Bricklayer to the Commissioners of Sewers; Joseph Thompson, who was the "City Painter"; and John Deeton, who was the keeper of the Greenyard and Fieldkeeper to the More Fields.

In the same year another pamphlet was published, entitled "City Corruption and Mal-Administration display'd, occasion'd by the Ill Management of Public Money in general." This refers to a tender of £19,170 which eventually became £16,975, and the writer wanted to know if there was any objection to Messrs Dunn & Co. This pamphlet also gives a list of the seven aldermen and 110 commoners who supported the higher tender.

The principal contractors for the Mansion House were all members of the Court of Common Council, including an alderman who had the bell-hanger's contract, and another alderman who submitted his bill for ironmongery. Of course such transactions have been impossible for many years. At that time all the members of the Court were paid; 2*s.* 6*d.* for an attendance at Committee being usual, although as much as 12*s.* was paid.

There was soon further trouble about John Cordwell, the contractor for carpenter's work. The following is an extract from the Court Minutes of April 17th, 1739:

Resolv'd, That it appears to this Court that Mr. JOHN CORDWELL, Carpenter, a Member of this Court, hath been concerned in forming a Combination to raise the Price of Piling and Planking the Foundation of the Mansion-House.

That the said Mr. Cordwell hath, by such Combination, grossly abused the Office and Trust reposed in him as a Common-Council-Man.

It is Resolved and Ordered, That a Bill be prepared and brought into this Court, To prevent any Member thereof from being Concerned in any Works belonging to this City or Bridge-House: And it is referred to a Committee appointed by this Court to erect a Mansion-House for the Use of the Lord-Mayors of this City for the Time being, to prepare and bring in the same.

These Proceedings were taken notice of by the author of *Common Sense* of May 26, in the following words, viz.:

By this Act (says he) they have shut their Doors against Corruption, they have not only forbid its Entrance there, but they have taken Care to clear that Court from the very Suspicion of being corrupt. "Such a Reputation once establish'd, must produce all the Effects which naturally flow from good Government." Such a Self-denying Bill, must give the World a most advantageous Idea of the publick Spirit of the Common-Council; and, considering the great Trust reposed in them by their Fellow-Citizens, if they did not Establish in the Minds of Men a Confidence of their Integrity, the City would be filled with Murmurs and Discontent. They are a little Parliament, they are elected by a great Body of People, their Equals; Such a Body being too numerous to manage their own Affairs, they have entrusted and empowered these few to act for the whole. (Whence this Gentleman asks) What must become of that City which is to receive Laws from a Faction determined against Truth and Demonstration? What can it expect but to see the Good of the Whole sacrificed to the private Interest of a Few?

At a Common Council held July 5 the above-mentioned Committee presented the following report and bill:

To the Right Honourable the Lord Mayor
Aldermen and Commons, in Common-
Council assembled:

We whose Names are hereunto subscribed, your Committee (among others) appointed to erect a Mansion-House for the Use of the Lord-Mayors of this City for the Time being, do hereby certify, That in

Pursuance of your Order of the 17th. of April last, we have prepared a Bill to prevent any Member of this Court from being Concerned in any Works belonging to this City or Bridge-House, which we have hereunto annexed, and submit the same to the Judgment of this Honourable Court.

WHEREAS Inconvenience may arise from Members of the Common Council being Concerned in any of the Publick Works belonging to this City or Bridge-House, Therefore for preventing the same, BE IT ENACTED, by the Right Hon. the Lord Mayor, the Right Worshipful his Brethren the Aldermen, and the Commons, in Common-Council assembled, That from and after the   Day of   No Proposals shall be received from, or Contract made with, any Member of the Common-Council of this City for the time being, for the Doing, Executing or Performing, any Publick Work belonging to, or for the Use or Service of this City or Bridge-House.

Which Bill being read a first and second Time, Mr. Sisson, a Common-Council-Man for Farringdon Ward within (a Gentleman who had been long thought superior to any private View) made a Motion that the Bill might be committed; which was rejected by 75 against 43. And what is very remarkable, Every one of the Commoners of the Committee who brought the Bill in, voted against it; and tho' Mr. Sisson Moved, that the Bill might be Committed, yet he Voted that it should not be Committed!

Quære 1. Whether these Gentlemen thought Mr. Cordwell blame-able, when, in consequence of his appearing to have grossly abused his Trust as a Common-Council-Man, they voted for a Bill to prevent the Inconveniencies attending such Combinations for the future?

Quære 2. Whether the same Concern for the Publick Interest of this City influenced their voting against the Bill brought in for that Purpose, as prevailed upon them to agree in the Motion for it?

Quære 3. Why, after it appeared to the Court that Mr. Cordwell had grossly abused his Trust as a Common-Council-Man, he was entrusted with the Execution of the same Business for which he had fallen under the Censure of the Court?

Quære 4. Whether a Desire to promote the Honour and Interest of the Citizens of London, abstractedly, from all other Considerations, was the Cause of these Gentlemen's appearing against a Bill brought in by an unanimous Resolution of themselves and all present? And,

Quære 5. What Inconvenience to the City, could have followed from passing the aforesaid Bill into a Law?

In 1738 the Commissioners of Sewers decided at the re-quest of the Mansion House Committee to construct a sewer so as to avoid going under the building; they proposed a

grate four feet square with a proper curb of oak at the end of Bearbinder Lane—and from thence to carry the sewer southward within seven foot of Walbrook Church and then to return westward till it issues into the common sewer in Walbrook at the south east corner of Bucklersbury

the sewer to be 3 feet wide and 5 feet 6 inches high.

Dance was instructed to inspect the drainage work carried out at the Lord Chancellor's house in Ormond Street, and also that of Lord Oxford's house in Covent Garden, "for his direction in making the Drains" at the Mansion House. Dance reported he found that it would be necessary that the ground "should be pyled and planked, in order to lay the Foundation," and he estimated the cost at £1337. 9s. 8d. Three tenders were obtained, the lowest being 1s. 4d. per cube and 4½d. per foot super for planking. Two experts were also consulted as to the advisability of the work.

It is often stated that springs were found when the excavation work was in hand and consequently the piling work was necessary, but I can find no authority for that statement; the subsoil was bad and the work was consequently necessary. The subsoil generally in the neighbourhood has been found very unsatisfactory. During excavations a stone dated 1442, with cross, inscription, etc., was discovered.

With regard to the tenders for the work the Committee strongly suspected collusion and reported to the Court, stating that Dance estimated the price at 1s. per foot cube. Fresh tenders were obtained and Cordwell's price of 10d. per foot cube for piling and 4d. per foot super for planking was accepted.

There was soon trouble about the bricks and many were ordered off the site as they were "not fit to be used."

The next tenders required were for "Smiths and Plumbers' work in the Cramps and Chains." Dance's estimate was £816. 11s. 0d., the material was to be the best "Swedish iron," and the lowest of six tenders was accepted, the rate being £1 per ton.

In March, 1739–40, there was one tender of 12s. 9d. per cwt. for pig lead; it was accepted.

Cordwell's bill for piling and planking was £1098. 17s. 11d.

Another member of the Corporation who executed work at the building was Mr Deputy Child, who was instructed to make a grate, and Mr Deputy Molyneux submitted a bill of about £400 for fixtures. Mr Deputy Horsenail was also a contractor for a considerable amount of work. In 1757 he cut down the cills of the Venetian windows of the Egyptian Hall. The balustrading was removed and the difference in the appearance of the windows of the Ball Room and the Egyptian Hall can be seen to-day.

On 19th October, 1739, it was decided that an inscription was to be engraved on a copper plate to be placed under the foundation stone, the wording to be first approved by the Lord Mayor and the Court of Aldermen. An inscription was considered on 23rd October and it was decided to ask Mr Creech, the head master of Merchant Taylors' School, to translate it into Latin, and it was to be inscribed on the plate in English and Latin, the ceremony to take place the following Thursday. It was also decided that Dance was to distribute 20 guineas among the workmen "as is usual on the like occasion" "that a piece of the several pieces of coin in Gold, Silver, and Copper, from a Guinea to a Farthing, that have been coined this Year, be laid under the chief corner stone." Mr Creech politely declined to translate the inscription and the Rev. Mr Reading was asked to do so. It was decided to invite the Lord Mayor to dine at the Crown Tavern, behind the Royal Exchange, his Lordship to go in his scarlet gown in his state coach with his officers; afterwards to dinner in his private coach. It was also ordered that "Mr Sleep One of the light Wayts of this City do add two trumpets to his Band of Musick and attend the procession to Stocks Market," and the Committee in their gowns attended. Mr Richard Sleep was paid £4 "for the City Musick," and the stone was duly laid on 25th October, 1739.

The coins that were deposited under the foundation stone were: one guinea, one half-guinea, one crown, one half-crown, one shilling, one sixpence, one fourpence, one threepence, one twopence, one penny, one halfpenny, one farthing.

The following is the account from the *Gentleman's Magazine*:

1739. 25th. October—The Lordmayor, attended by several Aldermen, Deputies, and with the City Musick, went from Guildhall, and laid the chief Corner Stone of the intended Mansion House, whereon is the following Inscription,—

This Chief Corner Stone was laid the twenty-fifth Day of October in the year of our Lord MDCCXXXIX, and in the 13th. year of the Reign of our Sovereign Lord George the Second, King of Great Britain, France, and Ireland. By the Rt. Hon. Micajah Perry Esq Lord Mayor of the City of London, (12 Commoners as on the Committee aforesaid) also

PLATE XXVIII

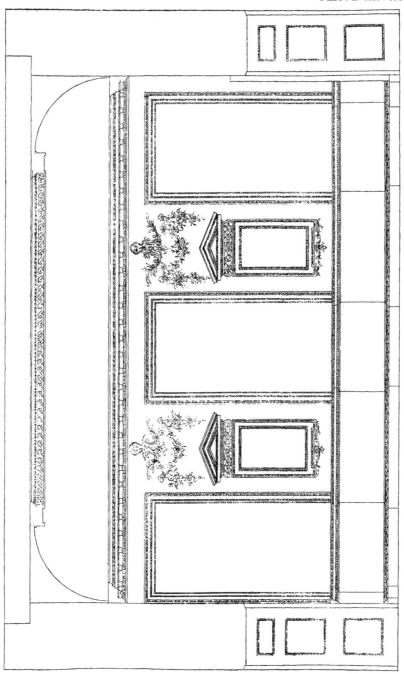

NORTH DRAWING ROOM
From Dance's original drawing

PLATE XXIX

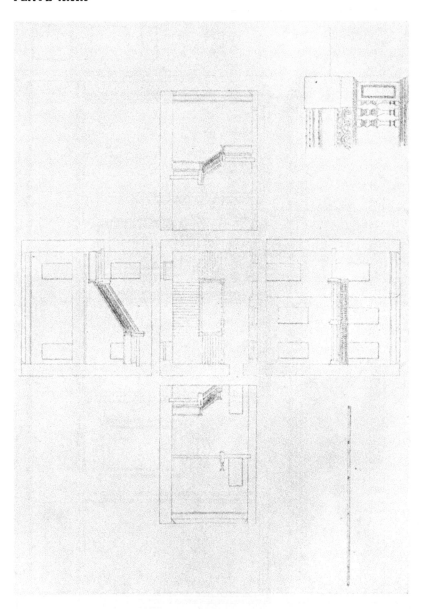

THE GRAND STAIRCASE
Now the South Drawing Room

Alderman Sir Francis Child, Kt., John Barber Esq, Sir Ed. Bellamy Kt., Sir John Williams Kt, Sir John Bernard Kt, Sir Robert Godshall Kt, being the Committee appointed by order of the Lord Mayor, Aldermen, and Commons of this City in Common Council assembled, to erect this Fabrick for a Mansion-House for the use of the Lord Mayor of this City for the time being.

George Heathcote Esq⎫ Aldermen
Sir John Lequesne Kt⎭ being Sheriffs
George Dance, Architect.

The *London Daily Post* also stated that the Lord Mayor gave 20 guineas for the workmen. The foundation stone has been covered over and the position cannot be traced to-day.

Lord Mayor Perry kept a diary, and the manuscript is preserved at the Guildhall[1]. It is interesting to read his account of the ceremony of laying the foundation stone. On the 25th October he wrote as follows:

I afterwards put on the Scarlet Gown and went to Stocks Market, attended by several Gentlemen of the Committee appointed to erect a Mansion House for the Lord Mayor of this City, in their Gowns, preceded by the City Musick and my Officers, with the Sunday Sword and Mace, and laid the chief corner stone of the said Mansion House, and placed therein a copper plate with an inscription engraved thereon, and afterwards returned home.

With regard to the model there was great trouble. On October 16th, 1737, Mr Cordwell, the "City's Carpenter," said it would be finished by Christmas. On February 17th, 1737–8, he said it would be finished by 17th March. On April 18th the Committee reported the model was finished and that it would soon be at the Royal Exchange for exhibition. On the 16th May Cordwell reported the model would be at the Royal Exchange in about two weeks' time, and a man was appointed at 10s. a week to look after it—he was to take no gratuities, to be on duty from 10 to 4 o'clock, and was not to allow "any Boys or Girls, or any rude or disorderly persons to view the same," the model to be on view for at least one year.

The bill for carving for the model was £192. 3s. 10d. and Cordwell's bill was £760. 18s. 8d. Dance's valuation was £210. 7s. 7½d. It was suggested that Dance should appoint two men, and Cordwell two men, to settle the amount. Cordwell

[1] Printed by Sir William Treloar, Bt., in his work, *A Lord Mayor's Diary*, 1906–7.

refused, and said that if he were not paid in full he would "take proper methods" to enforce his claim. The Committee called in Messrs Morris and Robinson, two experts, to advise them; they valued the model at £265. 5s. 6d.

In October, 1740, Mr Patterson, the City Solicitor, reported he had received a "special original Writ" from Cordwell for £1000. Cordwell's bill was exclusive of the carving. The City Solicitor paid £400 into court. When the case came on it was agreed to refer it to three arbitrators, Messrs James Gibbs, James Horne and John Smallwell; the City Solicitor was to pay each of them £21. The arbitrators awarded the sum of £450.

The City would have fared much better had they paid Cordwell's bill of £760. 18s. 8d. although it was far too high. The following was the bill they had to pay:

John Patterson Solicitor

To Cash paid Henry Branson the Carver	192.	3.	10
To Cash Awarded Mr. John Cordwell by the Arbitrators	450.	0.	0
To Charges of taking £400 out of Court	3.	8.	0
To Cash paid Mr. Dance's Bill of Expences paid Surveyors	78.	2.	5
To Cash paid Mr. Cordwell in full of his Bill of Costs of Suit	104.	3.	0
To Cash paid do on Arbitration	101.	3.	6
To Solicitors Bill for Defending the Cause	110.	18.	5
To Do Bill for Disfranchisements	42.	14.	0
To Do Bill on Arbitration	89.	0.	3
	£1171.	13.	5

The model was exhibited in the East Pawn at the Royal Exchange. There were shops on the first floor of that building and they were known as Pawns. The scale was 1 inch to the foot, so the model must have been about 16 feet long by 8 feet wide and 8 feet high, including the attic storeys.

Portland stone was used for the exterior of the building, and it has worn exceedingly well.

In February of 1741–2 Dance refers to the mason's work to the inside of "The Assembly or Dancing Room." His estimate for the gallery in Portland stone was £327. 10s. 0d. He was ordered by Committee not to show any of the particulars of his estimates to any artificers.

The rate for water used during the construction of the building was not to exceed £2 per annum.

In March and April, 1743, Cordwell was still very backward with the roof, it was finished in August, except over the Egyptian Hall. This roof with its large span gave great trouble; the principal timbers were specified as 18 inches by 10 inches, but Cordwell wanted to fix them of only 14 inches by 10 inches, and stated he could not obtain the larger scantling. Dance said the larger scantling could be obtained and it was.

In April, 1744, the lowest of several tenders was accepted for glazing the windows at the rate of 8d. per foot super, laying flooring at £1. 10s. 0d. a square, and frames and sashes at 1s. 7d. per foot super.

In May, 1744, the carving of the tympanum was considered. Mr Roubiliac produced a model and his estimate was £400. Mr Taylor, afterwards Sir Robert Taylor, who has been referred to above, submitted a sketch and the same estimate, and Mr Chair a sketch and no estimate. The Lord Burlington was asked to advise the Committee, but he "refused to intermeddle thereon," and in July Mr Taylor was instructed to proceed. Mr Roubiliac was paid 30 guineas for his trouble and Mr Chair £10. 10s. 0d.

In July tenders were considered for further flooring and £1. 16s. 0d. a square accepted for better class material, and £1. 11s. 0d. for the attics, eventually further tenders were obtained and £2. 7s. 0d. and £2 a square accepted.

In June, 1745, a tender of 2s. 4d. a foot super was accepted for the "Corinthian windows," and £1 a square for "sounding boards" to the floors.

In July Cordwell was again before the Committee and told he must proceed with the roof to the Great Hall or proceedings would be taken against him; but in the following December and again in April, 1746, he had not progressed any further and the Town Clerk was instructed to give him formal notice that he must do so forthwith.

In June, 1746, the posts in the front were to be constructed 14 inches square, 6 feet long and 3 feet 6 inches above ground, iron capped at a cost of £1. 9s. 0d. each.

In March, 1747, Cordwell had completed the roof of the Great Hall, and as "the late Act of Parliament had advanced the Price of Glass" the contractor refused to work at the old rate and fresh tenders were invited, eventually the same contractor was paid 12½d. per foot super.

In March, 1747, the public complained that there was no "Coachway from the Poultry to Walbrook," and that several people in the neighbourhood had quitted their houses in consequence. Dance suggested as a remedy that the house recently bought from the Duke of Bedford should be pulled down.

In April, 1747, Dance submitted drawings "for finishing the Inside of the Mansion House," he estimated the cost at £7900. The Egyptian Hall was paved with "Portland octagon paving and black marble dots."

In July, 1747, the Committee reported that they had spent on the purchase of property and on account of the work done, a total sum of £40,483. 1s. 4d., and that they considered it would cost £13,482 to finish.

In October, 1747, the contractor for mason's work applied for an allowance stating that on account of

the rupture with Spain and France, prices advanced 8s. per ton for Freight, in all about £1200—that this Extraordinary Freight has always been allowed in former wars and even in the present viz.:—The Board of Works, Westminster Bridge, Westminster Abbey and Greenwich Hospital.

The contract was £17,000 and the Committee recommended an extra for freight of £1143. 13s. 5d.

In May, 1748, Dance submitted plans and estimates for the four staircases, "the two grand ones whereof to be one Storey high, he said must be made of wood, and the two back ones he proposed of stone," cost £2000. It was agreed all should be made of wood. Inside work to basement to cost £1073, "without the Coach house and stables," which were then contemplated with an entrance on the west side of the building.

In May, 1748, Dance submitted estimates to finish the rooms on the principal floors as follows:

	£
The Vestibule	200
The Judicial Rm. now known as the Justice room office	187
The Young men's room now known as the room of the Lord Mayor's secretary	177
The Saloon, now known as the Hall	185

	£
The Withdrawing room now called the Venetian Parlour	500
The Sword bearer's room now called the Justice Room	199
The Great Parlour now called the Long Parlour	765
The Common Parlour now called the North Drawing Rm.	300
North Colonade Now part of the saloon	162
South Colonade	192
	Total £2867

The matter of finishings was considered so important that models were prepared. Dance submitted those for the principal storey and staircase (except the Great Hall) with an estimate of £4000, including the chimney pieces. An estimate of £1161 for the joinery for the same floor was accepted, and one of £905 for the plasterer's work, and £900 for mason's work. John Gilbert's estimate of £1843. 16s. od. for the carving was considered and it was decided to obtain tenders.

John Cordwell petitioned for an extra £169. 11s. 3d., principally on account of "the Extraordinary price of Materials occasioned by the Rupture with Spain and France." He was allowed an extra of £71.

In July John Gilbert's tender of £1665 was accepted for carving for the principal storey.

In November the contractors for the joiner's work were proceeding so slowly that they were called before a Committee and explained they could not get enough "freemen" to work and asked permission to employ "forigners."

In June, 1748, there was a petition by the churchwardens and principal inhabitants of the parish of St Mary Woolchurch because of "the great Distress and almost total ruin to which our Parish is reduced occasioned by the said building." The parish consisted of 58 houses and only 31 were occupied, "a number too small to bear the burden of its Taxes, and Support the Poor whose Numbers very near Equalls the Inhabitants."

In June, 1751, a tender of £1650 was accepted for the joiner's work "in the one pair of stairs and attic stairs," and £750 for the plasterer's work. In the carver's work for the same storeys John Gilbert's estimate of £1500 was accepted. The chimney pieces for the same storeys cost £350.

In July, 1752, it was announced the building would be completed by Michaelmas. There was trouble about the carving on the front of the building, particularly the regalia, and although the stone work is "bossed" out for carving over the main north entrance the work has never been executed. It is interesting to note that carving is shown in some views of the building.

About this date it was advertised that prices would be received for fixing "Marble Basins in the Water Closets...making and fixing Reservoirs and making and fixing an Engine to force the Water to the Top of the sd. Mansion House." The cost was £720.

In July, 1752, the Committee reported that, with the exception of the Great Hall, they anticipated the building would be completed by Michaelmas; also that the money spent on the building, model, and purchase of property amounted to £56,020. 4s. 0d. The Committee had authority to spend £4000 on furniture.

In 1752 another proposal was made to build a sewer in the passage at the back of the Mansion House, but the church-wardens of St Stephen objected as the sewer would be in "part of the churchyard where they have a right to bury." The proposal was

to fix a grate of four foot square with a proper curb of oak at the end of Bearbinder Lane—and from thence to carry the sewer southward within seven foot of Walbrook Church and then to return westward.

A Committee was appointed to look into the matter and simply reported that the sewer was being constructed as agreed in 1738, they made no reference to the claim by the church-wardens.

In September, 1752, the proposal for a stable in the building was abandoned and it was ordered that "Mr Dance do cause the divisions prepared for stalls in the place intended for the Stable to be altered into Bins for the Cocket Office," but in October it was decided not to fit the bins, etc., for the cocket office, but to pave the room with Purbeck marble.

With regard to the lighting it was decided

a lanthorn be provided for the Colonade, six brackets for the Vestibule, Eight lights for the Great Parlour and ten lights for the Great Staircase, according to Mr. Dance's drawings

cost not to exceed £260.

John Gilbert was ordered to supply

Eight rich carved frames with glass and branches...gilt with Burnish Gold for the Great parlour for Eightyfour Pounds also six Brackets richly carved for the Vestibule...for fifteen Pounds.

In October Dance was ordered to make a doorway between the stable and coach house, these names being still used.

In 1753 there was further trouble about the carving of the regalia over the windows in front of the building.

During this year Sir Crisp Gascoigne entered into residence.

In July, 1753, the Committee reported they had spent £4286. 13s. 5d. on furniture, and still more furniture was wanted. This sum was paid and a further allowance of £1000 was granted.

In December, 1753, Mr Chamberlain's account of demand for taxes was as follows:

Land Tax, half a year at Michaelmas 1753 @ 2s.	60.	0.	0
Window lights half a year at Ladyday 1753	5.	0.	0
Poor's Rate half a year at Michaelmas 1753	45.	0.	0
Church rate towards repairing the Parish Church of St. Mary Woolnoth	50.	0.	0
Scavanger's Rate one Year at Christmas 1753	5.	0.	0
	£165.	0.	0

It was decided that £30 p.a. should be paid in lieu of Poors Rate, and the Chamberlain was to appeal against the assessment of £120 for land tax.

In March, 1754, the churchwardens of the united parishes of St Mary Woolnoth and St Mary Woolchurch Haw attended the Court of Common Council and asked for £60 p.a. for Poors Rate and £33. 6s. 8d. towards the rate for repairing St Mary Woolnoth, being after the rate of £800 p.a. as settled by the Commissioners of Land Tax. It· was resolved that £33. 6s. 8d. be paid towards repairing the church, and that £46. 17s. 6d. be paid for Poors Rate, being after the rate of £625 p.a. and that in future the said house "shall be assessed after the rate of £625 and no more to all taxes."

In 1754 the Committee of the Managers of London Bridge Water Works applied for £5 p.a.; this was agreed to. The water rate now paid is £332. 19s. 8d. p.a.

In October, 1754, Dance delivered an account as follows:

The Worshipful Committee appointed to erect a Mansion House.

to

Dr.

Geo: Dance.

1754
Octr. 16th.

To £52,200 expended in the building the Mansion House at £5 p. Cent	2610. 0. 0	
Paid Bentleys Bill by order of the Committee	8. 0. 0	
Paid Mandeville's Bill by Ditto	3. 3. 0	
Paid for a pair of Hansers	0. 15. 0	
for Surveying making Drawings, and weighing, measuring, and taking an Acct. of all Materials, Goods, and Utensils, & seeing all Orders and Agreements with the Workmen duely executed the whole amounting 'to £4700	235. 0. 0	
	£2,856. 18. 0	
Recd. on Account	2,700. 0. 0	
	£156. 18. 0	

This account is of interest to architects, as Dance did work which would now be done by a quantity surveyor, who would be paid a percentage apart from the 5 per cent. paid to the architect.

The minutes of the Committee state that Dance was to be paid 5 per cent. on any furniture, not necessarily designed by him. It was also stated that Dance had spent £182 for a labourer for sorting and throwing out all bad bricks, seven years at 10s. a week, which he stated he was not obliged to do under his agreement. The Committee considered the work was included in their contract with him and refused to pay him. To-day a clerk of works would be paid by the employer and he would condemn any bad materials and the contractors would have to remove them; so Dance's 5 per cent. includes work as a quantity surveyor, and also as a clerk of works.

In 1755 the Chamberlain was directed to pay a sum of £2000 for completing the Great Hall.

In April, 1755, it was decided to fix

Iron rails...between the Dorick Columns in the area to prevent persons coming about the Justice Business etc., from going all over the House as now they do from whence great Inconvenience arises.

In June, 1755, Dance produced his designs for the "Joiners, Plasterers and Carver's Works for the Inside of the Great Hall which he...estimated at £1958." Tenders were obtained and the lowest were £600 for the plasterer's work, £437 for carver's work, "Masons work in fluiting the pillars" £450. John Gilbert, who did most of the carving at the Mansion House, estimated the work at £530. The estimate accepted was by John Nicholl and William How. Dance estimated the cost of painting the Egyptian Hall at £212. Horsenail, who was employed to flute the columns, was an alderman's deputy.

At a General Quarter Sessions held at Guildhall on February 13th, 1755, the assessment of the Mansion House was stated to be £40 for poor rate, it was agreed in April at £35.

In July, 1755, the Committee came to a decision which applies to-day, as follows:

THE Committee proceeded according to the Order of the last Committee to take into Consideration the Reference from the Common Council dated the Twelfth of June last of what Allowance should be made the Lord Mayor of this City for the time being to provide such Additional Furniture for the said House as may be Necessary during their respective Mayoralties, and after some time spent therein Resolved to Report, That this City should not for the future provide any more Furniture or be at any Charges in Mending and Cleaning the Windows, mending Cleaning & Repairing or Altering of Furniture, providing and keeping in Repair any Locks Keys Bars Bolts or Hinges or on any other Account whatsoever, But in Consideration thereof, there shall be paid to the Lord Mayor of this City for the time being Inhabiting the said House the Annual Sum of One hundred Pounds at the time of his quitting and yielding up to his Successor all the Furniture mentioned in the Inventory delivered to him at the time of his Entering into the said Mansion House in the same Plight and Condition he Received the same, reasonable Use and Wearing thereof only excepted, And the Draught of a Report being prepared was Agreed to and Ordered to be fairly Transcribed and presented to the next Common Council.

In January, 1757, it was found extremely inconvenient to have no entrance except under the front Portico, and it was suggested an entrance might be made into the lower ground floor storey on the west side of the building. Dance estimated the cost at £37. 3s. 4d. and he was ordered to carry out the work.

The idea being abandoned of having a coach house and stable as part of the Mansion House the Committee in 1757 decided "to consider of a proper place for Erecting a Coach House and Stable." In February of the same year an estimate of £137 was accepted for painting the Great Hall.

In September, 1757, all the work was finished except painting the Great Hall. The floor was in a very bad condition and it was necessary to spend about £300 on repairing the paving, and Mr Horsenail agreed to repair it "in the best manner and most reasonable terms he can." He was apparently given a free hand.

At Easter, 1758, the hall was used for dancing and the fitting up of the building including hire of furniture and lighting was about £142.

It was decided to spend £450 on three large chandeliers for the Great Hall and to buy six chandeliers at £180 each, and glass sconces costing a total of £100 for the Dancing Gallery.

In May, 1758, Dance charged 5 per cent. on £3450, further work which had been carried out since his last account, bringing the cost of the building up to £55,650.

In 1758 a site adjoining Leadenhall Market was considered for a temporary coach house and stables, three coach houses and stalls for 12 horses were to be provided at a cost of £588. Dance prepared the plans but the scheme was abandoned.

Deputy Horsenail was paid £284 for repairs to the floor of the Egyptian Hall.

In October, 1758, the Grocers' Company agreed to let their stables to the Lord Mayor. The Committee stated the Corporation had power to build but not to hire. The Committee thought that land at Leadenhall Market would be suitable for a temporary coach house. Dance estimated the cost at £558. 14s. 8d.

In May, 1759, six chandeliers were ordered for the Dancing Gallery at a total cost of 300 guineas.

A site in Elbow Lane was considered for a stable: the Dyers' Company were willing to let it on perpetual lease at £50 p.a. The Corporation offered £30, but the Dyers' Company would accept no less than £35 p.a.

In October, 1765, the Grocers' Company intimated they were about to "take down and destroy their Coach-houses and Stables, so that no future Lord Mayor can have the use thereof."

PLATE XXX

OLD BALL ROOM

PLATE XXXI

LONG PARLOUR

In 1765 a chandelier was provided for the Great Parlour at a cost of £145.

There was further search for a site for the stables: the Governors of Christ's Hospital would not part with any portion of Blackwell Hall for that purpose. Dance tried to find a site on Dowgate Hill and failed, and the Committee tried to find a site and were unable to do so: consequently in October, 1766, it was ordered that the

Town Clerk do wait on the Worshipful Company of Grocers with the Compliments of this Committee and to desire that they will permit the Lord Mayor to have the use of the Coach-house and Stabling for another year, at the same time to acquaint them, that the Committee will use the most expeditious means in their power to provide a place for that purpose,

and in November, 1766, Dance was ordered to build a temporary coach house in the Guildhall yard, at as little expense as possible, but as I can find no further reference to the matter it is exceedingly doubtful if the building was erected.

In 1767 the Corporation purchased the land for stables etc. in Whitecross St, the buildings were erected and are still used.

In March, 1768, several windows, lamps and chandeliers were damaged during the "riots and tumults," the chandeliers in the Egyptian Hall were considerably damaged, the cost of the repairs was £200. The mob was furious because the Mansion House was not illuminated to celebrate the election of John Wilkes as a Member of Parliament. At this date the Great Hall was referred to as the Egyptian Hall.

In 1771 two large glass lustres were bought for the Egyptian Hall.

Dance referred to the open area as the "Atrium or Court."

In 1773 Dance was ordered to prepare a design, and an estimate of £105. 10s. 5d. for a "Skreen to enclose and divide the great Vestibule from the Cortile" was submitted. In February, 1774, an order was given for it to be built and the service door was made from the staircase to the Egyptian Hall.

In 1774 certain alterations were evidently being carried out contrary to the wishes of the members of the Court of Common Council, for on December 2nd they passed resolutions calling attention to a resolution of August, 1755, that the Lord Mayor was to pay for all works included in his grant of £100, and that no alterations were to be made without the order of the Court, that works in hand were to be immediately stopped and the Justice Rooms restored to their former condition.

In 1775 Dance submitted his design for a Portico at the West door, a tender of £85 was accepted. This is the portico shown on Plate XV, but it was afterwards pulled down.

In the same year a new "Shore" was made in Charlotte Row and Dance attended the Commissioners of Sewers with reference to draining the Mansion House into it.

In 1776 it was agreed to pay an extra £5 a year for water.

In 1776 Dance reported upon his proposed sanitary improvements, there were three cesspools, which he called by a grosser name, he proposed to connect them by means of a brick drain, and to make a connection from the northernmost cesspool to the sewer in Charlotte Row. He further proposed to build "six such proper stink traps as will be sufficient to Prevent any Ill scent...and to introduce a proper quantity of water." His estimate was £160. Eventually £16 was paid for "2 Marble Basons for Water Closets" and £50 for "an Engine for Water Closet."

A reference was made in 1776 to the "£100 usually allowed the Lord Mayor at the end of their Mayoralty's in lieu of providing Furniture and keeping it in repair by order of this Court of the 15th. of August 1755."

In April, 1777, there were still cesspools under the building, and an account of £15. 12s. 0d. for clearing them on two occasions is shown. During this year "eight carved and guilt elbow chairs," two oval pier glasses and some sundries cost £341.9s.0d.

In December of this year it was

Ordered that the Venetian Parlour...be appropriated for the Swordbearer and officers of the Household to dine in; and that the officers below the Salt do after Dinner retire into the small Justice Room.

In December, 1777, the Committee decided that in their opinion the insuring of the Mansion House from fire was an unnecessary expense: and the City Lands Committee were allowed to have surplus gravel in consequence of making a new sewer at the back of the building.

In 1778 a room was formed in the basement for the servants to "dress their hair" in.

During the Gordon riots of 1780 an "Account of Windows" refers to "Windows Broke Bad 49 Midling 67."

About this time glazing was referred to as "Glassing Work."

On December 17th, 1784, the Committee reported that the insurance "was for £10,000 for the last 7 years," and to renew for "the like term with the additional Duty lately imposed by Act of Parliament will amount to the sum of £96. 9. 0." The Committee recommended that as the building was of stone it should not be insured. It was fortunate there was not a fire, as of course practically the whole of the interior is of wood construction.

In this year the Sheriffs' fines which were appropriated for building the Mansion House were in the future to be "applied to the purposes of Blackfriars Bridge."

In 1787 it was decided to erect a covered way across the Cortile of light woodwork covered with sail cloth at a cost of £67. 6s. 0d.

In 1789 Dance reported the roof of the Egyptian Hall "was in a ruinous state," and that in consequence of the orders of December, 1786, he had shored it up, but that the timber was quite decayed and a new roof was necessary.

Dance was ordered to prepare Designs and Estimates for covering the Court Yard, or area, and also of "covering the Roofs of the Egyptian Hall and Dancing Gallery": apparently this meant a new roof to each room: his estimate was £2895. He also submitted a design for a new iron railing in the front of the building at a cost of £249.

In December, 1789, Dance was ordered to repair the area or cortile at a cost of £30.

In January, 1790, it was agreed that the Town Clerk should be paid £350 p.a. for attending the committee and his two assistants £70 and £50 respectively.

In June, 1792, Dance reported again that the roof timbers of the Egyptian Hall were suffering from dry rot, and that the walls "above the great Entablature" were out of the upright, and "considerably bulged in the middle," that a new roof was necessary and he suggested that it should "spring from the height of the great Entablature": he estimated the cost at £600. See Plan 55.

In March, 1793, it was decided that the porch on the West side of the building was to be "extended the length of a coach on each side of the iron gateway."

In October, 1793, it was decided in the Court of Common Council that Dance should report upon the suggestion of removing all the columns in the Egyptian Hall. Dance reported against the proposal both from a structural and an aesthetic point of view.

In October, 1793, it was decided to sell the materials of the roof of the Egyptian Hall. The advertisements appeared in *The Times* of October 18th, 1793, as follows:

Guildhall London

9th. October 1793

The Committee for General Purposes will meet at Guildhall on Wednesday 23rd. instant, at Eleven o'clock in the forenoon to receive Proposals for making a new Roof to the Egyptian Hall of the Mansion House, agreable to Mr. Dance's Plan.

Also to sell by public Auction the old materials of the said roof in four distinct Lots. The Stone in one Lot, the Lead in a second Lot, the iron in a third Lot, and the Timber in a fourth Lot. The Purchaser of each Lot to remove it away at his own Expense.

The Plan & Particulars may be seen at Mr. Dance's Office at Guildhall aforesaid.   Rix.

There was considerable annoyance in the Court of Common Council because the roof was found to be rotten and the following resolution was passed

that it be referred to the General Purposes to consider of the expediency of erecting a New Mansion House for the residence of the Chief Magistrate of this City instead of a general Repair and Alteration of the present one

The Committee reported that it was "not necessary or expedient."

In 1794 Dance was ordered to prepare separate estimates "for lowering the Roof of the Egyptian hall, and also of the Ball Room, the covering of the Cortile or area and converting the same into a Hall." This question of a covering for the central area had been considered in 1787 and apparently a canvas covering was used, for in November, 1790, the Committee were asked to lend the awning for use at the Guildhall on November 9th, this was the awning ordered in 1787.

Dance's estimates were as follows:

(1) Lowering the Roof and Ceiling of the Egyptian Hall   £1500
(2) Lowering the Roof and Ceiling of the Ball Room   £800
(3) Covering the Centre Cortile & converting it into a Hall   £2500

Plan 56 is a scheme that was not executed.

In November, 1794, Dance reported with the following suggestions, which were all carried out, viz. the covering over of the Cortile, the formation of a second fire-place in the "great Dining Parlour," and the removal of the Grand Staircase. A reference to Plan 51 shows the original plan of the storey. Plan 56 is Dance's scheme. The Committee reported in favour, stating that the covering of the Court would furnish

a Noble and convenient access to the Egyptian Hall the great Dining Parlour and other apartments as well as rending the House free from that dampness which is accumulated in the Court as it now exists:

they stated the Grand Staircase was seldom used. Dance's total estimate for all the alterations was £426. An advertisement appeared in *The Times* of December 18th.

In 1794 it was considered whether the Staircase should be removed at a cost of £300 and the roof lowered and the gallery removed at a cost of £1200. See Plan 55.

In March, 1795, Dance certified for the Cortile and extra chimney at a total cost of £307. 17s. 0d.

The roof of the Egyptian Hall was shored up and in October, 1795, the Committee reported the construction of a new roof had been postponed from time to time according to the wishes of each Lord Mayor. Dance had made a fresh estimate of £1200 and they thought the work ought to be done as soon as possible.

They also submitted an estimate of £300 for the removal of the Grand Staircase and the formation of two rooms and made the same recommendation. This was agreed to in November, 1795.

In November, 1795, the Comptroller was ordered to prepare a Contract for lowering the roof of the Egyptian Hall at a cost of £1200, and for removing the Grand Staircase and converting it into two rooms, one on each floor, at a cost of £300.

The extras on the alteration to the Great Staircase and the formation of two rooms amounted to £203. 4s. 4d., this included alterations to windows, cutting away the old plaster decoration and extra work to the chimney pieces.

The extras on the second roof of the Egyptian Hall amounted to £252.

In April, 1796, the Committee considered the question of

the removal of the gallery in the Egyptian Hall: and decided to do so as

it would be a great advantage to the beauty, and much increase the lights of the said Room, leaving as much thereof over the door of the Entrance as is necessary for a music Gallery.

In October of the same year it was decided to remove the stone paving of the Egyptian Hall and lay wood flooring at a cost of £393. 16s. 6d.

In November, 1796, the awning of the covered way was again borrowed for the Guildhall: and Dance reported that three fire-places could be made in the South wall of the Egyptian Hall and suggested one as an experiment at a cost of about £32. 10s. 0d. All three were made and the flues can be seen to-day, they project from the external face of the wall.

Dance was ordered to prepare a design for a music gallery.

In November the question of furniture for the "new Upper Room" was considered, this was the room formed by taking away the staircase as mentioned above.

In November, 1796, it was decided to make the three fire-places, to lower the windows in the Egyptian Hall and put in new sashes, and an advertisement appeared in *The Times* of November 23rd as follows:

The Times Nov. 23rd. 1796

Guildhall London Nov. 17. 1796

The Committee of General Purposes will meet at the Mansion House on Thursday the 24th. inst. at 12 o'clock at noon precisely to receive Proposals for making three Fire Places, lowering the windows, making modern Sashes, and erecting a new Gallery in the Egyptian Hall at the same House. Also to receive proposals for making a boarded Floor on ground Joists in the said Hall. Particulars of the said works may be seen at Mr. Dance's, the City Surveyor's Office Guildhall aforesaid.

A description of the work proposed appears in the minutes of 19th October, 1796, the windows were to be

lowered down to the top of the Block Moulding on the outside, that the old sashes be taken out and new Modern Eldorado or Metal sashes be placed in their stead and that the Return of the Great Corinthian Cornice which now impedes part of the light be taken off and a flatt Moulding put instead thereof.

On November 24th, 1796, an estimate of £231. 15s. 0d. was accepted for the flooring of the Egyptian Hall, and an estimate of £187. 16s. 0d. for lowering the windows: and an estimate of £44. 8s. for the music gallery.

In May, 1797, the following accounts were paid:

£44. 8. 0 for erecting the Music Gallery
£187. 16. 0 for improving the large windows at the East & West ends
   of the Egyptian Hall
£231. 15. 0 for laying a boarded floor on the Egyptian Hall

In November, 1798, Dance advised as to lighting the building and recommended as follows:

Outside: 12 large lamps with double Lens burners, 7 with single Lens burners and 6 with common two spout burners:

Inside: 1 Patent Lamp and 4 two spout Lanthorns burning day and night and 1 Two spout Lanthorn in back staircase.

He recommended that the Patent Lamp should be furnished with "The best Spermaceti Oil and the rest with that kind or sort which will burn Dry." But the Committee thought double Lens and the lamps unnecessary.

In July, 1800, it was reported to the Commissioners of Sewers that the railing at the Mansion House was about to be set back two feet and the ground given up to the public, which would be a great convenience. Plates XV and XVI show the iron railing slightly in front of the steps, and we get the width from this entry.

Pine and Tinney's plan of the neighbourhood in 1742 is shown on Plan 14. Rocque of 1746 on Plan 15 and Horwood's 1799, Plan 16, show interesting alterations in the district during those periods.

Plan 50 is a photograph of the original Ground Floor Plan.

Plate XXIII is a photograph showing the front and side of the Mayor's Nest and Noah's Ark. Plate XXIV is the side elevation, Plate XXV is the Section, the great height of the Ball Room and Egyptian Hall will be noted, and Plate XXVI shows the exterior of one side of the Cortile, with the balustrade to the area. Plate XXII is a view of Cheapside, with the Noah's Ark and Mayor's Nest in the distance. Plate XVII is a view in 1830.

Chapter XII

Work during the Nineteenth Century

IN December, 1801, Dance submitted designs "for finishing the Saloon in a permanent way, including a boarded floor instead of the present Pavement" to cost £300; this work was finished in September, 1802, at a cost of £341. 3s. 10d.

In 1802 a scheme was submitted to warm the house by "a steam Machine" at a cost of about £350, but it was not agreed to.

In March, 1803, an estimate of £2097. 6s. 8d. was submitted for new furniture for the Drawing Rooms.

In 1804 there are references to several rooms, on the principal floor, "Venetian Parlour," "Dining or Wilkes' Parlour,"[1] "Swordbearer's Room" and "Long Parlour." On the "One pair Story" we read of the "Anti-room & Drawing Room," and in the basement the "Yeoman of the Cellars Office" and "Pewter-Room."

In 1805 the Lecturer of the united parishes of St Mary Woolchurch Haw and St Mary Woolnoth, submitted a petition and stated that in 1769 the Lecturer was allowed £10 p.a.: he asked for an increase as "many of the Necessaries of Life had nearly doubled in price and all have unusually augmented to such a degree as probably will never be known to an equal Extent in an equal Period." The sum of £10 p.a. is still paid to the Rector as evening Lecturer.

In the same year it was proposed to re-build the North-West staircase in stone "on an enlarged and improved scale." The Lord Mayor protested against the idea and it was abandoned.

In 1809 it was decided to have a better Justice Room, up to that date it had been the room now used as the Clerk's office, and the present Justice Room was the Swordbearer's Room.

In 1811 an additional entrance to the Ball Room was considered.

In March, 1808, it was recommended to advise the Court

---

[1] John Wilkes was Lord Mayor 1774–5.

that all "allowances for coachire and attendances should cease," and also that the expenses of Committees should be limited to £500 each "in lieu of all allowances, Dinners and other expenses." In February, 1810, it was decided that £200 be allowed to members of the committee as "Coach-hire" according to the number of attendances, this out of a grant of £500 p.a. Two sub-committees were to be considered equal to one grand committee; as there were about 20 members in the committee this would mean about £10 a year each.

There are many references to "the Dining *or* Wilkes's Parlour": this was the North Drawing Room. "The South Drawing Room," formed by taking away the staircase is referred to as the Swordbearer's Room. Dance estimated that the formation of folding doors between the rooms would cost £350.

In 1812 the Lord Mayor suggested that the two windows of Wilkes's Parlour facing the inner area might be blocked up and the window tax saved: this was agreed to.

In May, 1812, the Lord Mayor asked for a shower bath to be fixed, this was unanimously refused by the Committee, on the grounds that it was

unnecessary to erect a permanent Shower Bath in the Mansion House inasmuch as the want thereof has never been complained of; any Lord Mayor requiring the same for the accommodation of himself or family may easily procure a temporary and moveable bath at a small expense.

In 1814 the Gas Light and Coke Company offered to erect ten lamps in front of the building "with a stronger and better light than they now have, for the same sum"; at that time they were oil lamps.

In 1815 it was decided to light the interior of the building with oil and the exterior with gas. It was agreed to have two lamps at the private entrance each at £10. 10s. p.a. and six lamps in other places outside each at £5. 5s. p.a.

In January, 1816, it was suggested by Committee that the building should be lighted by gas, and that the chandeliers purchased for the Guildhall might be used, and in April the Committee considered the use of gas for the Egyptian Hall and Ball Room.

In 1820 there were many complaints about the gas, it was stated that about a dozen gas burners had gone out seven or eight times within a fortnight; between 8 and 9 o'clock.

In 1816 nine gas lamps were fixed in the basement each at £6. 6s. p.a. and another in the Hall at £10. 10s. p.a. The Lord Mayor was approached and said he had no objection to gas in the basement.

During the same year the Committee decided to approach the Court of Common Council and suggest the purchase of gasaliers at a cost of £400 for the Egyptian Hall, and the Gas Company were paid £154 for connecting up to the Hall where there were "14 gas light lustres" which cost £252.

In 1817 there were 15 inside and 14 outside lamps, lighted by oil and costing £161. 5s. p.a., and 11 inside and 14 outside gas lamps costing £147. 7s. p.a.

During the same year it was resolved that, with regard to the Ball Room, the doorway should be blocked up, and one of the adjoining panels on each side should be opened so as to give better access to the room and that the columns in the room were to be removed and the cornice set back, so as to give more space.

In 1820 there is a reference to the Chaplain's Rooms.

Apparently the present South Drawing Room was the Swordbearer's Room when the present Justice Room was formed, for in 1821 the Lord Mayor asked that the "Swordbearer's Room might be fitted up as a small Drawing Room with suitable furniture," and in 1822 there was an estimate for "forming Wilkes's Parlour and the Swordbearers Room into Drawing Rooms": the estimate was £370. 0s. 0d. and £912. 4s. 6d. for furniture. A plan of about 1798 has the North Drawing Room marked as "Wilkses's Parlour."

At this period the Clerks' Offices, formerly the Judicial Room, was the Vagrants' Room.

In 1822 it was decided that Mr Daniel should paint a picture to be placed over the fire-place in the Swordbearer's Room which is near the South Drawing Room. This was to cost not more than £50.

In 1827 a scheme to heat the Egyptian Hall was approved at a cost of £200. In the same year it was resolved that the annual lighting expenses should be limited to £300, and repairs to £1000: and that the external lighting of the windows of the Guildhall on Lord Mayor's Day should be discontinued.

In 1830 it was reported that there were 163 external lights, 12 interior lights and 4 skylights: it was stated that the building was formerly assessed to 200 windows and that the assessment now paid was for 171.

In 1832 it was decided "that a warm Bath be fitted up."

In the same year Montague the City Surveyor reported with reference to the lowering of the attic storey of the Ball Room: he stated there were many fractures and settlements and advised the attic storey should be removed and a new roof built to correspond externally with the Egyptian Hall. His estimate was £890.

About this period there was a mania for looking-glass, which was fixed even on the doors and door linings, and at a very heavy cost, luckily it has almost all been removed or painted.

In 1832 gas was apparently not very satisfactory, for the Lord Mayor wanted oil lamps substituted for gas in the Venetian Parlour. On December 19th Montague certified for the completion of works costing £3504. This was in connection with the general repairs throughout the building.

In 1835 the present standing order was passed, preventing members acting for or against the Corporation: doubtless the result of the scandals in connection with the erection of the building.

In 1835 Sir Robert Smirke reported suggesting the steps in front of the building should be set back and rearranged, so as to give an extra width of five feet to the pavement, the railed enclosure being moved, the steps to ascend to the Portico being the same in number but to commence at "each extremity of the Front." His estimate was £600.

It is interesting to note that in 1837 a contract was agreed with Messrs Thwaites and Reed to regulate the clocks at the Mansion House, they are still the contractors.

In 1839 the Committee suggested that the room then "appropriated to paupers and prisoners," should be fitted up as a Justice Room and the room under, then used as a Laundry, should be altered into a room for the accommodation of the public and for prisoners, and two staircases constructed to give access to the Justice Room above. The plate room adjoining the housekeeper's room was to be altered into a laundry, and part of the internal area in the basement covered in.

In 1839 the looking-glass mania was still in full swing. The Lord Mayor applied for "folding doors with Glass Frames" for the Vestibule.

In 1840 the exterior was cleansed by a "Steam Fire Engine," and the stonework repaired at a cost of £367. The method was advised by Mr C. R. Cockerell, the celebrated Architect, who had "washed" the Bank of England.

In 1842 the Committee were authorised to spend about £1000 in removing the Attic Storey to the Ball Room and the formation of a new roof to correspond in general character with the roof of the Egyptian Hall. It will be remembered that the latter roof was lowered in consequence of dry rot in the timbers, but the cause of the alterations to the Ball Room roof was not dry rot, but the weakness of the attic walls, these were found to be bulging outwards and were not strong enough to support the roof.

In 1845 Bunning reported on a proposed new entrance from Charlotte Row. The present Entrance Hall had been designed as stabling for eight horses, but never completed. In 1845 the space was used as "Coal Cellars, Knife House and Dust Bin," and it was proposed to convert the space into a Hall and "cut a communication through the Wall to the present staircase making the present entrance door into a window, providing a Stove for the Hall and erecting a Portico." The cost to be about £950.

In 1852 it was agreed to place certain sculpture in the building. The artists submitted models about 18 inches high, some of these are still at the Mansion House. £700 was paid for each piece of sculpture, they were as follows:

Genius	Mr Bailey
The Morning Star	„ „
Timon of Athens	„ Thrupp
Caractacus	„ Foley
Egeria	„ „
Griselda	„ Marshall
Comus	„ Lough
Leah	„ McDowell
Sardanapalus	„ Weeks
Britomarth	„ Wyon
The Bard	„ Theed
The Last of the Welsh Bards	„ „
Hermione	„ Durham
Alfred the Great	„ Bowring Stephens
Alexander the Great	„ J. S. Westmacott
Faithful Sheperdes	Miss Susan Durant

About this date there were still constant applications by the Lord Mayor for looking-glass in the doors and linings. There is also evidence of the mania for graining the woodwork.

In May, 1843, the lowering of the Ball Room roof was certified as complete, and the cost was £875.

Mr Montague died in 1843 and John Young certified for payments until Bunning was appointed Architect and Surveyor in the same year.

In 1842 it was agreed to spend £3000 on decoration, the columns of the Egyptian Hall were to be painted "in imitation of marble" and varnished. Bunning advised plain paint. Between 1824 and 1841 an average of £1276 p.a. was spent on decoration, etc.

In 1845 Bunning submitted an estimate for a new Porch on the West side of the building.

In the same year a looking-glass was purchased for £200 for the Egyptian Hall, it was 12 feet 6 inches by 7 feet 6 inches, and chandeliers were purchased for the Long Parlour for £121. 1s. 3d. "instead of paying £15 p.a. for hire and use."

In 1846 the oil lamps in the Drawing Rooms were described as being very old and the introduction of gas was discussed, but objected to by several aldermen, and it was decided to use candles.

In the same year, four schemes were considered for erecting a new Porch in Charlotte Row, the old Porch was further North, and is shown in Malton's view, dated 1798. The Committee decided on the scheme showing the present Porch and a tender of £1047 was accepted.

In 1846 it was decided to purchase land at the corner of Poultry and Charlotte Row for £800: the area is not mentioned but the scheme was to round off the corner where the National Mercantile Assurance Society were erecting a new building.

In December, 1848, Bunning reported on a proposal to form a new Justice Room "in the large room adjoining the present Justice Room," cutting away the floor of the Ball Room above to increase the light, "the present justice room" to become a room for affidavits, "and the public entrance made through the westernmost window, next the Entrance Hall of the Mansion House," increased accommodation for prisoners being formed in the basement "and a staircase formed from the Cages to the

Dock": an estimate of £467 was accepted and the work carried out.

In 1850 the fire-places were still used in the Egyptian Hall. In this year the Commissioners of Sewers complained of the "public sewer" under the building. The Committee said it was private and ordered it to be repaired. This year it was decided to appeal to Parliament for a repeal of the window tax: and an estimate of £595 was accepted for remodelling the kitchens.

In 1851 the Lord Mayor stated that in the event of loss by fire or burglary he would not be responsible, and the Comptroller stated that the Corporation did not insure any of their property.

At this time there was a well at the Mansion House, it was found the water was contaminated and it was suggested another well, farther from the urinal, should be sunk, cost to be £40. 10s.

In this year it was decided to purchase, at a cost of 50 guineas each, the busts of Queen Victoria, Prince Albert, William IV and the late Duke of Teck, all by John Francis.

In 1856 Bibles and Prayer Books "properly bound and stamped or lettered," were provided for all the Bed Rooms: different qualities for the various rooms.

In 1857 it was suggested the lower windows at each end of the Egyptian Hall should have curtains: later on looking-glasses of a very feeble design were unfortunately placed over the windows, they are there now.

The Chaplain's Rooms are referred to as late as 1858.

In 1859 a contract for three years was made for lighting with gas the outside lamps at £4. 10s. each p.a. and the inside lamps by meter at a cost of 4s. per thousand cubic feet.

As late as 1859 large sums were being paid for looking-glass, including the panels of doors.

In 1860 the craze for large sheets of plate glass was the cause of the removal of the old sashes on the principal floors, and "new Wainscot sashes" with "best plate Glass" were to be substituted: luckily the windows of the upper floors were spared.

In 1868 it was decided to remove the iron railings in front of the building, these railings are shown in several old views, see Plate XV. In the same year it was agreed to spend a sum not exceeding £8000 on strengthening the foundations.

In 1867 there were further settlements and iron ties were

inserted and a parapet was rebuilt. Tenders were obtained for coloured glass for the two large windows in the Egyptian Hall, Messrs Ward and Hughes and Alex. Gibbs were selected, the price to be £360 for each window.

In 1865 Bunning reported "the whole of the timber and piling immediately under the walls is found to be in a very advanced state of decay and in many instances completely rotten." He asked for authority to spend £1000 in addition to the £500 he had already spent.

In 1865 there was a request to alter the name of George St to Mansion House Place as that was the name of the continuation of George St which contained only one house. The applicant stated there were three streets known as George St, E.C., and twenty others in London, including similar names, such as Little George St.

In 1866 the Police Committee reported it was desirable to remove the iron railings in front of the building.

In 1868 it was decided the two windows in the Egyptian Hall should be as follows:

The Royal Window. The signing of Magna Charta, Arms of King John and Queen Elizabeth—Queen Elizabeth's procession from the City to Westminster. Royal Arms.

The City Window. Death of Wat Tyler at Smithfield, Arms of Walworth and King Edward VI. Procession of King Edward VI to his coronation. City Arms.

Alex: Gibbs to execute both windows: price £380 each.

In 1870 the Committee applied to various gas firms for schemes to illuminate the coloured glass windows, eleven estimates were received and varied from £70 to £469.

The same year it was agreed to spend £2790 on repairs to stonework and new external lamps: and one firm suggested electric light for illuminating the windows.

In 1875 it was decided to substitute pipe drains for brick drains: and to spend £1665 on lighting and heating.

In 1876 the lifts were erected. In 1879 the doorway was formed between the Venetian Parlour and the Secretary's room. In 1880 the lighting of the Egyptian Hall by electricity and the installation of a telephone were considered. In 1881 a scheme was discussed for the removal of the lavatories adjoining the saloon, estimated cost £500. The same year tenders were considered for the installation of electric light, a tender was accepted for £425 for one year and the option of purchase of the plant for £1171. 10s. 0d. The plant evidently included a gas engine and complaints were soon made about the failure of the light and the noise of the engine.

In 1883 the coverings to the ventilators in the basement were removed: they had been closed in consequence of an attempt to blow up the building.

In 1888 and 1889 extensive sanitary works were erected at a cost of about £2055.

In the *Daily News* of December 17th, 1891, it was stated that electric light was first used in the building on the previous day.

In 1901 there were slight settlements in consequence of the construction of tube railways and a small amount was spent on the building.

In 1902 flags were received from the various colonies and hung in the Egyptian Hall.

In 1905 the old and dangerous gas sunburners were removed from the Egyptian Hall, and a system of ventilation by means of electric fans and concealed inlets was installed by the author.

In 1909 a system of iron doors and fire escapes was carried out, by the introduction of the doors the building becomes divided into two parts, practically separate buildings.

At the close of the Exhibition of 1851, £10,000 was voted for statuary for the Egyptian Hall. Ten premiums of £15. 15s. 0d. each were paid for designs for statues.

The banners in the Old Ball Room, and some of the banners in the Egyptian Hall, bear the arms of the Lord Mayors who presented them during their term of office.

PLATE XXXII

IN THE LADY MAYORESS'S BOUDOIR

IN THE SOUTH MORNING ROOM

PLATE XXXIII

IN THE VENETIAN PARLOUR

IN THE NORTH DRAWING ROOM

Chapter XIII

The rooms in the Mansion House.
The Dance Family

A COMPARISON of Dance's design with the others submitted will show that the Corporation were wise in their choice. A photograph of George Dance the elder is shown (Frontispiece); this has never been previously published. There is a fine portrait of George Dance the younger in Sir John Soane's Museum, Lincoln's Inn Fields. He succeeded his father in 1768 and was in turn succeeded by William Montague in 1816.

As usual the building received the customary hostile criticism that important new structures are subject to, a practice that seems to increase as time goes on. Was it not Ruskin who described the Houses of Parliament by Barry or Pugin as "a triumph of modern confectionery"? Again, the Albert Hall and Albert Memorial have been referred to as a Twelfth-night cake, from which some giant hand removed the ornament off the top and deposited it on the other side of the road. Bentley's Roman Catholic Cathedral at Westminster has been described as "a gasometer and a water tower"; Garnier's Paris Opera House as "the mother of all gin palaces," and so on. In the case of the Mansion House it is impossible to print certain gross criticism, but in 1731 a book was published, entitled *A Critical Review of the Public Buildings of London and Westminster*, later editions give James Ralph as the author, but it seems clear that he did not write it[1]. The following is an extract:

> The man pitched upon, who afterwards carried his plan into execution, was originally a shipwright, and to do him justice, he appears never to have lost sight of his first profession. The front of his mansion-house has all the resemblance possible to a deep laden Indiaman, with her stern galleries and ginger bread work. The stairs and passages within are all ladders and gangways, and the superstructure at top answers pretty accurately to the idea we usually form of Noah's ark.

[1] See *Notes and Queries*, July 2nd, 1864.

I can find no authority for the statement that George Dance was a shipwright, and of course the building has no resemblance to an Indiaman, but when a critic wishes to be offensive, mere truth is insufficient for the occasion. The Grand Staircase, now a Drawing Room with a bedroom over it, must have been a very fine architectural feature of the building.

The design had not great originality, there are many examples scattered all over the country, of houses having for a central feature a portico raised on a podium. A reference to architectural books will show instances not only by Dance, but by Gibbs, Ware, Kent, Wood, Chambers and other architects of the eighteenth century.

The portico type of elevation governs the plan, for the Ground Floor becomes a low storey, and the First Floor is the principal floor. After all it is not a bad arrangement, the offices are on the Ground Floor, and not lowered into an area-lighted basement, consequently they are well ventilated. The kitchens at the Mansion House can compare favourably with any in London, they are lofty, brick vaulted and amply ventilated.

The type of porch as we see it at the Mansion House can be traced back to Grecian temples, it was adopted by the Romans, and although the Italian architects of the Renaissance shook off its influence and obtained a dignified effect for their buildings by simpler means, the less gifted architects of England did not do so, but plainly followed a model of which the Pantheon at Rome is a well-known example.

The Portico style is certainly suitable for the residence of the Chief Magistrate of London, and the building has been favourably criticised by competent authorities of to-day. It is typical of the pompous Georgian era, it is sedate, severe, churchy and dignified, a kind of Hallelujah chorus in stone.

The use the Mansion House is put to makes it perhaps the most remarkable building in the world, for I believe it is the only structure now existing which, like the palace of the Doge at Venice, is a residence, a court of justice and a prison. Guests little think that by opening a door they could pass into a London Police Court, with the dock handy, and cells below. The Police Court is still known by the old name of Justice Room.

There is a large collection of Dance's drawings at Sir John Soane's Museum and there are a few at the Guildhall: but the plan of the Principal Floor cannot be found, it was, however, illustrated in 1767 in *Vitruvius Britannicus*, together with the front Elevation and Section, and Plan 60 shows the plan as it is now. No closet is shown on either the Ground Floor or the Principal Floor as originally designed.

The following are some notes upon the various rooms, commencing with the highest or Third Floor.

In 1799 the Chaplain had one room, but in 1820 his "rooms" are referred to, and mention is made of his sitting-room in 1821, and fittings were provided for his surplices.

On the Second Floor the alterations have been few, bathrooms have been added and various structures built out over the central area. The principal room on this floor is the Ball Room originally called the Dancing Gallery. A section of this room is shown in Plate XXV. The removal of the attic storey was very detrimental from a point of lighting, but the windows have clear glass and the light is sufficient on most days. Plate XXIII shows Dance's original design, the clerestory had seven windows on each side and one at each end, the decoration was originally intended to be plaster, very similar in treatment to the rooms on the principal floor. There was one door in the centre communicating with the corridor on the South side: in 1817 this was blocked up and two doorways were formed. Although Dance originally proposed plaster decoration the room had wood panellings, and to get a few inches more space the columns round the room were removed and the cornice cut away: this was a most unfortunate mutilation and the marks of the breaks of the cornice can be seen to-day. The columns are shown in the Section (Plate XXV) which was published in *Vitruvius Britannicus*. This room was not like the Egyptian Hall, with the attic storey over the centre portion of the room, but the height of the whole room was about 56 feet. The present height to the top of the cornice is about 32 feet and to the top of the vault 38 feet. About the year 1880 the plaster figures of Leda and the swan were considered objectionable, and were covered over for some years.

On the First or Principal Floor are the important reception rooms which are as follows:

Egyptian Hall. This apartment was originally known as the Grand Hall, or Great Hall, and it has been altered more than any room in the building. It was originally well lighted, the attic storey had 20 windows and there were the two large Venetian windows, one at the East end and one at the West end, these have been filled with coloured glass. Below each of them, and below the gallery which formerly existed, was another large window, these still exist but unfortunately are covered over with mirrors of a very feeble design, one mirror can be seen on Plate XXVII. The result is the room is practically dark, even on a bright summer day. Artificial light must always be used with the result that the coloured glass is not seen, except when it is illuminated from the outside. It is an extraordinary thing that a large hall having three external walls should be dependent on artificial light, windows could, of course, be inserted in the South wall, and the room could be flooded with daylight, although at the West end of the passage behind the building, the church of St Stephen is very close, windows at the East end of the passage could receive light over the Church Yard.

There is nothing Egyptian about the architecture, but Vitruvius described a hall with columns and a clerestory above as an Egyptian Hall as follows:

In the Egyptian oecus, over the lower columns is an architrave from which to the surrounding wall is a boarded and paved floor, so as to form a passage round it in the open air. Then perpendicularly over the architrave of the lower columns, columns one fourth smaller are placed, above their architraves and cornices they are decorated with ceilings and windows are placed between the upper columns.

Lord Burlington was interested in, and a subscriber towards the erection of, the Assembly Rooms at York, where there is a Hall built "after the Egyptian manner." This still exists, it is longer but narrower than the room at the Mansion House.

There was originally a gallery on all four sides of the Hall, this can be seen in Plate XXVII. This gallery must have been very useful on occasions when large numbers of people were entertained, and as it formed part of the original design the reinstatement of the gallery might well be considered. Again, the removal has made the decoration of the high side walls somewhat difficult, the old lines still remain and look meaningless without the gallery, and further, the gallery, if reinstated at the East and West ends, would be useful as a division should the mirrors be removed and the lower windows re-used. The height up to the ceiling of the clerestory was over 80 feet, this is about double the height of the lower side of the main cornice from the floor level. Plan 55 shows Dance's proposal for the lower roof after removing the clerestory.

The Long Parlour was known as the Great Parlour and the Common Parlour, and had windows on both the East and West sides; the five windows on the East side overlooked the Cortile. These windows are shown in Plan 51, and the view across the Cortile must have been very charming.

The Venetian Parlour was known as the Great Parlour and is probably the room referred to as the Entertaining Parlour and the Dining Parlour. The doorways on the North side were made some years after the building was erected. The room immediately to the North and used by Sir William Soulsby, was known as the Young Mens' Room, the Lord Mayor's Parlour and the Breakfasting Parlour; it had a very fine chimney piece, unfortunately a portion of the room is cut off and used for lavatories. It had three windows facing North.

The Vestibule is in the centre of the North front, a few years ago it was disfigured by a partition which was recently removed, this room is perhaps the most charming in the building; some of the models of the sculpture are shown, they are on artistic little brackets.

The room at the North-East corner is similar in size to the Young Mens' Room, it was originally known as the Vagrants' Room, later it was known as the Judicial Room and the Outer Justice Room: it is now used for offices in connection with the Police Court work. Adjoining to the South is the Justice Room with communication to the cells below. This fine apartment was originally the Swordbearer's Room: and as the Swordbearer was instructed to draw up the particulars of the architectural competition he naturally looked after himself and his successors in office. But the room was soon used as a Vagrant or Prisoners' Room: and as the Judicial Room last described was found too small the room under consideration was fitted up as the present Justice Room.

Immediately South of the staircase and facing East are the two Drawing Rooms. The North Drawing Room was originally designed as a Drawing Room, later it was known as a Dining Room and for very many years it was called Wilkes's Parlour, after the celebrated Lord Mayor. This was originally a charming room, Plan 52 shows the Plan and four elevations, it will be noted how symmetrical the room was, there was no large opening on the South side, simply a doorway to correspond with the doorway to the staircase, there was a large panel in the centre and the South side corresponded with the North side; and there was a chair rail on each wall: unfortunately, a portion of the chair rail has recently been removed, pilasters have been introduced with the caps immediately under the cornice. As Dance's drawings still exist, it would be a happy idea to restore the room according to his design. In this room three windows overlooked the Cortile.

The South Drawing Room was originally the Grand Staircase, it was soon found that it was unnecessary. Plate XXIX shows the plan and elevations. The staircase was removed, and on the Ground Floor a Drawing Room was made and a fire-place with flue constructed. On the floor above the staircase became a bedroom. The spacing of the windows is not so symmetrical as in the North Drawing Room, and the apartment has been disfigured with pilasters.

There remains the Cortile, it is strange to think that this was built with an open colonnade on the North and South sides and that guests had to pass into the open air to reach the main entrance to the Egyptian Hall. Plan 56 shows a sketch by Dance for constructing a barrel vault over the Cortile, and it is to be regretted it was not carried out. The architectural effect of the original Cortile must have been very charming, but after the colonnades were enclosed it was found that further floor space was required and the Cortile lost: the architectural details can be still seen from the upper windows. On the North side of the Cortile there is a Hall which fortunately has not been altered. Plan 53 shows the original design.

Plan 50 is the plan of the Basement as originally designed, it shows an area around the central portion which supported the Cortile. It also shows P a "Stable for eight horses," Q a "Coach House for 2 Coaches," R or "Room for hay." It has been shown in previous pages that the Stable and Coach house were never finished for the purposes originally proposed, but were used as stores for documents, etc. It will also be noted that the staircases were built with square ends, and not circular as shown.

PLATE XXXIV

RULES OF THIS HALL
SWEAR NOT. LIE NOT
NEITHER REPEAT OLD GRIEVANCES
WHOSOEVER EATS OR DRINKS IN THIS HALL
WITH HIS HAT ON, SHALL FORFEIT SIXPENCE
OR RIDE THE WOODEN HORSE.
Witness USHER of the HALL.

John William Dykes Hall Porter to the Rt Honble Tho Challis Lord Mayor 1853

George Roberts Porter to ye Rt Honble Sr Crisp Gascoyne Lord Mayor 1753

Fireplace in the
Servant's Hall.
Mansion House.

Showing the "Wooden Horse"
— on the right —

R. Randoll
1917

Reproduced by kind permission of Sir William Treloar, Bt.

The coach house is now the Plate Pantry, the stable for eight horses is now the Private Entrance Hall, the Cocquet Office is now partly used as the Swordbearer's Room and partly as a Manservant's bedroom. The Porter's Lodge is now the Affidavit Room, the Housekeeper's Room is now used for cells, etc., the Larder is now the Housekeeper's Room, the Store Room for Pewter is now used for stores and as a larder, and the Scouring Room and Kitchen for Housekeeper are now one apartment, the Still Room. There is no South-East Staircase, I believe it was never built, the space is now used as a Butler's Room. The open areas have been covered over and are used as lavatories, etc. with ventilation over.

Under this Ground Floor there is a basement with the usual cellars.

With regard to the exterior Plates XIX, XX and XXI are some views. The front steps were altered so as to give more room for the public, and although the panel over the main entrance door is shown carved, this work has never been completed, the panel to-day remains "bossed" and ready for the carver. There was a balustrade between the large columns, two of the obelisk posts that stood at the street level are now fixed on the sides of the main entrance.

Anyone interested in the architecture of an old town will find the specimens of ancient work in the poor parts of the town, the main streets get rebuilt or "improved," and the same thing happens in many old houses, the principal rooms are "improved." This has happened at the Mansion House: all the old sashes with their fine wide bars have been replaced by large squares of plate glass most objectionable as regards surface, and not in keeping with the architecture, but the upper storey still shows the old sashes, and some day they may make their reappearance in the principal windows. This would be a great improvement of the exterior.

Plate XXIV shows the original design for the West elevation. The balustrade to the large window of the Egyptian Hall has been removed, and might well be restored and the external lighting and reflectors removed. The doorways are shown for the stable and coach house. Malton's view, Plate XIV, shows the early porch in 1798, this was removed, the door was made with a window lighting the staircase and the porch rebuilt further South, this has been enlarged and might well be extended still further South, so as to become a central feature.

On the South side are shown the three flues which were made when the fire-places were formed in the Egyptian Hall.

Plate XXVII is a view of the Egyptian Hall, with the roof lowered, and as it is now, but the objectionable mirrors at the ends are not shown.

THE DANCE FAMILY

The Dance family was celebrated, many of the members became famous in different vocations as in the case of other families like that of Wren, Wilberforce, West-Ridgway and Pollock. George Dance the elder had two sons who were Royal Academicians, and his descendants included Commodore Sir Nathaniel Dance[1] and Colonel Sir Charles Dance. James Dance the Dramatist was an elder brother of George Dance the younger: an account of these men is included in the usual books of biography, etc. but very little is published about George Dance's ancestors and the author has made a search.

In the *Gentleman's Magazine*, 1751, p. 332, in the list of deaths for the year 1751, we read "July 6th. Giles Dance Esq. father of the city surveyor, aged 87"; this would give his birth in 1664, which was probably too early: for in the Freedom Records of the Corporation of London there is one entry, "Giles Dance, Son of James Dance of the City of Winchester, Carpenter, was apprenticed to William Gibbs, Citizen and Merchant Taylor on the 15th May, 1685, for 8 years." If he was born in 1664 he would then have been 21. The registers of St Maurice Winchester contain an entry in 1670, "Gyles the sonne of James Daunte (Dance) carpenter was baptised Monday the fifth of September Ao 1670." If he was born in 1670 his age would have been 15 when he was apprenticed and 81 when he died. The entries at Winchester are a little confusing, apparently there were two men named James Dance. For one James Dance was a turner and married "Sarie Walldone" in July, 1664, but "James the son of James Dance" was baptised on 4th June of the same year: again Elizabeth the wife of James Dance was buried on February 3rd, 1708: however,

---

[1] (See James' *Naval History of Great Britain*, etc.)

the following is a list of the children of James Dance who was described as a "Carpenter":

1668	Elizabeth	baptised	13th September.
1670	Gyles	"	5th September.
1672	Frances daughter	"	26th January.

The children of James Dance, without any note of trade are as follows:

1664	James	baptised	4th June.
1675	James	"	28th November.
1678	Mary	"	20th October.
1686	Elizabeth	"	30th May.

Robert Dance, a carpenter, is also mentioned in 1674.

Again, there are entries in the Coffer Books in the Winchester Archives stating that several payments were made to Robert Dance the Carpenter, between the years 1682 and 1686.

Giles Dance was made free of service on July 5th, 1693, he was "bound to William Gibbs and turned over to John Wray, per Mr. Wray of Holborne, Mason" and on July 2nd, 1713, he was admitted to the livery of the Merchant Taylors' Company.

Giles Dance was living in the parish of St Leonard, Shore-ditch, when he made his will in 1749, he referred to his wife Sarah, his son George, and his daughter Hester Horne, and his grandchildren Giles, John and Elizabeth Tottingham: the Executor was Richard Horne of the Navy Office. No occupation is given but mention is made of "copartnership between my son George and me." The *Gentleman's Magazine* stated that he died on July 6th, 1751, but that was not correct as the will was proved on July 5th.

In the records of June 2nd, 1725, of the Merchant Taylors' Company is the following entry:

George Dance Stonecutter Moorfields, per Patr: son of Giles Dance Liveryman.

This entry is valuable and contradicts the statement in the *Critical Review* that George Dance "was originally a ship-wright." He was admitted to the Livery in December, 1730.

It is interesting to note that Giles Dance was apprenticed to William Gibbs, for James Gibbs (1683–1754) was the cele-brated architect and a competitor for the Mansion House: but there is no evidence of relationship.

There is some uncertainty about the date of birth of the

Architect of the Mansion House. It is given as 1695, and also as 1700 by certain authorities.

With regard to the death of George Dance the elder, the *Gentleman's Magazine* states it was on February 11th, the *London Magazine* of February, 1768, states it was on February 16th, and the *Dictionary of National Biography* states it was on February 8th. He was buried at St Luke's Church, Old Street, but the only record that can be found is the entry in the register "George Dance, a man. Buried February 17th, 1768." The tombstone cannot be found.

There was another Dance interested in the building trade in the eighteenth century, for in the *London Magazine* of 1733, p. 426, we read, "Mr. Dance, an eminent Surveyor and Master-Builder, who built Guy's Hospital in Southwark," died during August, 1733. The following are extracts from the Minute Books of the Hospital:

14th. April 1725 "Resolved that Mr. Dance be continued in the Employment of Surveyor of the Buildings necessary to this hospital on the same conditions and with the same salary of Fifteen Guineas per Quarter as was agreed on with him in the Lifetime of Thomas Guy Esq."

Also in an account of the Executors of Thomas Guy's will passed by the Court of the Hospital on 29th October, 1725, we read as follows:

Paid Thomas Dance for 3/mo Salary as Surveyor of Mr. Guy's building in Southwark, due at Xmas last £15. 15. 0.

Thomas Dance left considerable property, in the record of his will he is described as living in the parish of St Paul, Covent Garden, a plaisterer; the will was dated December 8th, 1732, it mentions his brothers Richard, William and Joseph, his nephew, Richard Dance, and there were many charitable bequests.

It is interesting to note that the Dance interest in Guy's Hospital was continued at a later date, for in 1764 George Dance designed the West wing of the entrance front and the stone façade of the centre building.

George Dance was instructed to supply the place of George Smith, who was dismissed from his office as Clerk of the City's Works on February 19th, 1733; he was appointed to his office by the Court of Aldermen on December 2nd, 1735. He resigned on February 2nd, 1768, and the same day his son was appointed successor in the office, he was known as the City Surveyor.

Appendix I

Sheriffs' Fines

WITH reference to the Sheriffs' fines, although it was decided on 30th April, 1730, that any fines *in the future* should be used to pay for the building, the Court of Common Council decided on 29th June, 1731[1], that "moneys which *are* or *shall be* paid...as fines" were intended to be so used.

Looking back into history, I find that in the reign of Edward III a man was fined £100 for not serving the office, the money being paid to the man "chosen by his default in his place," and he also lost his franchise for ever[2]. In the reign of Henry VIII the amount was raised to £200, half that sum was paid to the Chamberlain for "the use of the Commonalty" and the other £100 to the man who served the office in his place. And it was also decided that the Act passed in the reign of Edward III whereby a man lost his franchise was "utterly void and of none effect" as far as the loss of franchise was concerned.

In the year 1530 Robert Amadas, described as "King's jeweller" to Henry VIII, was elected Sheriff and asked to be excused, but twelve "substantial commoners" went to the King "beseeching him"...to "command Amadas" to serve the office. The record is that "Henry answered that his pleasure was that "as Amadas was master of the jewels that he should be clearly "exempted": the result was that Ralph Chopping was appointed and Amadas paid no fine[3]. In one case half the fine was allocated for the use of the poor in the poor-house of Smithfield[4].

In Elizabeth's reign one man paid £500 to the Corporation to be exempt from the offices of Alderman and Sheriff, stating his health was bad, but he was not exempted from serving "the offices of his Drapers Company[5]."

In the same reign it is decided that "Mr Gunter at the request of the Earl of Leicester and Mr Secretary Cecil is

---

[1] *Journal* 57, f. 234.   [2] *Ibid.* 13, f. 25.
[3] *Ibid.* 13, ff. 242–4.   [4] *Ibid.* 16, f. 203.
[5] *Ibid.* 18, f. 338.

discharged from the offices of Alderman Sheriff and collector of XV[ths.] for the find of £400[1]." The following year Queen Elizabeth wrote asking for the exemption of Mr John Brameche from the offices of Sheriff and Alderman, but it "was in no wise agreed unto[2]."

An Act of Common Council was passed on 1st August, 1582, stating that unless a man elected for the office of Sheriff could "swear by his own corporal oath and that of six other citizens of good fame" that he was not worth 300 marks, he was to be fined £400, £200 (less expenses) to go to the man serving in his place, £100 "to the Chamber of the City," and £100 to the poor of St Bartholomew's Hospital, and unless he paid the £200 within three months, there would be a further £100 to pay the Chamberlain[3].

In 1609 it was recorded one Alderman gave "£500 to the Salters Company and £2500 to the Chamber of London for the City's use is discharged from being elected Sheriff for ever[4]."

In the reign of Queen Anne the fine was £400 to be paid "into the Chamber of London for the use of the Mayor Commonalty and Citizens," the man fined to be exempted for ever from serving the office[5].

In 1720 the fine was fixed at £400 and "20 marks more towards the maintenance of Ministers of the several prisons according to another Act of Common Council of 3rd December, 1656." This fine was continued until the Mansion House was built.

In 1777 six men were fined £615. 6s. 8d. each; from 1778 until 1836 the fine as a rule was £413. 6s. 8d., but there are a very few cases of fines of £413. 6s. 8d. being paid. In 1852 three men were paid £400 each, and no fines have since been imposed.

Mr Beaven in his history of the Aldermen of the City of London refers to the statement so often made that the Mansion House was built "from fines imposed by a tyrannical corporation upon persecuted Nonconformists"; he states "it is a simple travesty of fact to assume the persons fined were all Nonconformists."

[1] *Journal* 19, f. 215.   [2] *Ibid.* 19, f. 239.
[3] *Ibid.* 21, f. 226.   [4] *Ibid.* 27, f. 385 b.
[5] *Ibid.* 54, f. 473.

Appendix II

The Re-building of London after the Great Fire of 1666

IT is interesting to note that when John Evelyn prepared his scheme for rebuilding the city he provided a site for "The Lord Mayor's House," and a site for a house for each of "The two Sheriffs." There was a great rush to prepare plans and Evelyn wrote in a letter dated 27th September, 1666, "Everybody brings in his idea: among the rest I presented his Majesty my own conceptions, with a discourse annexed. It was the second that was seen, within two days after the conflagration; but Dr Wren got the start of me." When I read my paper at the Royal Institute of British Architects on 20th December, 1919, on "London Town-planning Schemes in 1666," I stated that I had been unable to find Evelyn's "discourse," although I had made a careful search, but by 20th September, 1920, I had succeeded in finding a MS. copy of it, and it is printed in the *R.I.B.A. Journal* of that date, for the first time. After referring to the Guildhall he states: "Near unto this might be designed a magnificent house for the Lord Mayor and others for the two sheriffs of London; which being erected at the publick charge, ought to be the constant residence of the Gentlemen who bear that office *pro tempore* and would therefore be contrived accordingly." The whole discourse is a carefully considered document and full of interest.

Three drawings made by Dr Wren for rebuilding London are preserved in the Library of All Souls College, Oxford, and I am indebted to the authorities of that College for allowing me to have two of them photographed and reproduced for the first time.

Plan 61 shows the fire boundary, and the principal streets within that area are marked by a single line, Newgate Street, Cheapside, Watling Street, Cannon Street and Thames Street, etc., are shown, and St Paul's Cathedral, the Royal Exchange, the Guildhall and a few other buildings are indicated.

With this plan before him, the great architect apparently prepared Plan 62, it has been cut out with a pair of scissors or a sharp knife; a photograph of the well-known final plan is published in the *R.I.B.A. Journal* with the lecture above referred to. It is interesting to note that Plan 62 does not agree with Wren's final ideas in certain particulars, the sketch plans for St Paul's Cathedral vary slightly; again the first scheme differs from the final scheme in that the minor streets around the Exchange are straight and not at right angles to the longer streets; in the latter they have an angle in the middle of the length. The plots immediately East of Ludgate are set back in the first scheme, adding importance to the Gateway, and the narrow blocks of buildings along the embankment were added in the final scheme. The Custom House is not shown in the first scheme and the roads in the neighbourhood are consequently different, and the planning just north of Billingsgate varies considerably. The only buildings that are marked by a reference letter on Plan 62 are the proposed Guildhall and Doctors' Commons. The site plan for a new Exchange is sketched in the same way in both schemes.

The basis of Wren's plan is the formation of two wide roads from the East, one from Leadenhall Street in the direction of Aldgate and one from the neighbourhood of the Tower; they meet at Ludgate, and St Paul's Cathedral is in the acute angle of the junction: it would have occupied quite a small portion of the present site. Apparently Wren was willing to sacrifice a large cathedral for his angular scheme, for St Paul's Cathedral would only have had about the same area as the Mansion House: had a large cathedral been built on the ancient site then the road plan was impossible. It all shows a rush, and even if the scheme had been approved the question of a large cathedral must have arisen and prevented the development of the idea. The plan strikes one as the first effort of a great man; prepared in so few days it could not possibly have had careful consideration.

With regard to St Paul's Cathedral it is much to be regretted that to-day we get no general view of it from any main street East of the cathedral; the curve of Cannon Street gives us a charming view of a small portion of it and a view is obtained along Watling Street; but had Wren's plan for rebuilding London been carried out this defect would have been worse, for a reference to the plan will show that nothing could have been seen of the cathedral from any point East of it.

Had Wren's plan been carried out parochial and ward boundaries would have disappeared, some of them having existed since Norman times. A pamphlet of 1667 gives the number as "Eighty-nine Parish Churches, besides Chappels, burnt." Certainly at least 86 were destroyed or severely damaged. Wren only provided for the re-erection of 17 churches. Six chapels were burnt, but Wren made no provision for their re-erection, and the scheme made no provision for the preservation of the old burial grounds which would have been desecrated.

When we examine Wren's proposal and compare it with a plan of the city the first thing to strike one is his absolute disregard of the old streets. This is what was to be expected from Wren's first sketch, Plan 61. Not one single old thoroughfare remains, a little St Paul's occupies part of the site of the present cathedral, the Guildhall and the Royal Exchange would both have had different sites. Among others the following old buildings would have disappeared: The Guildhall, with its magnificent crypt; the Crypt of St Mary-le-Bow; Merchant Taylors' Hall; St Alphage, London Wall; every old church in the city within the fire area—many of them, although partly destroyed by the Great Fire, still retain small portions of the medieval buildings. This also applies to certain Halls of the City Companies. Except in the case of St Paul's no attempt was made to place a new church on an ancient site, and every little green spot would have disappeared, for it was arranged for "All Church-yards, Gardens and unnecessary Vacuities...to be placed out of the town." The city would have been one of bricks and mortar. If Wren's scheme had been carried out what an uninteresting place the city of London would be to-day, and how we should condemn our forefathers for gross acts of vandalism.

Now let us see what a gigantic Utopian scheme Wren prepared. Four hundred streets, numbering 13,200 houses, had been burnt down, and, say, 66,000 people were homeless. No doubt parts of the walls remained and there was subsequently little difficulty in marking the boundaries of the properties. On the old sites the people could get back very soon, some properties were certified early in the following spring; but Wren wanted to "scrap" all the old streets and to form new roads of a length of over 21 miles; the roads were to be run through the remains of houses and churches only partly destroyed, and which, of course, would have had to be razed to the ground. Then he would have had to fill up old basements and cellars and form foundations for his new roads and then make the roads; the old supply pipes for water would have been useless, and a considerable portion of St Paul's Cathedral would have had to be removed as it would have blocked up his two main thorough-fares. It was, indeed, a colossal scheme; it would have taken years to carry out, and the cost would have been enormous; in the meantime the people would have been homeless, and the trade of the city would have been stagnant, for until the new roads were made, no warehouses or business premises could be erected. No wonder the King's advisers came to a quick decision and rejected the idea.

On the second plate prepared by Evelyn it is stated that the plan showed 25 churches on their old foundations, and all the principal streets almost in the same position. All the schemes show a street opposite the east end of St Paul's Cathedral, and views were arranged from various other directions. Evelyn worked to improve the city for traffic and at the same time to preserve the ancient sites and all that was of interest to an anti-quarian: a great ideal, requiring much time and thought, and it is not to be wondered at that his great competitor, acting with very different ideas, proceeded quicker, and so Evelyn wrote he had made his scheme "but Dr Wren had got the start of me."

Evelyn's ideas were carefully worked out, traffic problems were considered, and proper respect was shown for historic landmarks, etc.

Chapter VIII deals with the surveys made after the fire. The disputes that arose were settled by Judges appointed for that purpose. In the British Museum there are 19 volumes[1], bound in parts, making 41 volumes in all; they are 9 inches by 1 foot 1 inch, and about 2½ inches thick, the bindings are modern; they contain on paper the drafts or "minutes" of the decrees of the Judges corrected by them and signed; at the side

[1] Add. MSS. 5063–5103.

of these cases is the word "entered"; this evidently refers to the final decisions beautifully written on parchment in nine volumes at the Guildhall. Each volume is about 15 inches by 18 inches and 4 inches thick, each has the original binding and there is an index. The decisions are signed, usually by three or four Judges.

At the commencement of vol. 1 is written "The First Book wherein are Recorded definitive Orders, Judgments and De-crees made by the Justices of the Courts of King's Bench and Common Pleas and the Barons of the Coife of the Exchequer by virtue of an Act of Parliament Intitled An Act for erecting a Judicature for determination of differences touching houses burned or demolished by reason of the late Fire which happened in London, begun at Westminster the Eighth day of May Anno Dni. 1661[1]. In the Thirteenth yeare of the Reigne of our most gracious Sovraigne Lord Charles the Second by the Grace of God of England Scotland France and Ireland King defender of the Faith &c. And then continued by several prorogations to the eighteenth day of September 1666 and then continued to the Eighth day of February following And thence prorogued to the Tenth day of October 1667."

The first case is dated 27th February, 1666, and was signed by four Judges, and the last is dated 18th February, 1675, and was signed by three Judges, but this is followed by two earlier cases.

The old index to the volumes at Guildhall only gives the names of the parties concerned; the total number of cases tried was 1584. At the British Museum there is a valuable index made in 1843; this gives references to the Wards and Parishes.

There is also at the Guildhall a volume dealing with the Southwark fire, the first case is dated 8th June, 1677, and the last 5th October, 1677.

---

[1] This date is the year of the commencement of the Parliament referred to in line 10.

Index

PLANS

A

PLAN I

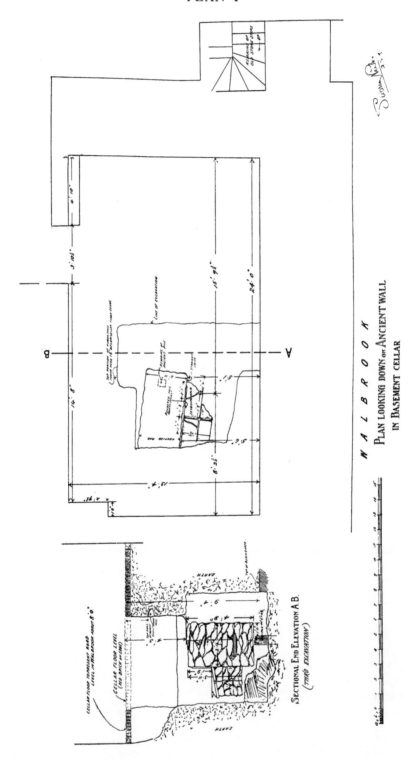

WALBROOK

PLAN LOOKING DOWN ON ANCIENT WALL
IN BASEMENT CELLAR

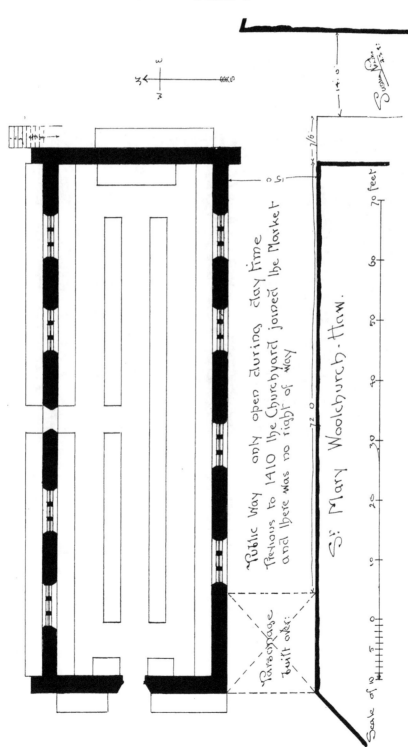

Plan of Stocks Market building as reconstructed from dimensions given in deed of 1357

PLAN 3

Portion of Braun and Hogenberg's Plan, 1572

PLAN 4

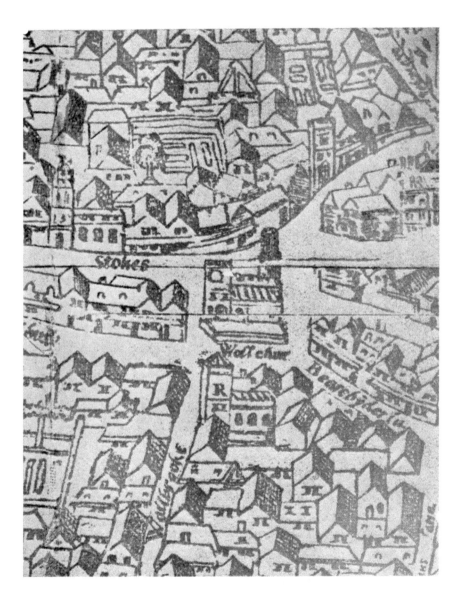

Portion of Agas's Plan, c. 1570

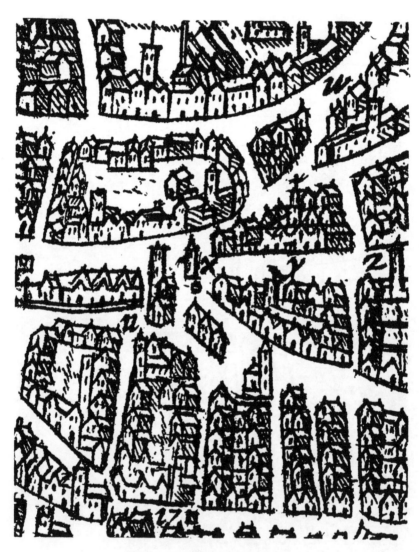

Portion of Norden's Plan, 1593

PLAN 6

Portion of Faithorne and Newcourt's Plan, 1658

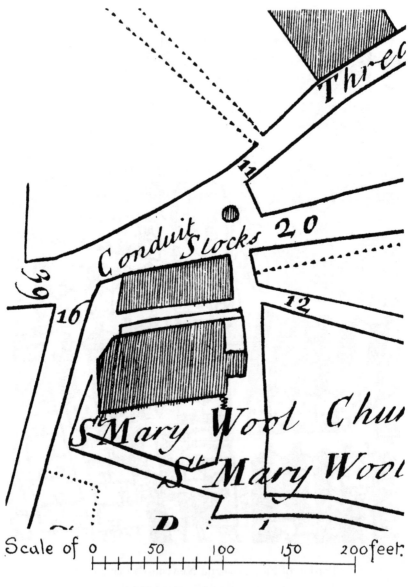

Portion of Leake's Plan, 1666

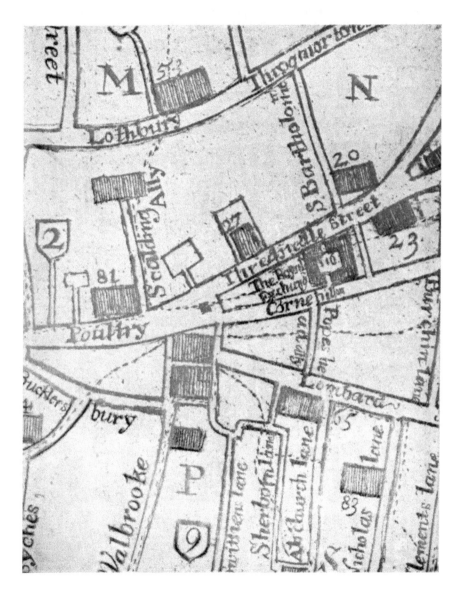

Portion of Pricke's Plan, 1667

Portion of John Overton's Plan, 1676

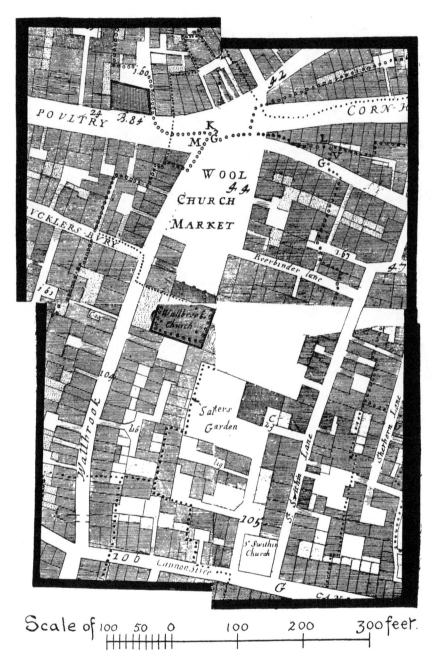

POVLTRY *24 B.84*

CORN-H

42

K
M G

WOOL
44
CHURCH
MARKET

L
N
G

VCKLERS-BVRY

Beerbinder lane

167

161

47

Walbrooke Church

104

Walbrook

126

Salters
Garden

C
23

119

St Swithin Lane

Sherborn Lane

105

St Swithin
Church

106 Cannon Strete

G

CAN

Scale of 100 50 0   100   200   300 feet.

Portion of Ogilby and Morgan's Plan, 1677

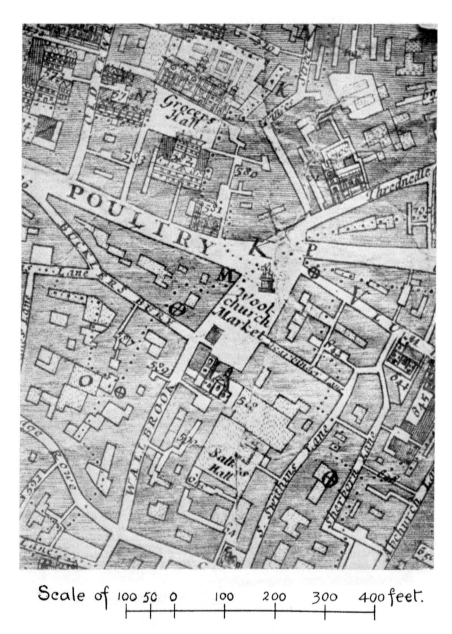

Scale of 100 50 0 100 200 300 400 feet.

Portion of Morden and Lea's Plan, 1682

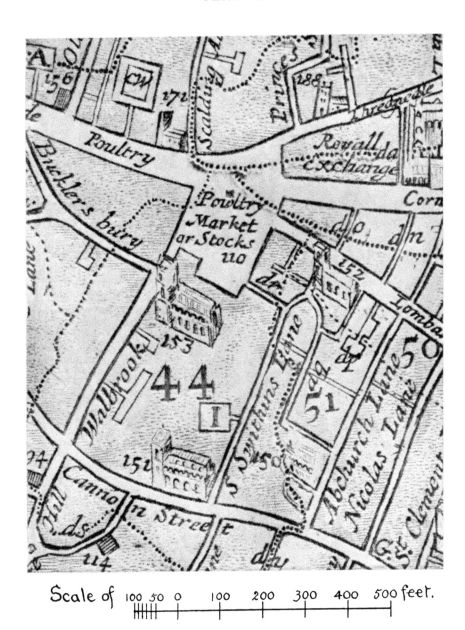

Scale of 100 50 0   100   200   300   400   500 feet.

Portion of Lea and Glynne's Plan, 1690

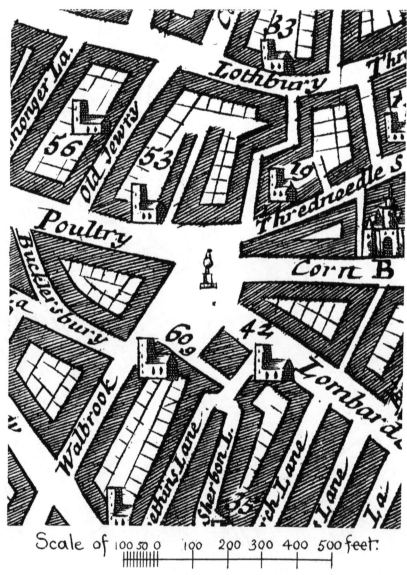

Portion of Overton's Plan, 1706

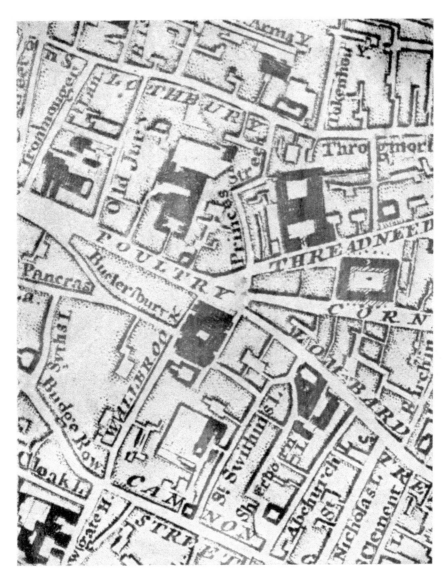

Scale of 100   0   100 200 300 400 500 feet.

Portion of Pine and Tinney's Plan, 1742

PLAN 15

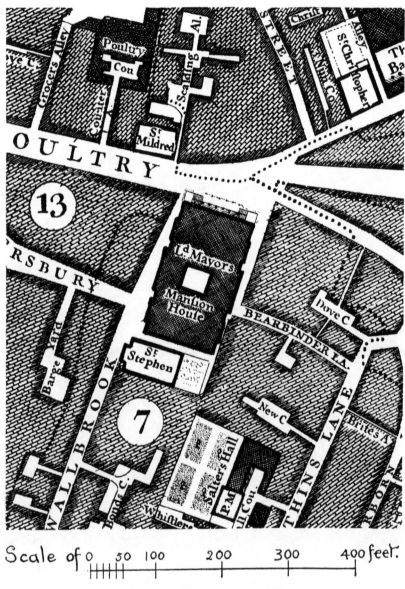

Portion of Rocque's Plan, 1746

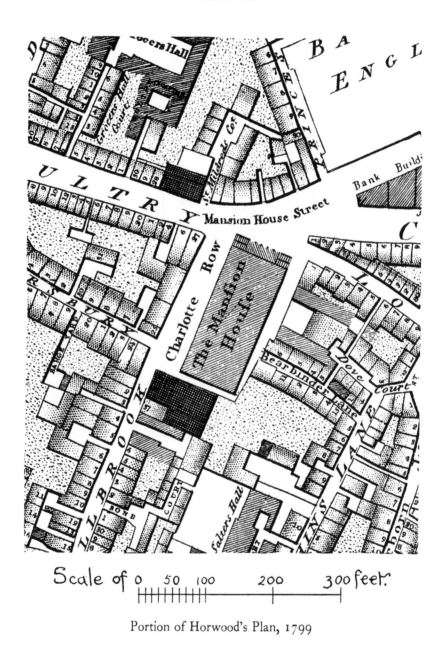

Scale of 0   50   100   200   300 feet.

Portion of Horwood's Plan, 1799

PLAN 17

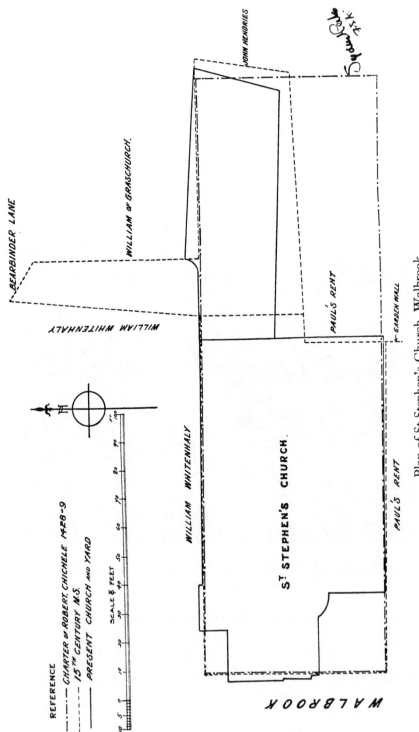

Plan of St Stephen's Church, Walbrook

PLAN 18

*Churchyard passage 4 ffoot 10 in. Wallbrooke at South end of the building 19 ffoot
wide and as much at North end Mr Wayte's ground*

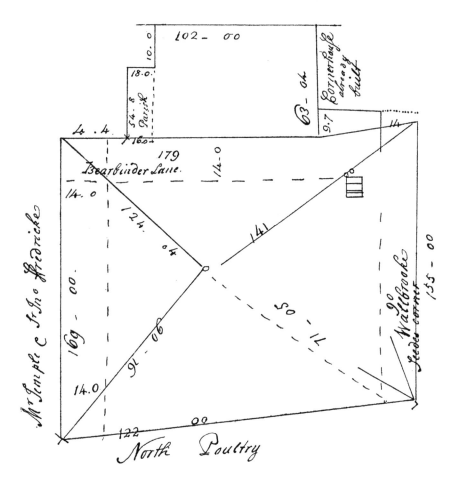

Plan of the Stocks Market from Oliver's *Survey*, vol. 2, p. 5[b], probably 1669

B2

Mr Pulford one ffound sett out 17th March 1668 at corner of the Poultry as designed below and there is cutt of 11 ffoot at East end and 16 ffoot 6 inch at West end for 18 ffoot at length

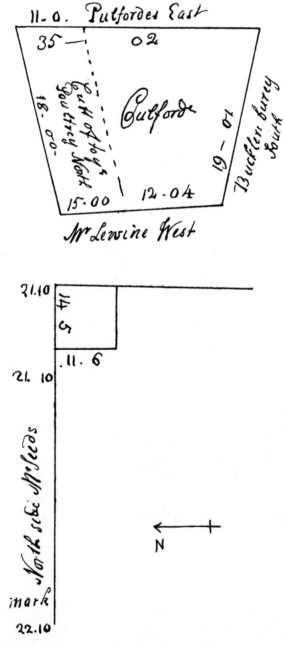

Mr Pulford's property in the Poultry, Oliver's *Survey*, vol. I, p. 136ᴮ

I sett out 1 ffound for Mr Rich. Clay in the Poultry the 16th of September 1670 as designed below

I sett out one ffound for Mr Arthur Smithson in the Poultry 14th of May 1669

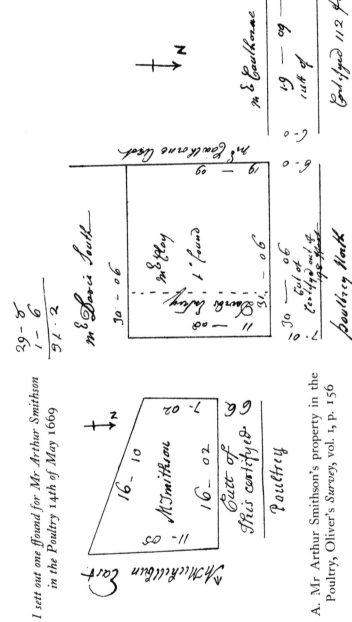

A. Mr Arthur Smithson's property in the Poultry, Oliver's *Survey*, vol. 1, p. 156

B. Mr Richard Clay's property in the Poultry, Oliver's *Survey*, vol. 2, p. 61

PLAN 21

I sett out one foundation for Mr Jeramy Royston in Wall Brooke which was the ould Church of St. Steven as designed on the other side this 20th May 1674

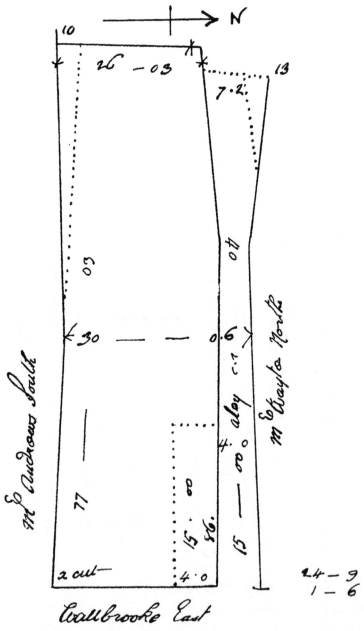

Mr Jeramy Royston's property in Walbrook, Oliver's *Survey*, vol. 2, p. 172

I sett out one ffoundation for the Lady Alice Vinor on the back of the Old Change
the 25th July 1670 as designed below

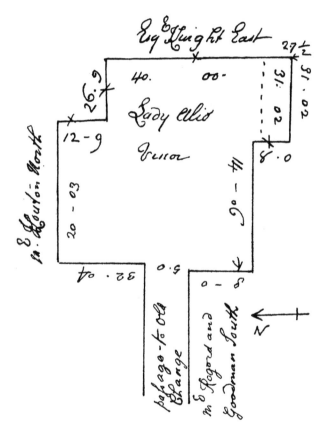

The Lady Alice Vinor's property at the back of Old Change, Oliver's *Survey*,
vol. 2, p. 51

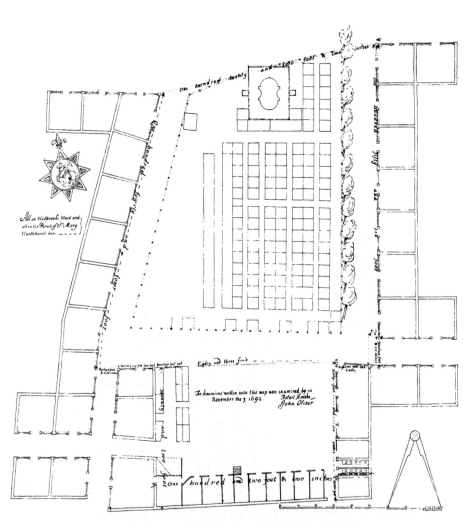

Plan of Stocks Market from old plan on parchment
(Probably a scheme of reconstruction) (1692)

PLAN 24

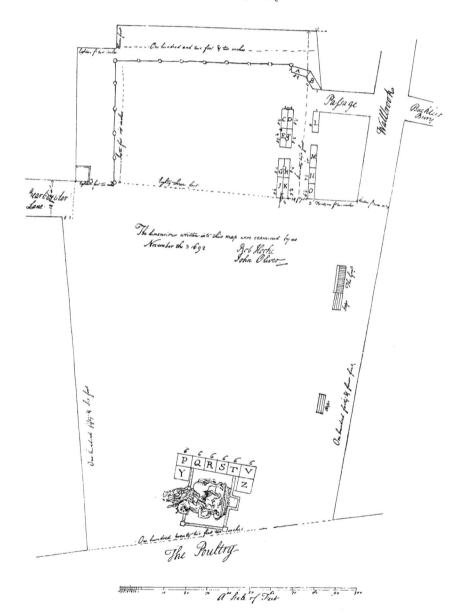

Plan of Stocks Market from old plan on parchment (1692)

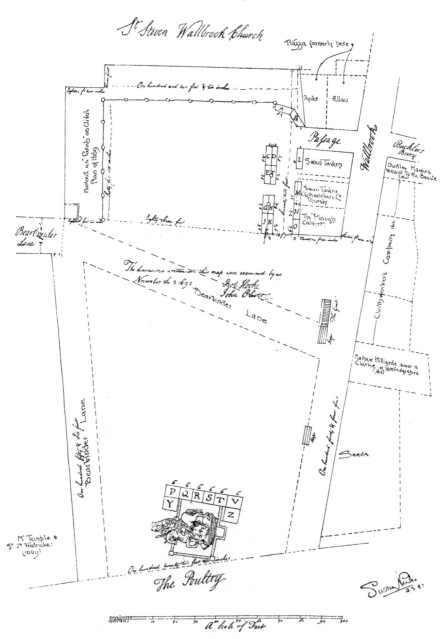

The Stocks Market. The Plan of 1692 with contemporary details added

PLAN 26

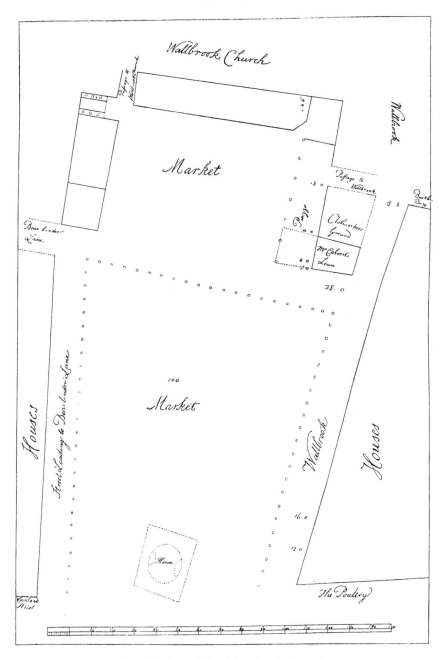

Dance's Plan of the Mansion House site

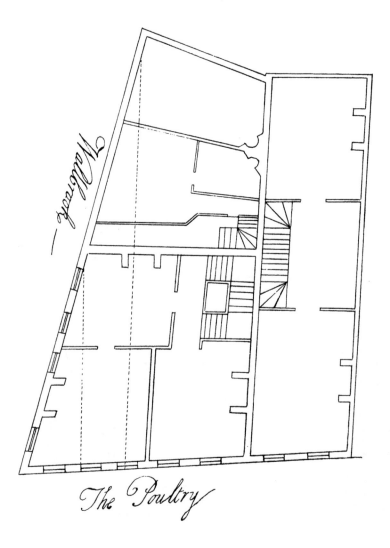

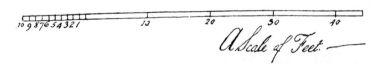

The Duke of Bedford's property at the corner of Walbrook and
The Poultry

PLAN 28

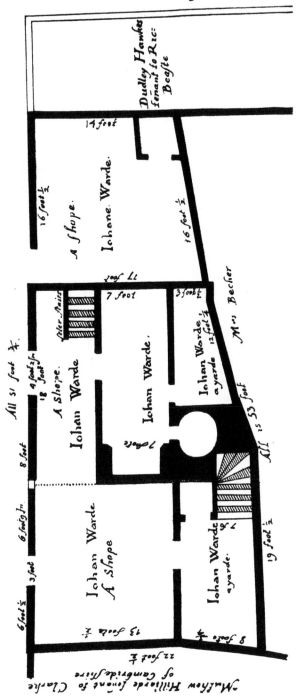

Property of the Clothworkers' Company in Walbrook, 1612

PLAN 29

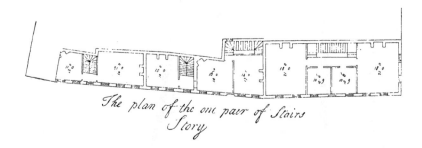

The plan of the one pair of Stairs Story

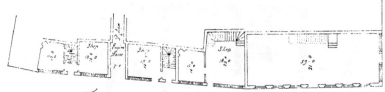

The plan of the ground Story

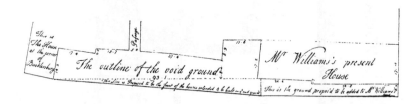

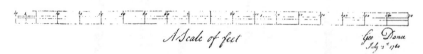

A Scale of feet

Geo Dance
July 3d 1760

Proposed buildings on the West side of Walbrook (1760)

PLAN 30

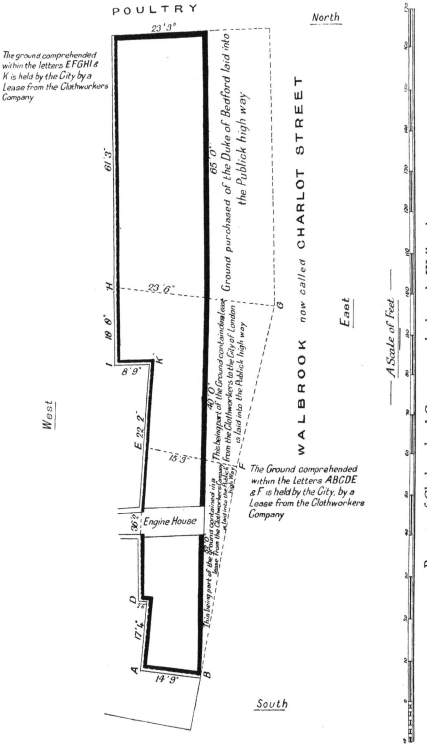

POULTRY

North

The ground comprehended within the letters EFGHI & K is held by the City by a Lease from the Clothworkers Company

Ground purchased of the Duke of Bedford laid into the Publick high way

WALBROOK now called CHARLOT STREET

East

23'3"

61'3"

65'0"

23'6"

10'0"

8'9"

E 22'2"

40'0"

15'3"

36'2" Engine House

This being part of the Ground contained in a Lease from the Clothworkers Company to the City of London is laid into the Publick high way

This being part of the Ground contained in a Lease from the Clothworkers Company is laid into the Publick high Way

The Ground comprehended within the letters ABCDE & F is held by the City, by a Lease from the Clothworkers Company

West

D 2'6"

17'4"

A 14'9" B

South

— A Scale of Feet —

Property of Clothworkers' Company and others: in Walbrook, 1775

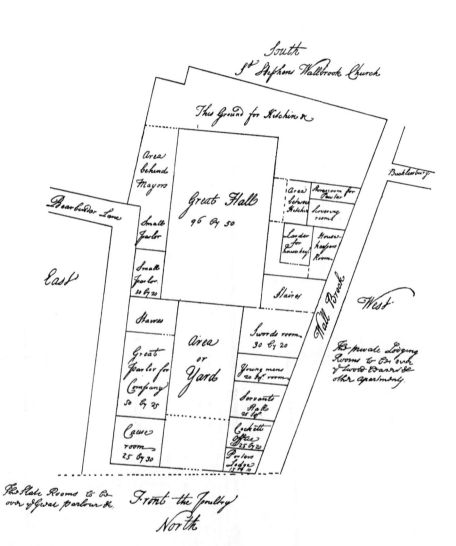

South
S⁴ Stephens Wallbrook Church

This Ground for Kitchin &c

Bucklesbury

Area behind Mayors

Great Hall
96 by 50

Area between Kitchin

Scorving room

Dearbendor Lane

East

Small Parlor

Larder for housekeep

House keepers Room

Small Parlor
30 by 20

West

Stairs

Wall Brook

Stairs

Area or Yard

Swords room
30 by 20

Great Parlor for Company
50 by 25

Young mens room
20 by

To private Lodging Rooms to be over y⁴ Sword Barrs &c other apartments

Servants Hale
25 sqⁿ

Cause room
25 by 30

Cockett Office
25 by 20

The Plate Rooms to be over y⁴ Great parlour &c

Porters Lodge
17 by 10

Front the Poultry

North

The Common Crier's Plan showing the requirements of the proposed
Mansion House

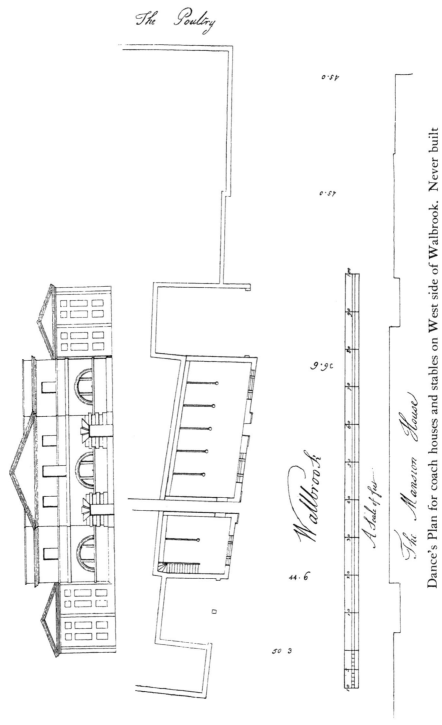

The Poultry

Walbrook

The Mansion House

A Scale of feet

Dance's Plan for coach houses and stables on **West** side of Walbrook. Never built

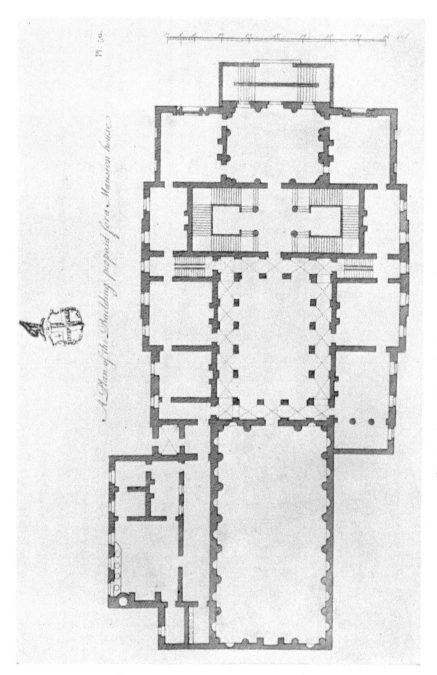

Plan by Isaac Ware for Stocks Market site

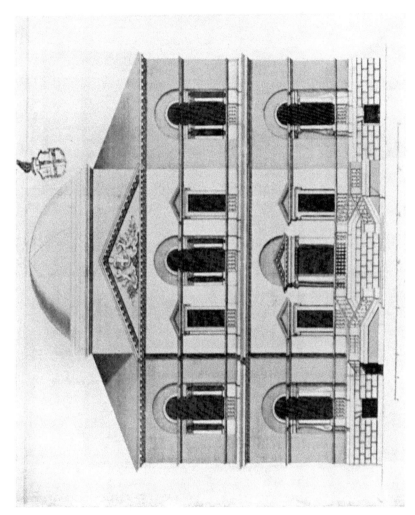

Ware's Elevation for Stocks Market site

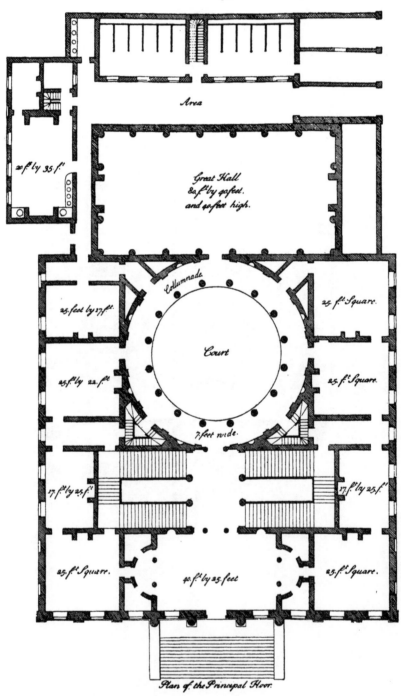

Area

20 f.^t by 35 f.^t

Great Hall
80 f.^t by 40 feet
and 40 feet high.

Columnade

25. feet by 17 f.^t

25. f.^t Square.

Court

25 f.^t by 22. f.^t

25. f.^t Square.

7. feet wide.

17. f.^t by 25 f.^t

17. f.^t by 25 f.^t

25. f.^t Square.

40. f.^t by 25. feet

25. f.^t Square.

Plan of the Principal Floor.

Plan by Isaac Ware for Leadenhall Street site

PLAN 36

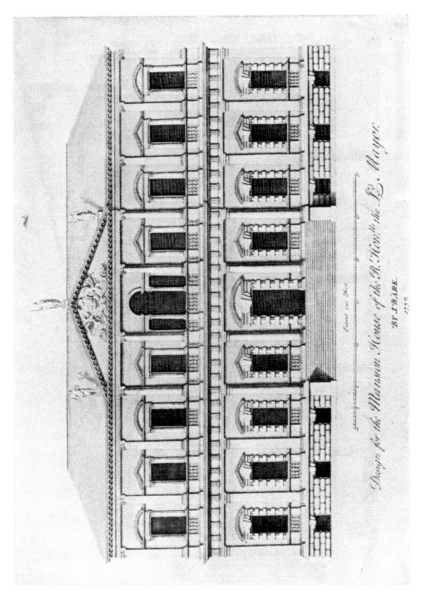

Ware's Elevation for Leadenhall Street site

PLAN 37

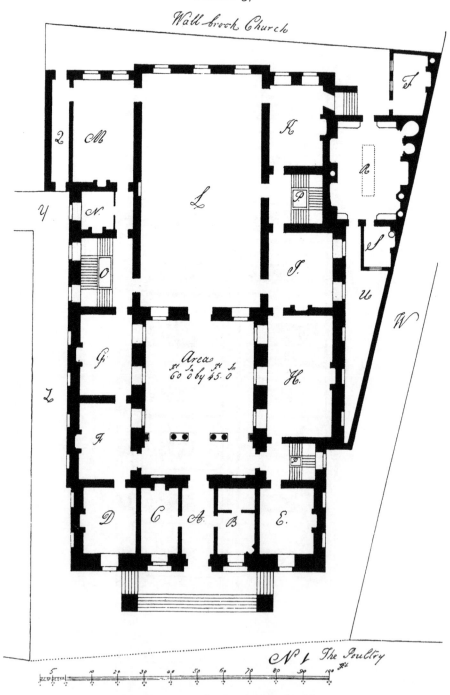

Plan by James for Stocks Market site

PLAN 38

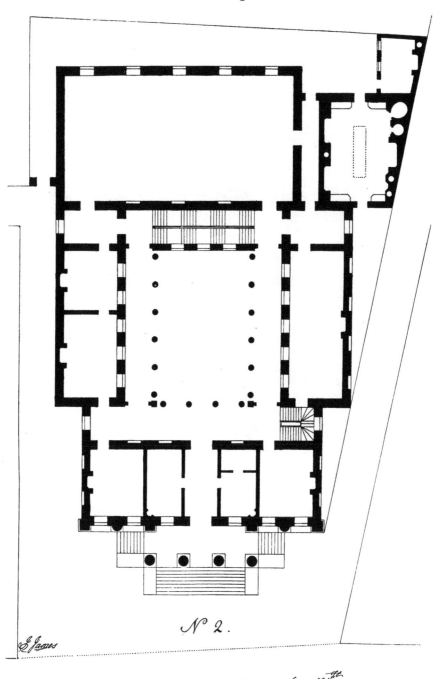

N° 2.

Alternative Plan by James for Stocks Market site

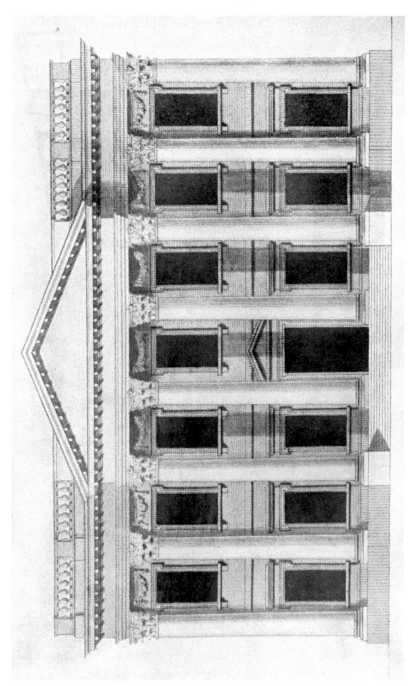

Elevation by James for Plan 38

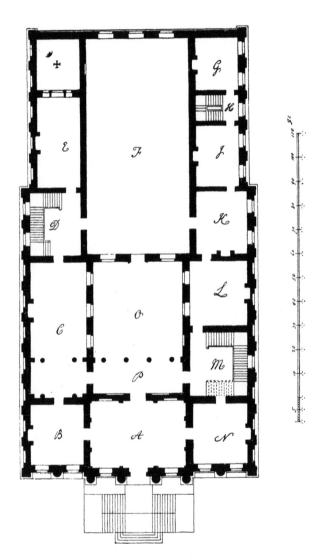

A third Plan by James

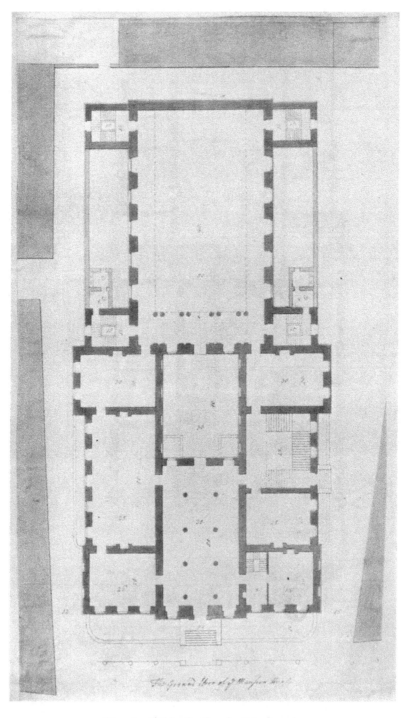

Plan by Gibbs for Stocks Market site

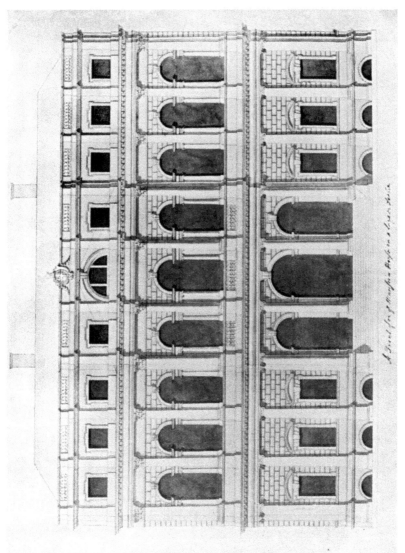

Elevation by Gibbs for Stocks Market site

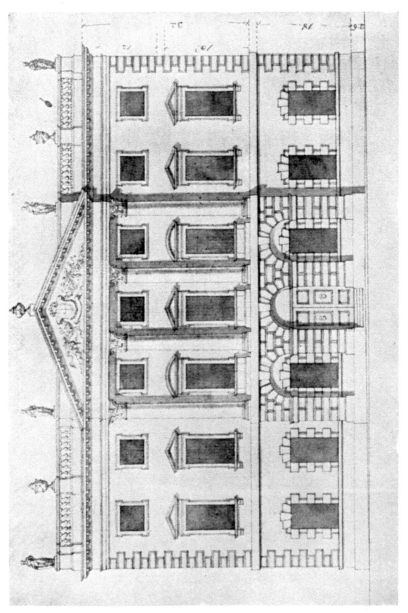

A second Elevation by Gibbs

PLAN 44

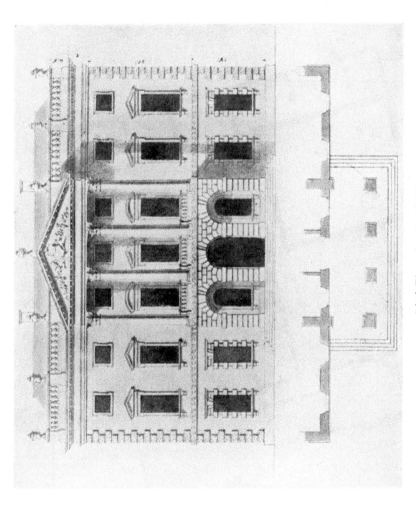

A third Elevation by Gibbs

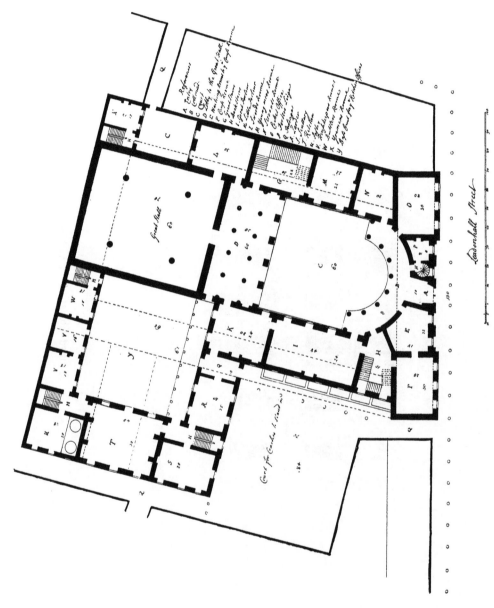

Plan by Gibbs for Leadenhall Street: ground floor

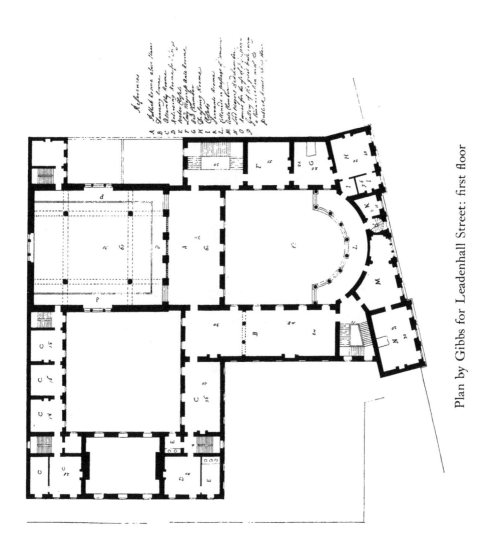

Plan by Gibbs for Leadenhall Street: first floor

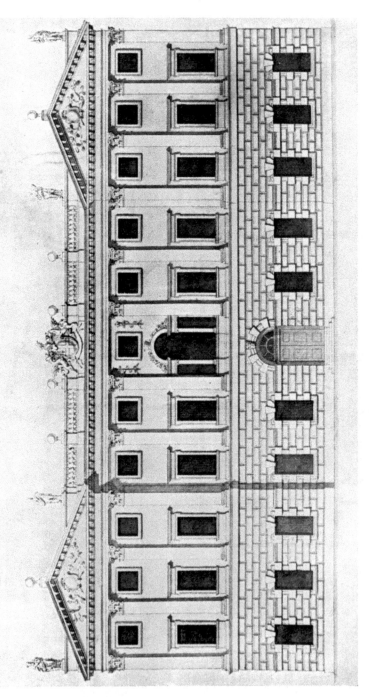

Elevation by Gibbs for Leadenhall Street site

PLAN 48

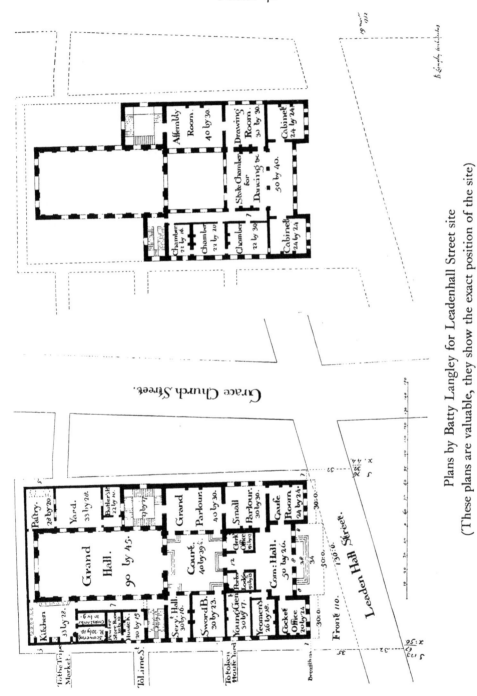

Plans by Batty Langley for Leadenhall Street site

(These plans are valuable, they show the exact position of the site)

P. M. H.

D

PLAN 49

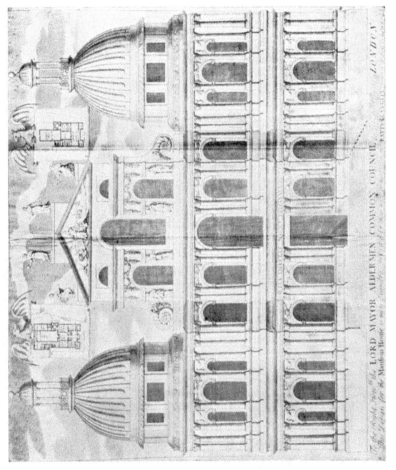

Elevation by Batty Langley for Leadenhall Street site, dated Aug. 26, 1735

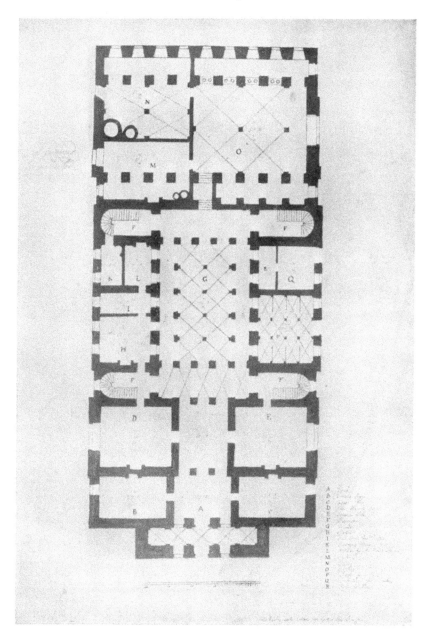

Dance's original Plan of the Ground Floor of the Mansion House

PLAN 51

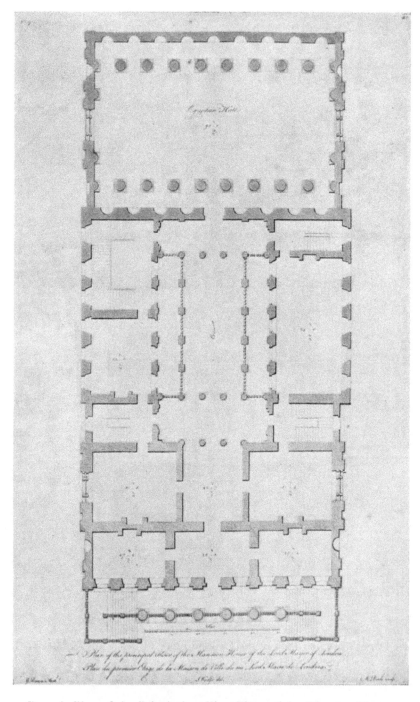

Dance's Plan of the Principal or First Floor of the Mansion House
From *Vitruvius Britannicus*

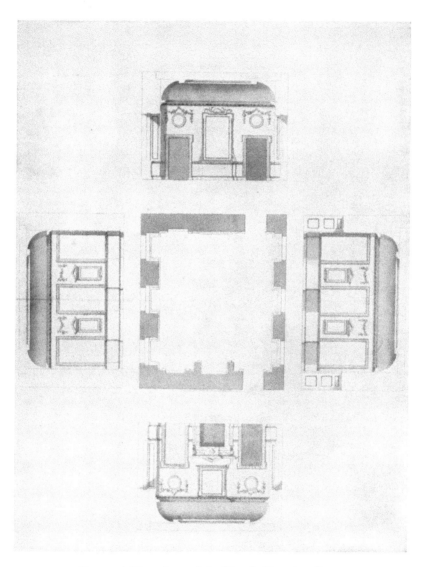

Plan and Elevations of the North Drawing Room

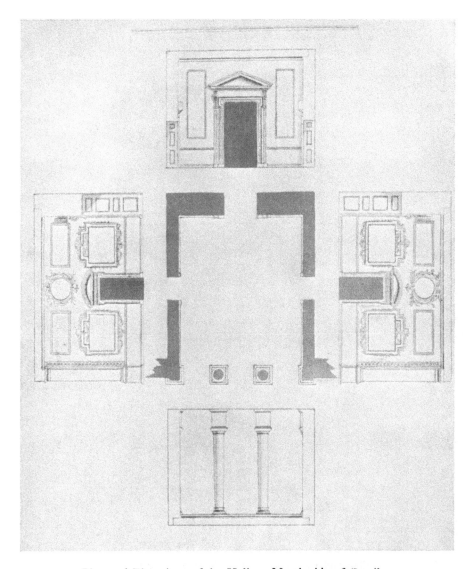

Plan and Elevations of the Hall on North side of Cortile

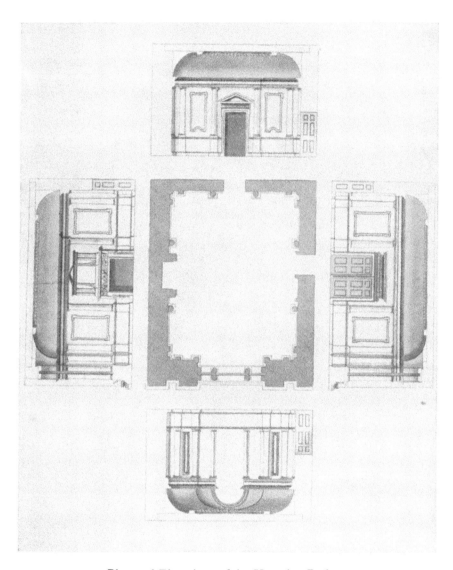

Plan and Elevations of the Venetian Parlour

PLAN 55

Section of the Egyptian Hall showing proposed reconstruction of the Roof

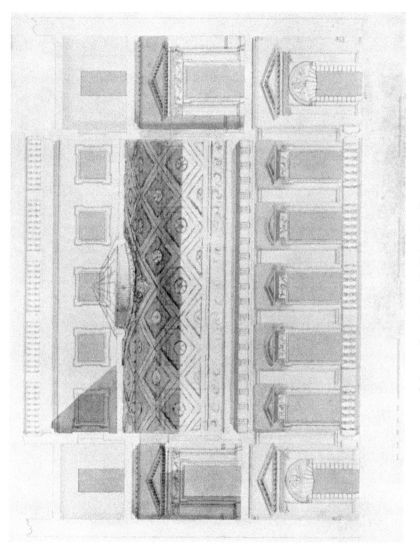

Scheme for the Roof of the Cortile, 1794

PLAN 57

Plan of Ceiling (not carried out)

Plan and Elevation of Fireplace (not carried out)

PLAN 59

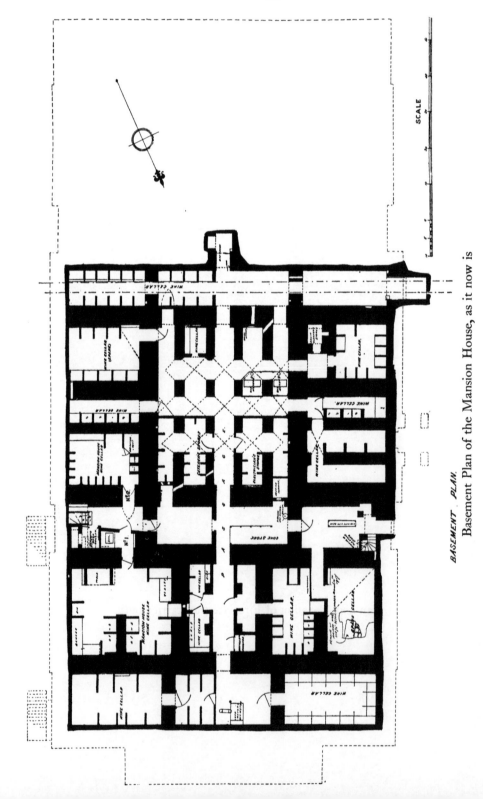

SCALE

BASEMENT. PLAN.

Basement Plan of the Mansion House, as it now is

PLAN 60

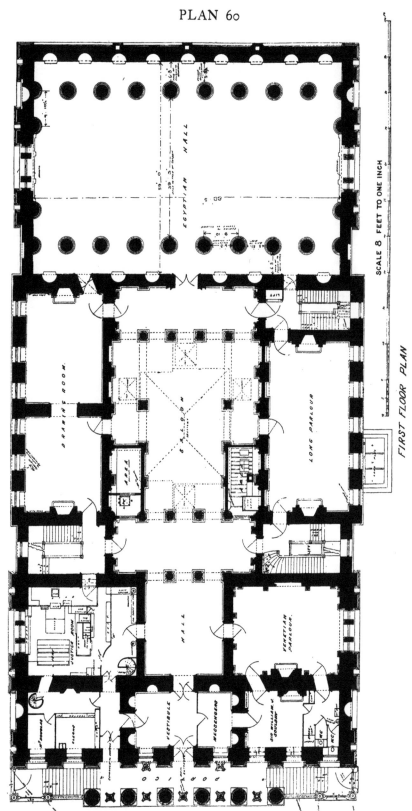

FIRST FLOOR PLAN

First Floor Plan of the Mansion House, as it now is

SCALE 8 FEET TO ONE INCH

PLAN 61

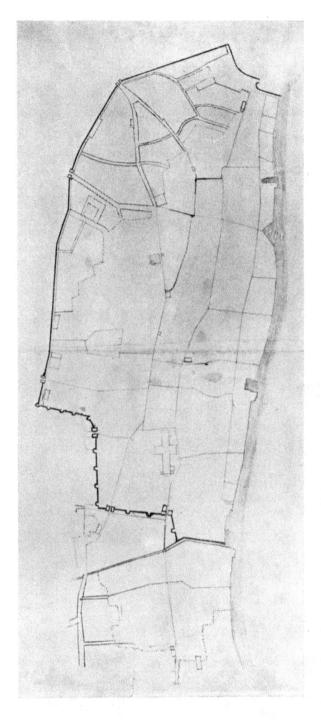

Wren's Plan of the City (1)

PLAN 62

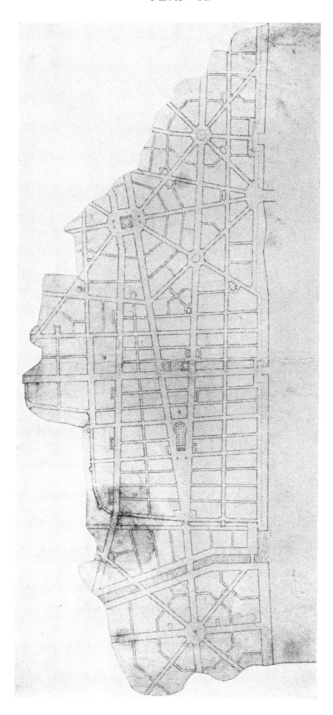

Wren's Plan of the City (2)

For EU product safety concerns, contact us at Calle de José Abascal, 56–1°,
28003 Madrid, Spain or eugpsr@cambridge.org.

www.ingramcontent.com/pod-product-compliance
Ingram Content Group UK Ltd.
Pitfield, Milton Keynes, MK11 3LW, UK
UKHW030859150625
459647UK00021B/2741